THE GENIUS OF
WILHELM BUSCH

Franz von Lenbach, *Ölskizze von Wilhelm Busch* (Oil Sketch of Wilhelm Busch), probably 1877. With the kind permission of the Wilhelm-Busch-Gesellschaft, Hannover.

THE GENIUS OF

Wilhelm Busch

COMEDY OF
FRUSTRATION

AN ENGLISH ANTHOLOGY

Edited and Translated by Walter Arndt

University of California Press
Berkeley · Los Angeles · London

University of California Press
Berkeley and Los Angeles, California

University of California Press, Ltd.
London, England

© 1982 by
The Regents of the University of California

Printed in the United States of America

1   2   3   4   5   6   7   8   9

Library of Congress Cataloging in Publication Data

Busch, Wilhelm, 1832–1908.
  The genius of Wilhelm Busch.
  Includes index.
  I. Arndt, Walter W., 1916–   . II. Title.
PT2603.U8A22   813'.8   79-63545
ISBN 0-520-03897-5

To Oscar, Fritz, Kate, Lisbeth, and Kurt Arndt,
who will enjoy this wherever they are,
and to Fiff Arndt, for years of prenatal care
generously given the book

Contents

Acknowledgments

The editor and translator thankfully acknowledges the support of this project by a fellowship award from the John Simon Guggenheim Memorial Foundation in 1977–78. He further wishes to express his grateful appreciation to Dr. Friedrich Bohne of the Wilhelm-Busch-Gesellschaft at Hannover for his active and ever kindly advocacy of Busch in English since 1961; to Dr. Herwig Guratzsch and the staff of the Wilhelm Busch Museum for furnishing illustration materials and permitting reproduction of several items in their collection; and to Erich Heller of Northwestern University, Gert Ueding of Oldenburg University, Dr. Lisa Diekmann of Hamburg, Dr. Michael Praetorius of Munich, as well as Doris Kretschmer, Peter Dreyer, Marilyn Schwartz, and Chet Grycz of the University of California Press, who helped in various important ways to make this book possible or to improve it.

Introduction

Wilhelm Busch—painter, draftsman, comic poet, and unwitting originator of the modern comic strip—was born in the village of Wiedensahl near Hannover in North Germany on April 15, 1832, the day of Bismarck's birth and the year of Goethe's death. He died in the hamlet of Mechtshausen in the Harz Mountains on January 9, 1908, a year of crisis in Europe which foreshadowed the Great War in which Bismarck's Germany collapsed.

Busch was sensitive, moody, withdrawn, and publicity-shy all his life, yet hardly the icy recluse he enjoyed playing. He had been starved in childhood for signs of affection and approval and developed habits of self-deprecation, self-punishment, and reserve uncommon perhaps even in his own time and sphere. An intermittent seeker of guidance from philosophy and a practiced cynic out of thwarted idealism, he seems, like many in the two generations between Thomas Buddenbrook and his creator, to have taken to Schopenhauer in middle life as to a bitter but bracing drug. A secluded life in a rustic environment was his refuge in any crisis, satisfying his extraordinary need for privacy and furnishing the characteristic settings and human types of his art.

He took up first mechanical engineering, then the study of painting at Hannover, went on to attend the academies of art at Düsseldorf, Antwerp, and Munich, but began to make his mark in his late twenties not in painting but by increasingly original experiments in graphic narrative by the ancient art of the woodcut. A frequent contributor from 1859 on to the humorous periodicals *Fliegende Blätter* (*Flying Leaves*, or *Broadsides*) and *Münchner Bilderbogen* (*Picture Sheets from Munich*), he first won resounding acclaim with the now classical ancestor of the lowly comic strip: the morality tale in colored woodcut, *Max und Moritz* (1865). This, quite possibly the most universally cherished and quoted work of art in the German language, is a rustic tale in verse of evil gusto, sardonic bathos, and ultimate grotesque. It features two "bad boys," their seven misdeeds against the righteous philistine torpor—the Gogolian *poshlost'* of *Dead Souls*—of the adult order, and their surreal end by a parody of the drastic and cautionary retribution so common in the German fairy tale.

What the *Charivari* was to France and *Punch* to England between 1841 and World War I, *Fliegende Blätter* for a decade or two after 1844 was to Munich and ethnic Germany—not yet cajoled and bullied into a makeshift empire by Bismarck. The hundreds of sparsely captioned or wordless woodcut anecdotes contributed to this journal, in part collected with fresh additions in the album-format vehicle called *Münchner Bilderbogen*, first brought Busch notoriety and steady royalties. The saga of the two rascals Max and Moritz, although as yet stark and flamboyant in line and color in the manner of anti-Bonapartist broadsides, marked his breakthrough to real fame.

Max und Moritz, crudely imitated in the United States in the nineties,[1] was

[1]Upon W. R. Hearst's suggestion, Rudolph Dirks (1877–1968) began in 1897 to draw on *Max und Moritz* for inspiration and the "role models" of his primitive but durable

not only the origin of the worldwide newspaper cartoon strip, but the first example of a dual art form developed by Busch and never successfully practiced after him. Over the next twenty years, he produced fewer than a dozen far subtler illustrated verse tales, or more properly, duets for word and sketch, which wreak a similar devastation of satire in an adult bourgeois world, this time predominantly in urban or small-town settings. The second of his genres, then, this one truly novel, is the mock-naive, comic-philosophic morality tale, fraught with visual mayhem and verbal acrobatics. It became the chief public vehicle of his middle years, and it has certainly remained the foremost glory attached to Busch's name, despite the steep rise in the attention and esteem accorded his hundreds of small paintings in recent decades. For while his numerous small landscapes and bucolic genre sketches in oil remained little known in his lifetime, they are now carefully collected and much discussed. He ultimately became a painter of haunting originality, who in statically violent, often hypnotic land- and face-scapes developed a spontaneous post-impressionism of his own, inspired, from the looks of them, by late Rembrandt, clearly by Frans Hals and Brouwer.

Busch was an artist of a quite peculiar and, in its way, unexampled versatility. As a lyric, satiric, aphoristic, and comic poet, and simultaneously a graphic genius of motion, gesture, and physiognomy, he attained a Shakespeare-Webster-and-the-Bible sort of household stature in German-speaking countries, and renown wherever his verse was well translated elsewhere. This last condition was met, as far as *Max und Moritz* and one or two later picture tales are concerned, in some Slavic and Germanic cultures, but not at all in Anglosaxony, where his mature, understated comedy should have found a ready home in a congenial existing tradition. Mark Twain's country, at least, would have relished the fused effects of stripped-down draftsmanship and now baldly vernacular, now mock-solemn diction, sparkling with Pudd'nhead Wilson aphorisms in the popular form of racy couplets.

Busch gave to Europe a half-century's worth of unforgettable, emblematic drawings, fused in the mind with lapidary verses that by themselves would fill a thesaurus of quotations.

comic strip, *The Katzenjammer Kids*, naturalized during World War I as *The Captain and the Kids*.

To see this treasure-house rifled like grandma's box in the attic, and a few snippets of the famous drawings used for casual marginal decorations, as has been the carefree practice of the *New York Review of Books* for the last seven years or so, is to witness a tribute of a sort, perhaps.[2] But the practice strikes many a continental European as comparable in taste to using John Tenniel's illustrations of Lewis Carroll (mediocre and stiff by comparison) as, say, lampshade decals for the Soviet trade. For you can take a hookah-puffing centipede out of his nook in a vagrant dream far more easily than one of Busch's graphic *trouvailles* out of its *pas de deux* with comic verse more familiar by now to its home public than the Bible. These drawings, it should be realized, did not illustrate another writer, nor did they merely minister to Busch's verse. They sprang full-armed out of the same dubiously genial brow as the brilliantly zany, booby-trapped verse of which they were both spark and tinder. Few in Germanic Europe, save perhaps for the luckless total-war batch born between 1935 and 1950, would need to look up the true context, pictorial or textual, of those exiled "vignettes," or a hundred others by the same unmistakable hand. Their memory would instantly restore it, and they would start reciting.

Two generations after Busch's death as a laureate of all-European fame, his work still awaited naturalization in English.[3] Yet by 1908 his tales had gone through countless printings from Prussia to Russia, from Holland to Hungary, and his name was more of a household word there than Carroll's or Beatrix Potter's were by the 1920s in England. His charac-

[2] A superior recent tribute, marking a significant step in the introduction of Busch to the English-speaking world, was Erich Heller's humane and penetrating essay "Creatures of Circumstance," in the *Times Literary Supplement* of October 7, 1977.

[3] At least twelve English and American items may be found in the eight shelf-feet of translations of individual Busch picture tales in the Wilhelm Busch Museum collection at Hannover. Of these, some are British or German-British of pre–World War I vintage. Others, on internal evidence, appear to be the labors of love of sesquilingual enthusiasts in the Grune- and Wienerwälder of the New World, including, incidentally, the late Nobel laureate in physics Max Born. The British (Museum) Library in London lists only four English renderings, two as early as 1868 and 1874. The latter of these is entitled *Naughty Jemima: A Doleful Tale*. (It is.)

ters—homespun, harassed, jockeyed by their ruthless progenitor from the shabbily and safely familiar into the disgraceful and macabre—were and are among the most vividly evocative culture uncles (Aldous Huxley's term) of Germanic civilization, in which much of England in his time was, after all, more at home than ever before or after. That he remained untranslated into English is the more curious as his amalgam of two unique talents is not only unrivalled in his own country—which has produced perhaps only one other outstanding humorist of light verse, Christian Morgenstern—but unmatched even in the homelands of his kind of humor, the English-speaking world.

Busch shares with his elder contemporary in France, Honoré Daumier (whose work he came to know), some of the latter's Breughelesque vision of the beast in bourgeois man. But Busch's settings are less metropolitan than Daumier's, and his scorn is both earthy and metaphysical, rather than civic and esthetic. He leveled at the stuffy mores and morals of low and middlebrow Germany a satire that was the more insidious for being couched in terms of bland mock-approval, and the more acute for venting the self-hatred of the accomplice, the native son. He aimed his cuts at the official pieties and rituals of Catholicism; at pseudo-scholarly bombast; and, throughout, at the hollowness of authority, the facile self-righteousness of the smug burgher on the defensive against the rebel principle in the shape of animal, child, or free-questioning spirit. In sketch, verse, and prose he mirrored the moral squalor of yokeldom and (not always consciously, perhaps) the profound inner conflict, still unresolved today, between safe but repressive authority and the half-stifled yearning for self-assertion, if not for civil and political liberties attainable only at the price of revolution. He is clearly far better understood in the new German republic than he was during the Empire: cultural self-definition has become an acute problem and, for two decades now, the boundaries between freedom and anarchic violence and between social cohesion and reactionary bourgeois stuffiness have demanded redrawing. The seventies have seen a great deal of newly gathered material and new writing on Busch, following a rush into new editions when the copyright lapsed on the fiftieth anniversary of his death. But these still leave one hard pressed to imagine for the benefit of strangers to Busch a constellation of talents for comparison that might convey, without absurd fulsomeness, something of the pictorial marksmanship, synchronized with verbal bite, of Busch's double weapon. The grisly, addled folksiness of Gogol's "Two Ivans," caught by Daumier's pen and freely seconded by Pushkinian verse of the "Tsar Nikita" vintage? Ogden Nash and Thurber rolled into one, enhanced by the pen of a thoroughly de-Bunkered, freshly inspired Al Capp? Perhaps; but the product of such fancied unions remains unimaginable. Meanwhile, one looks in vain, for example, for a foreign parallel to *Fipps, der Affe*, the odyssey of a picaro monkey, who is initially a stylized picture-book rogue of a picture-book Africa. Kidnapped off a coastal palmtree and brought to the civilization of Bremen and parts inland, he increasingly becomes *simia sapiens*, or perhaps *homunculus liber vitiosus*. It comes his way to fill, with disastrous originality and panache, and all-but-ultimate success, a series of delicate commercial and domestic positions; and in the end he is executed, in what would be fun to prove one of the few genuinely tragic scenes in German literature, by a moronic peasant with a shooting-iron left over from Waterloo.

There is similar trouble with poor Baldwin Bahlamb, or Clement Dove, whom Gogol's Akaky Akakyevich, Dostoevsky's Devushkin, and Dickens's Traddles would all have pitied and stood a half-pint if they had had a shilling among them; but who derives from Hoffmann's Anselm by way of bores like Ludwig Richter and Moritz von Schwind and wafts, a little sadly, the parochial frowst of decaying German romanticism. And *Tobias Knopp*, the centerpiece of that six-pound folio wholesomely named Busch's *Home Thesaurus of Humor*? Perhaps Goncharov's *Oblomov*, minus his few stirrings of energy and ambition, offers an analogue in labored prose of this swift canter, verse and sketch driven two-in-hand, through a life of aimless self-procreation. *Klecksel* (Squirtle? Dollop? Blotchit?), companion piece to Bahlamb-Dove, treats the comic tribulations and self-afflictions of a dabbling young painter whose bourgeois lusts prove stronger than his talent or tenacity. Its feckless hero, whose name is a verbal blob or blot of paint and who happens to look exactly like another dabbler, then aged sixteen, who called himself Maxim Gorky, subsides ingloriously into what may be called the Bavarian way of life; here at least Mr. Permaneder, Toni's last husband in *The Budden-brooks*, stands ready as a more cosmopolitan descendant.

Some of Busch's most poignant tragicomic creations treat a theme uncomfortably close to home: aspiration or ambition, noble or absurd or both, foiled by petty circumstance; the malice of inanimate things; and human inadequacy. These works abound in wry, endlessly "quotable" aphorisms, and in verbal-graphic slapstick with startling enclaves of black humor and shockingly cold-blooded grotesquerie. Yet most are cast in the homely settings and trivial circumstances with which Busch pretends to be (and his reader is easily lulled into feeling) totally at home and in some atavistic sympathy. Thus the reader's recognition is assured and his unconscious defenses against the ensuing estrangement (or "defamiliarization") effects undermined. These aesthetic tactics point to the surrealist modes of Busch's English coeval, Lewis Carroll, and his younger contemporary, the inspired fantasist-parodist Christian Morgenstern (1871–1914). In some sallies prompted by Bismarck's war against France and his *Kulturkampf* against the Roman Catholic influence in German politics, however, he used his genius for lampoon and caricature-by-allegory with a coarse partisanship that still hurts feelings after the lapse of a century. Some of these sallies involved his publishers in bans and lawsuits; and in some backwaters even *Max und Moritz* was thought subversive enough of adult authority and pedagogical principles to justify official injunctions as late as the 1920s.

It may perhaps be gathered from the Knopps, Bahlamb, Kuno Klecksel, and company that Busch laid himself open, perhaps not without a degree of cynical connivance, to fraternizing cooption by the German Babbitts—the counterparts of those misty-eyed quaffers of the Rockwellian home brew in the United States, the sensa-yooma and yoomin-nature fans. This false affinity saddled him with cozy and all too durable sobriquets like "the laughing sage of Wiedensahl." But watch the sage of Wiedensahl improve his razor claws, and welcome little children in with gently smiling jaws: where they are pickled and preserved, or recovered "unusable" like Gogol's dim drunk policeman, or fed as grist to some cheerful clattering mill which feelingly preserves their granulated outlines like object lessons or vague messages of distress to passing dirigibles!

Parts of Busch's work, and occasional asides, have lent a semblance of plausibility to suspicions of anti-Semitism and (more than a semblance here) of virulent anticlericalism. In *Plisch und Plum* anti-Semitism, one might feel, alarmingly jerks its stiff arm. One of the painful *contretemps* which befall Fittig, the sweet-natured, harassed father to Paul and Peter (in their turn set in authority over the two raffish puppies, Plisch and Plum, so uncannily like their masters), confronts him with a rumpled, curly-all-over, baroque-nosed, shuffling ol'-clothes-man. Busch blatantly names him Schmulchen Schievelbeiner. This is roughly like "Little Ikey Bandylegs": on the face of it a crude provocation to the recently emancipated Shoileys and Seymours of Busch's time and place. Schmulchen is as striking a model (yet hopelessly remote and superior as a graphic feat) for the yid of the Nazi gutter press, as quintessential a decoction of age-old complacent prejudice, as exists in German graphic art. He has the seat of his hard-to-credit pants ripped out by the instinctively hostile Aryan mongrels and with a groveling whine threatens to sue Herrn *von* Fittig; he has quickly ennobled him, you see, to flatter him in his obsequious, typically *ostjüdisch* manner. . . . But how ambiguously Busch captions this Hitler's dream of pure crystalized "racism":

> Black his soul and suit of clothes,
> Curved his walking stick and nose,
> Here comes Shmulie Shnozzle-Hooking—
> (We, thank God, are better-looking.)

Busch takes the nasty-genteel anti-Semitism (which was endemic in the middle and upper classes of the Western world until the martial triumphs of Israel) ad absurdum by dragging it shamelessly into the open and seeming to indulge it: a hoary device of satire. But to some angry observers, after World War II more often than in his lifetime, such neuralgic spots have made Busch seem an uncomfortably gifted avatar of the complacencies and biases of the Bismarck era and its conservative and "national-liberal" establishment: anti-Catholicism, anti-Semitism, Teutonic chauvinism. Clearly there was a streak of such homegrown prejudice in the young Busch. It is surprising, though, how much of the evidence one may admit, as a veteran deplorer of most of Bismarck's works and many marks of his epoch, without the least detriment to one's approval of Busch, the prejudice-mongering magician. The reason must be that

Busch is here being challenged on a plane that is essentially not his own. One takes in the inspired contrapuntal dance—the double line of stylus and verse—and not the opinion or phobia it might be thought to promote or be instinct with. Clearly Busch himself knew by age forty that his mind and his line had outgrown automatic respect for household gods old or recent.

The inner habitat of his art—the region in which, or on the margin of which, hovers the Busch who is a stranger to most of the new values of imperial Germany—is that of the true grotesque. The grotesque is estrangement, the dissolution of the familiar into unsettling chaos. Wolfgang Kayser, the distinguished aestheticist of *Das sprachliche Kunstwerk* (*The Linguistic Artifact*), dipped in a gingerly way into some of those shifting quagmires of literature and painting in his essay "The Grotesque" (1960). He cites Busch as crediting physics and nature with a pervasive, inherent malice akin to Vischer's famous "malice of the object"—a virulent "liveliness down to the smallest unit." In a letter to Franz von Lehnbach (the John Sargent of Germany, who did the best-known portrait of Busch), Busch says: "He who has ever caught the flashing eye of that energetic bestiality will harbor the terrible suspicion that . . . a single devil may be stronger than a whole heavenful of saints." The principle of the proto-grotesque, estrangement, placed by many at the root of all humor, is the combination of incompatible elements. The incompatibility may lie in a conjunction of concrete objects or circumstances, or it may flow from the reaction of a character or narrator to a situation. "We approach the grotesque," Kayser suggests, "when that combination really cannot take place, when it overreaches what man can undergo or grasp, when it becomes, in a word, 'inhuman.'" We lose touch with the firm ground beneath our feet, we suffer nasty, quickening lurches out of the cozy, adoptable, and chuckleworthy, as in such idly gruesome, eerily Gogolesque stories as *Der Eispeter* ("Iced Peter"), which appears in the present collection as "Potted Peter."

In the record cold spell of 1812 (we are solemnly told) Peter goes skating in defiance of all warnings. He starts by tearing out the seat of his pants, frozen fast to the boulder he sits on, gets soaked in a water hole, but skates on till his stiffening clothes and spiky carapace of icicles weld him in place like a "frozen porcupine." He is discovered hours later, carried home amid stylized lamentations, and propped against the stove to thaw out. Presently, the Lord be praised, the melting ice begins to yield Peter's lineaments; but, tsk, tsk, the melting process continues steadily, the toffee oozes away with the wrapper, until the whole figure, still preserving a tenuous Petrine affinity in the masterly Buschian manner, becomes a puddle on the floor. This is decanted into a crock, of course, what else would occur to anyone?

> Yes—a crock, a twenty-liter,
> Serves for the preserve of Peter.
> Who, originally hard,
> Later turned as soft as lard.

We are then shown a cellar, bare of figures, featuring three crocks in startling close-up. The ones left and right are labeled "cheese" and "pickles"; the middle one, unpleasantly spotlighted and seemingly fastened at the top with special care to forestall spoilage while it awaits its turn, is labeled "Peter," with three crosses scratched beneath the name.

As the last great practitioner of the mock epic, a horrified gourmet of the grotesque, and the lone master of his private genre, the picture tale, Busch stands out as by far the most productive, successful, yet elusive and ultimately enigmatic humorist that Germany has produced. As for the poetic rank of light verse, and the quality of his in particular, one can hardly do better than to quote from A. A. Milne's remarks on the subject in *Year In, Year Out* (1952):

> Light Verse obeys Coleridge's definition of poetry, the best words in the best order; it demands Carlyle's definition of genius, transcendent capacity for taking pains; and it is the supreme exhibition of somebody's definition of art, the concealment of art. In the result it observes the most exact laws of rhythm and metre as if by a happy accident, and in a sort of nonchalant spirit of mockery at the real poets who do it on purpose. . . . It is a precise art which has only been taken seriously, and thus qualified as an art, in the nineteenth and twentieth centuries. It needs neither genealogical backing nor distinguished patronage to make it respectable. . . .

Boxwood and Canvas

Until well past the middle of Busch's thirty years as an active draftsman, his medium was the woodcut. By the mid-seventies, the centuries-old craft, associated with chapbook and broadsheet, devotional literature, and early block-printing, was at length technically outclassed as the prime disseminator of line drawing; first, gradually, by etching and engraving for book illustration and reproduction of paintings, later definitively by zinc plate and electrotype gravure. By that time the woodcut with its characteristic constraints, economies, and stark virtues had decisively set Busch's graphic style. The pictorial work of *Knopp II* and *III*, the first to be transferred from drawing directly to zinc plate (1876), is freer and airier, here and there more extenuated and daringly fugitive with finials and dots, than that of *Knopp I* just before. But there is really little in these or in later tales that in subtlety and targetry of line goes far beyond the capacity of the artist who for twenty years had himself transposed his sketches onto boxwood blocks and supervised, excoriated, and corrected the work of the "xylographer."

The craft and estate of the professional woodcut artisan, not necessarily himself a creative artist, is a datum of cultural history which, only a century from its passing, has perhaps been largely forgotten. Even Busch's persistent use of it until 1875 may strike one as something of an anachronism, since, among other pictorial printing techniques, lithography had been available for decades and might have lent itself quite well to his purposes. The explanation probably lies not merely in a sure artistic instinct, warning him against interrupting the slow but sure development of this "melody" part of his double instrumentation, and in a certain conservatism, evident also in his reluctance to authorize photomechanical modes of reproduction when the time came, but in the pull of a four-hundred-year-old European tradition with a peculiar simplicity and breadth of pictorial appeal.

The woodcut as a major art form, represented in Germany rather transiently but splendidly by Dürer and the elder Cranach, Burgkmair, Altdorfer, Beham, the younger Holbein, and many others, declined there in early modern times in favor of etching and engraving. The archaizing tendency of the Romantic age revived it and surrounded it with a somewhat artificial aura of retrospective idealization, as it did most aspects of the feudal order and its craft guilds. But the nostalgia for the imagined mystique of happy, ennobling handiwork on the part of intellectuals fearful of industrialization marked its de fac-

to demise as surely as, say, the state-sponsored recording and collecting of live oral tales and epics in early Soviet times marked—and possibly accelerated—the doom of folk literature in Russia. The first of the periodic post-romantic revivals of quasi-medieval craftsmanship—which punctuated the advance of modernization in the 1850s, the 1880s, around 1910, 1930, and 1960, with attendant antiquarian fads and drawing-room integral-lifery—was powerfully inspired and led by William Morris in England, Busch's close contemporary. But in Germany the tendency had already caused Biedermeier artists of idyllic-pastoral and historicizing tastes like Alfred Rethel, Adolf von Menzel, and Ludwig Richter to seize upon the woodcut again and make it the medium of meticulous pictorial chronicling (Menzel), revival of medieval motifs (Rethel), or rather saccharine tableaus of storytelling shepherds, pious children, happy countrymen at their age-old tasks, and soldiers decoratively dying for Old Fritz of Prussia. Crisper and more forward-looking uses, of course, were found for it at about the same time by French illustrators and satirists of genius like Grandville, Daumier, and Doré. It was Daumier who, unlike any other foreign graphic artist of his time, came to Busch's attention and clearly influenced some of his early drawing, as has been convincingly shown by Fritz Novotny.[4] Ludwig Richter became an acquaintance of Busch's during one of his sojourns in Bavaria, and there are in the latter's earlier output several quite Richteresque fairy-tale plates, illuminations for children's books, and the like. But the sentimentalization of old-world Germany was fundamentally alien to Busch's ruthless veracity: he knew far better than Richter did the actual nature of old-world village life, red in tooth and claw.

Busch, as we know from numerous hints to be found in his correspondence and between the lines of his autobiographic prose, suffered through most of his life from a sense of defeat over a certain faintheartedness which had stunted the painter in him. It was not fully hidden under that dour, self-deprecating resignation he had allowed to become second nature to him under Schopenhauer's influence. As a dutifully cowed product of his Protestant upbringing and a lifelong dweller in

[4]Fritz Novotny, *Wilhelm Busch als Zeichner und Maler* (Vienna: Anton Schroll, 1949).

Lutheran parsonages, he disguised his disappointment as a salutary awareness of limitations and defended it stubbornly against the attempted encouragement of lady friends and successful society painters like Lenbach and Kaulbach—themselves, by then, lionized producers of whiskered portraits and battle scenes, picturesquely ennobled by sovereigns and enshrined in German art histories—who admired and befriended him. The compulsion to paint was very strong in him; three separate times he set forth—with what fervor of resolve we may only guess from short diary entries and letters to intimates—to master and adapt to his thematic world the broad brushwork, bold manipulation of light and shade by way of planes rather than lines, the wondrous color harmonies and artless sensuality of the Flemish school.[5] Overawed, he failed, or so he thought, and tried to deny and renounce this yearning, fleeing into infirmities, hindrances, and distractions rather than summoning up the uncongenial impudence to persevere. It was then, it may be conjectured, that he threw himself back into the old art of the woodcut, with its long, homely, utilitarian artisan tradition, its affinity for the caustic and bizarre, and its proximity to workaday craftsmanship, which in his masochistic frame of mind must have appeared properly humble and sobering. It is hardly fanciful to detect a note of relief in his embracing a confining, familiar technique, combatting refractory materials and the imperfect skills of subordinates. It was an art, moreover, which to the curiously parochial purview of his compatriots seemed for sundry reasons—one doubtless being Dürer—even more "German" than did (and still do) most manifestations of European thought and civilization. The German version of the old saw, "*In der Beschränkung zeigt sich der Meister*" ("mastery manifests itself amid constraints") may well be considered the unspoken motto and alibi of Busch's conscious life as an artist at most times; only he would have preferred a phrase like "modest achievement" to "mastery."

This conclusion is rendered the more cogent by the fact that in the seventies the painter in Busch began to work his way to the surface once more and intermittently, but with a new ease and abandon, produced interesting work that belongs to the

[5]See the entry for 1851–52 in the Biographical Chronicle.

Wilhelm Busch, *Trüber Tag* (Dreary Day), late 1880s. With the kind permission of the Wilhelm-Busch-Gesellschaft, Hannover.

twentieth century. By then he no longer, it seems clear, felt forced to succeed in painting lest in his own estimation he should have failed altogether as an artist. The moment his national and European renown, earned solely by the picture tale, was so telling that it could no longer be quite argued away even by his own distrustful mind; when he had incontrovertibly become preeminent among the four Busch brothers, the famous uncle, the brilliant recluse of Wiedensahl, a hunted celebrity only too painfully subject to the flattery, the temptations, cooptions, and invasions of privacy which that estate is heir to; only then was "the heat off" Busch the painter: very little now rode on his proving himself in that field. It was then that he was able to hint in letters at the predatory old addiction. In a letter of late 1876 to Lenbach he speaks of seeking an "intermediate position" for himself as a painter. By this he meant two kinds of independence in accommodation: a situation of balance between his native sphere of bucolic genre miniatures and a naturalized status in the grander, plusher world of the painting metropoles; and an independent position be-

Wilhelm Busch, *Ländliche Prügelszene* (Peasants Quarreling), right side of a diptych, early 1870s. With the kind permission of the Wilhelm-Busch-Gesellschaft, Hannover.

liberate and defiant insufficiency, the congenital fragmentariness, as it were, of his efforts—was perhaps the outcome of perspicacity, not blundering. To the retrospective view of the present, it appears as a valid artistic reflection of a truth that was both epochal and individual: that painting had, for his generation, come to a dead end. Gerhart Ueding diagnoses fragmentariness as the necessary artistic principle of that time, arguing that:

> Busch utilized the fragment as an artistic possibility and engaged in a planned endeavor to perfect this form of expression. . . . his vision in this matter had just been sharpened, after all, by Schopenhauer's philosophy, which had taught him to comprehend the existence of things in the imagination as merely accidental, as a husk concealing what is essential, and hence in itself fragmentary like a shell without kernel. . . . Given this conviction, fragments and sketches cease to be mere evidence of subjective failure and perforce become independent forms of aesthetic expression which are alone capable of making the nature of the world manifest; at least in the sense of leaving it meaningfully blank. The fragment *signifies* the essence phenologically denied to all men and things. . . . his picture tales and pictorial episodes are fragmentary in that they seize upon single stations within a process of change, neglect entire chains of justification (why do Max and Moritz take such inadequate cover as to be instantly discovered by the farmer?), arrest what is momentary, allow tensions to arise between picture and text and the author's arbitrary whims to show through the fabric throughout. The very techniques of Busch the draughtsman and graphic artist themselves everywhere betray his choice of expressive fragmentation.[6]

The more Busch freed himself from any trace of envy of the would-be painter princes and renaissance men, Makart and Lenbach at Munich and Kaulbach at Vienna, the more boldly fragmentary his oil sketches became. All Flemish realism, all discernible psychological, symbolic, or historical "content" are thrown to the winds, plot and representation are reduced to pure gestation and randomly arrested movement. "Those glimpses caught of broad plains, those tree-ringed forest clearings as well as harvest scenes and human subjects . . . exist entirely in terms of an excited, rapidly flowing . . . brush script which allows any individual forms (even where it is really

tween his own blend of naturalism with advanced impressionist techniques and the overripe neoromanticism in painting which was sweeping the academies of Europe.

This should probably not be taken to mean that the Gordian knot which the lures and quandaries of painting presented to Busch's psyche was now cut, but rather that the paralysis of personal failure was ended. He had gained the necessary distance between himself and the predicament of the art in the nineteenth century generally to understand that the blind alley was not his but the epoch's. The "failure"—that de-

[6]Gert Ueding, *Wilhelm Busch: Das 19. Jahrhundert en miniature.* (Frankfurt a/M: Insel Verlag, 1977), pp. 361 ff.

"close-ups" which are involved) no time whatever to form and crystallize."[7]

The Quotable Uncle Doctor

Busch has added a great store of saw-edged two-liners to the domestic medicine chest of the educated: sham-didactic maxims, lead nuggets of loaded homiletics, dressing-gowned or togaed apothegms in the folds of which a chill agnostic contempt for placebos kicks like a pig in a sack. In the tidy preserves of German civilization and among those long intimate with it, those pat lines delivering the wide-eyed ferocity of a "horrid" child, often in a child's telescoped or short-circuited grammar, have for a century assisted the needy perhaps more than Goethe's mellower dicta or the sublime-turned-comic of some of Schiller's solemnities. If nothing else is remembered about the brilliant *Knopp* trilogy of a superannuated bachelor's sowing, reaping, and withering, it is an observation one would back for recognition against anything but one or two of the Commandments: *Vater werden ist nicht schwer*; *Vater sein dagegen sehr*; which may be approximated, without comparable bite to be sure, by "To become a father's rather / Fun compared with being father," or, as in our text, "Being father is a thing / Harder far than fathering." The inroads of age for a moment lose their pathos, and junk sculpture some of its dispiriting weight on the soul, when one reminds oneself that *Des Lebens Freuden sind vergänglich*; / *Das Hühnerauge bleibt empfänglich*: "Life's joy and zest are soon outworn; / What stays responsive is a corn"; or when one muses over the insidious line from *Dove* which tries, and no doubt always fails, to discourage talentless yearners for "artistic expression": *Er fühlt, er muss, und also kann es*; "He feels he must, and therefore can." From *Helen*, as from some forebear of a Bellow or Malamud character, comes *Es ist ein Satz von alters her*: / *Wer Sorgen hat, hat auch Likör*; "From ancient times it has been true: / He who takes licks, takes liquor, too." *Painter Squirtle* contributes, to say the least, the opening lines, *Das Reden tut dem Menschen gut*, / *Wenn man es nämlich selber tut*; "Much

talking never wearies us, / Unless it's someone else who does"; perhaps also the shrewd observation on profile sketches by children, much quoted as a deterrent by teachers in the days when drawing was still taught: *Zwei Augen aber fehlen nie*, / *Denn die*, das weiss er, *haben sie*; "Two eyes, though, always are in view; / *He knows* that people come with two." From *Fips*, besides the disarming remark about the sartorial simplicity of African life, "one is black, and that is that," it is probably the neuroelectric shock of fractured syntax which makes this other tag memorable: *Es lebte dort ein schwarzer Mann*, / *Der Affen fing und briet sie dann*; "There dwelt those parts a dusky man / Caught monkeys for his frying pan." At least as famous are these moral hangover distillates from *Helen* and elsewhere: *Das Gute, dieser Satz steht fest*, / *Ist stets das Böse, das man lässt*; "Our good, let no one question this, / Is but the bad we give a miss"; and *Enthaltsamkeit ist das Vergnügen* / *An Dingen, welche wir nicht kriegen*; "Self-abnegation is believing / In the delight of not receiving."

A good many tags and tag-ends are not consciously quoted, but have permanently enriched the colloquial language with proverbial sayings and exclamations (anticipating, but likely to outlast, various comic-strip noises and comedians' by-lines in American), which are not always traceable any longer by their users. *Erleichtert fliegt das Vöglein weg*—"Relieved, the little bird takes wing" from *Bählamm/Dove* provides a handy comment, scatological, ribald, or innocent. The gloating war cry *Klickradoms von Medici!* (from the cat chase in *Helen*) springs to the lips, baffling the uninitiated, when something fragile and possibly pretentious (preferably not belonging to oneself) falls into noisy ruin. *Autsch, nun ist ja offenbar* / *Alles wieder wie es war*, "All is now, alas! once more / As it used to be before" mourns patient endeavor totally undone, as when a tire toilsomely pumped up by hand is next seen flat again. The stark, pseudo-biblical phrase *angefüllt mit dem was übel*, "fullcharged with that which is noisome," from *Knopp I*, ninth episode, serves, for example, as a warning about a dubious piece of pastry, or a bad review passed on to an author by a friend. Similarly, Debischitz's cool, nicely enjambed diagnosis (*Knopp I*) *Dieses aber scheint mir ein* / *Neugebor'ner Spatz zu sein*, "This, in turn, I could have sworn, / Is a sparrow,

[7]H. W. Petzet, "Wilhelm Busch als Maler," in the 1964–65 *Wilhelm Busch Jahrbuch* (Hannover: Wilhelm-Busch-Gesellschaft), p. 49.

newly born," is applied to the discovery of an amorphous foreign body in a drain, or an unwanted organ in a Christmas turkey. And *Aber siehe, es gelingt / Schneller als ihm nötig dünkt*, from *Eight Sheets*—"But behold! one has succeeded / More abruptly than was needed"—fits any of the family of upsets akin to that of the topmost stair that is not there.

Verse and Sketch in Counterpoint

There is no ready English equivalent for the name which Busch gave to the hybrid genre he developed in the seventies. It is not *Bildgeschichte*, which might suggest "image tale" or "picture history," a symbolic story or the history of a painting; nor *Geschichte mit Bildern*, an illustrated tale. It is *Bildergeschichte*, a compound which leaves open or merges the semantic options of a tale of, in, or with pictures. For this, neither a "tale of pictures" nor a "pictorial narrative" will quite do. "Picture tale," first member in the singular, will be handy enough in English; and the ready association with "picture book," as with *Bilderbuch* in German, is quite acceptable. This is not to say that the genre exists in English. Even in German it had not quite evolved from a mixed ancestry before Busch, and it was to perish by 1888, twenty years before its master's death.

Busch's style as a draftsman has influenced cartoonists, of course, and some graphic artists of rank, particularly Alfred Kubin and Max Slevogt. The Buschian form and vein of light verse, leaving the graphic partner aside, produced myriads of humbler imitators. It may in fact have ingested, coopted, or stifled much subsequent talent in this field, leaving only Christian Morgenstern, and possibly Joachim Ringelnatz, to play an independent role. A bastard descendant, the slogan in rhymed tetrameter couplets, has infested German advertising ever since Busch. But the fully hybridized mode of verse-and-sketch was clearly far too exacting to have permitted any "school" to form. A dual gift of this rank, let alone the blithely mordant mind which attends to the blending and mutual goading of the two voices, could hardly have been expected to arise again short of a miracle, even if the cultural moment for this art form had not clearly elapsed (we may assert in retrospect) by the end of the nineteenth century.

In Busch's post-1870 narratives, the graphic and the verbal element are binary rather than dual. The media operate separately, in an arguable, commonsensical way, yet they are functionally fused over the long stretches of each tale, whether their statements or comments in the short run coincide or diverge. This binary voice, which makes Busch's picture tale the polyphonic and often equivocal vehicle it is, may be thought to reflect a given datum of his psychic condition. It is both duet and duel, and, to a degree, both source and premier device of the complex comedy of sympathetic guilt and hyperbolic retribution through which the artist's existential conflict finds expression and relief.

The graphic and the verbal element must be distinct, i.e., neither may be taken merely as illustration or caption, respectively, of the other, for they belong to different idioms of art and are each continuous, though elliptic by themselves. The subtler, and essential, function of either, nevertheless, is to be one of a pair of live wires between which comic-grotesque discharges occur. Picture and verse exist in mutual tension, they contrapuntally confront and mock, rather than complement one another. For the pithiest effects, the voices must blend, clash, or alternate in a changeful part song, each alone being incapable of as powerful an ambiguity or as poignant an irony as the two in counterpoint. Thus (to attempt an analogy) in the best of the *Lieder*, a verbal work of art with a potent and often intricate esthetic of its own is not "set to music": it is remade like a masterly verse translation into another language and emerges enriched by an additional dimension.

The ironic tension created by one-sided reticences or by contradictions, cunning or blatant, between narrative and gestural messages is the hallmark of the mature Busch. A comparison of the work of the seventies with *Potted Peter* or *Max und Moritz* (crudely powerful and balladesque, but of course already mock-naive in the manner of the recited but no longer painted north-German morality tales of around 1800) reveals that it is the source of far defter, sparer comedy than the follies of bucolic or bourgeois humanity as such, or the pratfalls prepared by the spite of the inanimate—that apparent grand conspiracy of malign objects against nervous or nonchalant man. By Germans, incidentally, the discovery of this conspiracy—well-known to Sterne, Aristophanes, and probably Prakrit comedy in India, is invariably credited to one Friedrich Theodor Vischer's dreary sketch of a philistine monomaniac, *Auch Einer: Eine Reisebekanntschaft* (1879), whose hero is a country cousin to the antiheroes of *Notes from Underground* and *The Kreutzer Sonata*, as self-engrossed as the former and as humorless as the latter.

What makes, for example, the honeymoon at Heidelberg in *Helen* a sardonic little essay on the marriage of convenience rather than merely felicitous graphic slapstick is, for one thing, the dour, sullen heave of Schmuck's toiling backside up the steep castle slope, accompanied by the comment *Wie lieblich wandelt man zu zwei'n / Das Schloss hinauf im Sonnenschein* ("How blithely two ascend as one / The Schlossberg in the noonday sun"); for another, Schmuck's ruthless dragging of a backward-sloping, romantically ruin-gazing Helen into the more congenial alcoholic shades of the Great Tun of Heidelberg: a scene which snidely belies the urbane neutrality of the *Auch* in the line "*Another* thing one likes to see is the Great Tun . . ."; for a third, similar touch, the obvious fatigue and mutual pique conveyed by the fine snapshot of the honeymooners slumped in opposite corners of the cab after such discordant sightseeing; accentuated by the notice-nothing, tour-guide tone of the jaunty phrase *Alsbald so sitzt man froh im Wagen . . .* ("Presently the cheerful tourists sit in the coach . . ."). One would not wish to labor the point, but for the pleasure of recalling, say, the determined man-of-the-world air of unconcern with which both Knopp and the subscribed couplet ignore the blatant goings-on of his philandering friend Mücke (Knaeppi) in the "cozy restaurant"; or the if-I-don't-look-it'll-go-away expression (achieved by four minute lines) on the dairywife's face in "A Chilly Affair" (*Eight Sheets in the Wind*) when she notices the crystalized Master Tweel; while the text blandly records: *Frau Pieter kommt, die Millichfrau* ("Frau Pieter comes, the milk-wife").

The damning resemblance between Cousin Franz and Helen's newborn twins which puzzles the young reader as he watches him congratulate Schmuck on the arrival of "two friendly little colleagues" is only the most reckless example, on a scale of shocks from faint hint to bald scandal, of the drawing pen's giving some of the show away. It may intrude a graceless Alfred E. Newman grin; it may scribble a smooth outrage

between lines where the verbal narrator leaves a sanctimonious blank and tiptoes on with a bogus nil nisi bonum air; it may merely plant an inconclusive suggestion of something more, or other, than meets the reading eye. Among the coarser instances of this graphic leering in *Helen* are the dot and tiny squiggles which alone disclose Helen's grief at her porcine mate's flopping into bed with no attempt at nuptial attentions; and later, the equivocal piety conjured into Cousin Franz's unsubtle features as Helen walks in his company ("all alone, so to speak") to the fertility shrine of (a verbal sneer here) "Chosemont de Bon Secours."

At other times the graphic extras are not so much cynical "oh, yeah's," slanderous contradictions, or suspect shadows smuggled into the story line as they are gratuitous comments which deepen the moral perspective or open social vistas denied elsewhere. Here belongs the insolent familiarity on the waiter's face when Helen has to instruct him to ignore her besotted bridegroom's further orders; the palpably drawn, yet (even here) ironized misery of cripples and ragamuffins at the distribution of Helen's bath wine to the lower orders; perhaps the episode where the hardbitten little *Ostjude*, Schmulchen, of whom more below, (with "Jewish cunning"?) improvises an arresting cynomorphic pose to deter further canine attack. For although verbal and graphic narration here speak in unison, and the popular ethnic stereotype is played up to, it is deliberately and farcically overdone, as argued elsewhere. Among other fine "throwaways" is the vignette of maidenly self-effacement by Mrs. Fittig, who has just rid her lap of its grotesque burden and stands averted as Schmulchen exhibits the "ruination" the dogs have dealt him "underneath"; and in *Dove* one recalls the wonderful primness displayed by the children (all but the smallest, who is not yet trained to Protestant inhibitions) as their parents blatantly embrace on the platform.

When one of the twin narrators is fastidiously elliptic or silent, the other may be explicit and earthy; when one waxes philosophical, elegiac, or lyrical, it is often the signal for the other to turn pat and mundane; when one takes a genial, debonair, all's-well-with-the-world tone, the other stands ready with the banana peel or the split in the trouser seam. Their respective roles, though, do not seem to be fully reversible. It is the verbal agent which typically acts Don Quixote's or Mr.

Micawber's part, the graphic one which tends to play Sancho or Mr. Dick in his forthright moments. The long wordless sequence of sozzled Knopp's trying to light matches in the cellar is certainly pure burlesque, the quintessential struggle with petty demons by Sancho Panza, not the don. But when, conversely, the graphic narrator is silently waiting in the wings, as in the long introductions to the great tales, it becomes plain that all such comparisons are lame. Even the don's flowers of rhetoric then show the worm at their roots or are ribaldly exposed as culled from the kitchen garden. Fine verbal ascents sadly crash through missing stairs, the tone is one of mock-heroism, an idealism which collapses in obsequious bows to the philistine to caricature itself; emotion which hastens into farce for fear of rebuff and ridicule. The noble afflatus even, with no Sancho Panza to puncture it, echoes as the cracked voice of a Quixote who has been bruised too much, invites failure in order to enlist himself among the mockers rather than the mocked, and pathetically distorts its ideals like a Dostoevskian buffoon.

The Mar-Peace and His Destruction

The "mar-peace" or troublemaker, his challenge to law and order, and his destruction are a persistent topic of Busch's in the picture tale and picture anecdote; a second one, closely related to the first, is aspiration and fiasco. The deep ambiguity of his treatment of the first holds the key to his split personality and an explanation of the extraordinary power of some of his humble and bathetic tales: he functions as the instigator of small-scale nihilistic pranks by the unruly, but in the summarizing and (however parodically) moralizing verbal frames to each story rallies to endorse, if only with a histrionic shrug or a ruefully wagging forefinger, the "slave morality" which hugs its chains and relishes the annihilation of rebels. The mental and moral labor of ascertaining and judging the author's stand and ostensible lesson is a vital part of that cooperation in the making of the literary work which here as elsewhere determines the aesthetic experience. His "paper theater," as he often called it, is frequently a rustic stage where his *Phantasiehansel*, his "fancyjohnnies," act out the crime and punishment of original sin, the natural cussedness and cussed naturalness of the defier of authority. "Troublemaker" here

has connotations and implications precisely similar to those we are familiar with in the classical usage of this term by such as town fathers, sheriffs, labor bosses, and employers. The mar-peace, in the form of the dangerously vital, untrained, "unacculturated" child, animal, or rebel, by his enviably uninhibited actions—and, in an important sense, his mere existence—challenges and ridicules the established order and the morality precariously constructed to sanctify and uphold it. Political quietism, social docility, sexual repression, tidiness of thought and manner are the chief elements of a way of life which, after the libertarian deliria and cautionary horrors of the French revolution, commended itself in Restoration Europe, particularly in Germany, as the proper human condition. The precariousness of this order, its ethical dubiety, and the subconscious jealousy felt by many of its never-quite-conditioned members for the audacious challenger produced (then as in the sixties of our century) the characteristic righteous hatred of the latter, and the furious overreaction which tries to smash what it cannot tame and assimilate. Gerhart Ueding's study, noted in the Bibliography, directs the most searching gaze to date at the cultural matrix of the Busch phenomenon. Ueding traces the changing European image of the child from Rousseau's *Emile* and golden-age innocence to the unfathomed, slightly uncanny, shockingly precocious, and even, at length, "congenitally wicked" young savage who intrigued the Romantics and haunted the era and setting (close to early Victorian in period and flavor) which may be called the Protestant Prussian Biedermeier. The exemplars by which these little demons were to be exorcised or transformed were children as presented (surely more wishfully or wistfully than hypocritically) by family journals, primers, and anthologies of poesy: well-groomed groups of dreamy-eyed little charmers in pastoral tableaus, framed in blossoming foliage against backgrounds of spinning grannies and contented ruminants. Ueding presents a highly original, unflinching analysis, which suggests corollaries for German political history and social psychology far broader than his immediate subject. It appeared, in fact, threatening enough to cherished shibboleths for conservative reviewers to attempt to shrug him off as a doctrinaire Marxist and Freudian.

A fine distillate of mid-nineteenth-century idées reçues on the nature of "the child" and the essence of pedagogy is provided, with a characteristic wry ambiguity in the author's tone, by the celebrated "progressive education" chapter in the picture tale *Plisch und Plum* (not included in this anthology). Thanks to a triumph of mutual ironization of picture and text, the matter has probably nowhere else been as succinctly and mordantly stated. On the morning after a scene of bedlam, in which the boys mingle and vie with their close canine counterparts in outrages offered each other and the domestic comity, at last drawing even the parents into a painful forfeit of decorum, the pups find themselves on foot-long chains, and the boys are committed to a private tutor:

Here sit Plisch and Plum, dismay
In their hearts, and growl away.

Chains, extremely short ones, leave
Little scope for joie de vivre.

Fittig, too, is woebegone.
"This," he groans, "must not go on.
Virtue wants encouraging!
(Vice is a spontaneous thing)."
Hence these scholars sitting there
In Preceptor Willow's care;
Who, all kindliness, sees fit
To explain his mind; to wit:

"Beloved pupils, I am delighted
To welcome you here, resolved (and invited)
Through ears that hearken and eyes that see
To fasten all faculties firmly on me.—
Let us read, then, and write; let us strive as we're able
To master the multiplication table;
It is by virtue of thus having striven
That men win honor and earn a living.
Yet—secondly—where would the profit be
Without breeding, good manners, and courtesy?
For one who addresses his neighbour ill
Reaps chiefly unpleasantness, not goodwill.
Thus, in conclusion (for this is my way),
I urge, and entreat, and solicit you: pray,

Have you determined, deep down in the heart,
To take my instruction in gracious part?
If so, please look up and join hands with me,
And say: "Aye, Master Willow, thus shall it be!"

Paul and Peter burst with joy:
(Oh, is that your way, old boy?)

They evince no wish to please,
Snorting merely rude tee-hees.
Willow, whistling softly then,
Mildly takes the floor again:
"Since you are minded, to my chagrin,
To harden your hearts and persist in sin,
I for my part am persuaded I should
Reverse you across this lectern of wood
And utilize your receptive position
In an effort to soften your hard condition."

Like a sabre from its sheath,
He has whipped from underneath
His surtout the slender, slick,
Lissom, limber willow stick,

Seizes Paul's and Peter's necks
Jointly by their jackets' slacks,

Grips the loose and whips the trim
Till it seems enough to him.
This done, he resumes with a jovial brow:
"My gay little charges, how say you now?

Does my reasoning strike you as sweet and true?"
"Yes! Yes! Master Willow!" their answers flew.

Such is Master Willow's bent.
That it works is evident.
People marveled, many said:

"Paul and Peter—how well-bred!"
Swiftly, too, for Plisch and Plum
Education time has come,
The encouragement of wisdom

By the Willow Training System.

Soon the two delight those parts
By their mastery of arts;
And—the simple justice of it!
The result of art is profit . . .

This World Is an Error, and the Joke Is on Us

The sensation of a missing topmost stair has a wider and deeper significance to Busch's feeling about life and men than accords with a mere wariness of pratfalls or even "snafu" raised to an axiom: if anything has a chance to go wrong it will. Underlying the sloppy *Gemütlichkeit* of his milieus and the stagnant reign of lowly common sense in them—seemingly so stable as to cry out for his farcical jolts—there lurks a sense of the profound unreliability of all that appears benevolent, secure, and reassuring. Placid Aunt Nolte, ludicrous and dimwitted, granted, but surely kind, goodnatured, and cozy (the child's wishful or willful view is taken here, as throughout the early chapters of *Helen*), turns into a hissing Xanthippe at night on minor provocation. Knopp, a middle-aged romantic petit-bourgeois with a rentier's tastes, flabby of body and soul but (this is part of the point) no worse than most, suddenly stares at us full-face as a gorging, swilling pig. "Good" Uncle Fritz in *Max und Moritz*, trotted out as deserving of the automatic courteous deference youth owes to maturity, goes berserk over some june bugs and "tramples and smashes all to death." Children prey on animals and each other, and adults on children, even as nature and malignant objects lie in ambush for all; *denn der Mensch als Kreatur / Hat von Rücksicht keine Spur*: "Love of kind, by nature's plan, / Is no part of basic man." Matrimony, as often as not, is internecine war underneath or beside smug and unpleasantly sultry domesticity. Salvation is rendered suspect as too expedient an evasion of our ill deserts, life after death a dubious option, if available, by the kind of company one must expect in heaven. The following is a letter of December 1880, from Busch to Hermann Levi, translated in full except for the closing sentences. With its Manichean doubts, its staccato leaps of logic and abstruse style, it recalls Busch's prose fantasy, *Edward's Dream*. It is hardly less crotchety, in the Hoffmannesque manner, but more revealing than most of the personal testimony which Busch vouchsafes us:

Dear Levi!

The cold winter wind is rushing the rain through the rustling trees. I still walk along the river, smoking, Schopenhauer in one pocket, Darwin in the other, on the putative way to the sea where, perhaps, lies the ship which sails, as they say, to the Isles of the

Blest. "The saints are already there," says Schopenhauer. But since the Will is indivisible, they would have had to take me along, willy-nilly, and I should already be "where I am not" [the allusion is to the Schubert lied's eponymous *Wanderer*, whose fruitless quest for happiness is finally answered, in a "ghostly whisper": "happiness is where you are not"]. Darwin says: "There is an evolution"; let us assume, from minus x by way of zero to plus x. Man would then be sitting at No. 0, while the ape would be scampering somewhere near -1. The progress made from -1 to 0 is evident: the recognition is dawning that this world is an error. We already talk of death and salvation, very prettily and edifyingly; then we go off to the pub, to the theater, to our sweethearts, or stay at home as good householders and cuddle with our wives. The meat we need is supplied by the butcher. We also make laws, found churches, railways, hospitals, orphanages, and more of the sort.—Well and good!—Meanwhile all that had been at zero dies off and is absorbed by $+1$, where it immediately, in the light of new intellects, steps into the old mixed inheritance as its own heir. There was progress up to zero. Good optimists that we are, we hope of course that it will go on like this. The *energy of depth*; the *drive towards variation*, perform their part too.—In short, $+1$ is brighter and better than 0.—On with it.—Here we are, already at $+10,000,000$. A lot of head, little body. No more canines, no more cartilege whorls in the outer ear. Food: vegetable. Procreation: as hitherto. The fat head still cannot force the skinny body into reason.—Onward!—Plus ten billion. Food: air. Procreation: by phlegmatic autogenesis. The man of No. 0 has long been extinct and out of mind.—The end!—Plus x. Almost all head. Bare residue of Will. Procreation: none. The intellects, floating about bubble-fashion, thoroughly see through everything. That speck of Will is easily negated, and all sound dies away, as we musicians are wont to say, in a reconciling chord.—Alas, alas! He who has ever seen the flashing eye of energetic bestiality is stealthily assailed by the dread intuition that a single outlandish scoundrel on Uranus might arrest salvation, that a single devil might be stronger than a whole heaven full of saints. Are the Christians right? Do the incorrigibles go to hell in the end? Can the individual raise a loan in the amount of his share in the collectively contracted debt, put the money on the table, and say: Good-bye, forever!?

Yonder, on the other bank of the river, stands Saint Augustine. He nods to me earnestly: here lies the boat of faith; mercy is the ferryman; he who calls insistently is brought across.—But I cannot call; my soul is hoarse; I have a metaphysical cold. . . .

THE PICTURE TALES

Potted Peter

When winter came so hard and cruel
In eighteen twelve, with dearth of fuel,

The prudent stayed indoors, and glad to;
But Pete went skating (he just had to).

Outside—unheard of! from the freeze
Dead crows were falling from the trees.

"Don't try it, Pete, no good today!"
His uncle Keeper bids him stay.

Hard by the roadside there appears
A rabbit grounded by the ears.

1864

Bad Peter shrugs a merry shoulder
and dons his skates upon a boulder.

But when he rises to his feet
The stone is welded to his seat.

Worn is the cloth and great the need,
The center gives and Pete is freed.

There, now! he skates (I could have told
    him)
Into a place which cannot hold him.

Quite wet, he clambers from the slough;
The cloth cap must be written off.

Though rather little yet, there grows
An icicle along his nose.

The cone is soon as large as life
And sharper than a butcher knife.

The crystals cluster and advance;
The jagged spike becomes a lance.

"A frozen porcupine, I swear,"
The passing viewer might declare.

At home they eye the clock in fear:
"Dear us! why isn't Peter here?"

Then Uncle calls as they are waiting:
"The good-for-nothing's out there,
    skating!"

With timber axe and silent woe
They look for Peter in the snow.

Here they detect with fear and loathing
A frozen piece of Peter's clothing.

But how much greater grief they knew
When the remainder came in view!

They haul him off by head and heels;
The father weeps, the tear congeals.

They gently propped him up and strove
To thaw him out against the stove.

Hurray! forgotten all chagrin—
The water runs, the crust grows thin.

But then, how singular and cruel!
The whole young chap dissolves to gruel.

Into a crock they sadly scoop
This half-familiar Peter soup.

Ah, yes! this pipkin is allotted
To Frozen Peter, duly potted.

Who, originally hard,
Later turned as soft as lard.

Max and Moritz

1865

Preface

Ah, the wickedness one sees
Or is told of such as these,
Namely Max and Moritz; there!
Look at the disgraceful pair!

Who, so far from gladly reaching
For the boons of moral teaching,
Chose those very rules to flout
And in secret laugh about.—
But designs of malefaction
Find them keen on instant action!
Teasing folk, tormenting beasts,
Stealing fruit for lawless feasts
Are more fun, as one can tell,
And less troublesome as well,
Than to sit through class or sermon,
Never fidgeting or squirming.—
Looking at the sequel, though:
Woe, I say, and double woe!!—
How it all at last came out
Chills the heart to think about.
That's why all the tricks they played
Are retold here and portrayed.

First Trick

Many women labor hard
Caring for a chicken yard.
Firstly, for the eggs supplied
By the worthy fowl inside.
Secondly, because a hen
Means fried chicken now and then.
Third, because their feather fluff
Is of value, too, to stuff
Squabs or pillows for one's head
(No one liking drafts in bed).—

Take Frau Bolte, here, a granny
Hating drafts as much as any.

In her yard three chickens dwell
And a lordly cock as well.—
With this state of things, what ought
One to do? the rascals thought.—
Why not get a heel of bread
(Carried out as soon as said),

Cut four equal pieces, quick,
Each a little finger thick;
These one joins with sewing thread
Length- and crosswise (one per head)
And lays out in hopes of fun

In the widow's chicken run.—
Granny's rooster at the sight
Starts to crow with all his might:

Cock-a-doodle-doo! A crumb!!
Pitter, patter, here they come.

Hens and rooster, when in reach,
Peck and swallow one bit each.

But when sense resumes its sway,
None can rightly get away.

Right and left and rear and fore,
They conduct a tug of war,

Flutter up into the air,
What a desperate affair!

Gracious me, all tangled now
And suspended from a bough!—
Their laments grow keen and keener,
And their gullets lean and leaner;

One last egg is laid apiece,
Then comes death and brings release.—

Widow Bolte from her bed
Hears the goings-on with dread.

She steps out in nameless fright
Oh, the horror of the sight!

"Flow, my tears, then, scoring, burning,
All my comfort, hope, and yearning,
All I dreamt might come to be
Dangles from this apple tree!"

Sorrow-stricken, bowed by gloom,
She has reached the place of doom,
Cuts the victims off their strings,
Lest they hang there, slack of wings,

And, despair in gait and mien,
Bears the tragic burden in.—

And was this the last trick? Wrong!
For the second won't be long.

Second Trick

As the widow on the morrow
Was reviving from her sorrow
She reflected, still distraught,
That a fine and fitting thought
Was that they (so young in years
Ravished from this vale of tears)
Should in solemn, silent pride
Be ingested, nicely fried.—
True, it brought her fresh despair
Just to see them, limp and bare,
Lie in state upon the hearth,
Who before that day of wrath,
Full of life and scratching hard,
Used to strut in walk and yard!—

Ah, once more she has to cry,
While her Spitz, bemused, stands by.—

Max and Moritz caught the scent.
"Up the roof!" their thinking went.

Through the chimney, gay and reckless,
They can see them, plump and neckless,

Browning nicely in their batter,
Grace the frying pan and spatter.—
The bereft just then repairs
To her scullery downstairs

With a ladle to scoop out
Just a dab of sauerkraut,
Which she has a passion for
When it is warmed up once more.—

Up above the fireplace
Other plans mature apace.

Max would hardly overlook
Bringing fishing rod and hook.—

Allez-oop-da! Nice and soft,
Chicken one is borne aloft.
Presto! number two and whee!
Swiftly rising, number three.
Now for number four, the last:
Easy—there! we have it fast!—
Spitz astonished, watched them soar
Bow-wow-wowing more and more.

But already thieves and prey
Have decamped and got away.—

How contentment will be shattered!
Widow B., returning, scattered
Sauerkraut and stood as rooted
When she saw the skillet looted.

Every single chicken gone!
Spitz it was she turned upon.

"Oh! Just wait, you wicked cur!!
I will have your sinful fur!!!"

And she dusted Spitz's wig
With the ladle, hard and big;
Loudly sounded his lament
As he pleaded innocent.—

Max and Moritz, though, are resting
In a shady grove, digesting.
Of the whole delicious theft
But two single legs are left.

And was this their last trick? Wrong!
For the third comes right along.

Third Trick

All the village, willy-nilly,
Knew the name of Tailor Billy.

Weekday jackets, Sunday coats,
Tapered trousers, redingotes,
Waistcoats bordered with galloons,
Woolly greatcoats, pantaloons—

Any garment, tight or loose,
Billy knew how to produce.—
Were it only darning, patching,
Shortening, perhaps, or stretching,
Or a pocket wrongly angling,
Trouser button lost or dangling—
What or where the flaw might be,
Fore or aft, to wind or lee,
He removes or remedies,
For he's pledged his life to these.—
Hence all people of the place
Show this man a pleasant face.—
Only Max and Moritz plot
How to aggravate his lot.—

Past his dwelling, one must know,
Rushing, roaring waters flow,

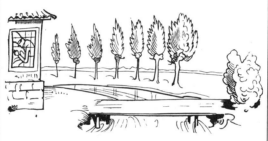

With a bridge of planks to guide
People to the other side.

Max and Moritz, full of spite,
Saw with mischievous delight
Reeker-rawker, heartless prank,
At the plank from bank to bank.

When the pitfall is prepared,
Loud and jeering shouts are heard:

"Bah! Come out here! Tattercoat!
Tailor, Tailor Billy-Goat!"
Almost any kind of jest
He could stand and not protest.
But when such a taunt was yelled
His immortal soul rebelled.

In one swoop he cleared the stoop,
Ell in hand: Again a whoop
Of protracted bleating smote
On his ear, and "Billy-Goat!"

He is crossing at a dash;
No! A crash, and then a splash!

Gleeful bleats and whoops, a snort—
Plop! We are a tailor short.

At this crisis of the piece
There approach a brace of geese.
Billy at his dying gasp
Seizes them with viselike clasp,

And is fluttered back to land
Shrieking goose in either hand.

What with all the stress of this,
One's physique may go amiss.

In Herr Billy's case the frolic
Netted him a painful colic.

Meet Frau Billy at her best:
For a heated iron pressed
To the belly with a will
Soon repairs the raging ill.—

Hear them up and down the street:
Billy's back upon his feet!

And was this their last trick? Wrong!
For the fourth comes right along.

Fourth Trick

From on high it is ordained
That the human mind be trained.—
Not alone the ABCs
Elevate it by degrees;
Nor does writing competence
By itself make men of sense;
Nor will 'rithmetic in season
Satisfy aspiring reason:
Moral precepts, too, are needed—
To be heard with zeal and heeded.—

Teachers see this wisely done.
Master Lampel here is one.—

Master Lampel's gentle powers
Failed with rascals such as ours;
For the evilly inclined
Pay preceptors little mind.—

Lampel, now, this worthy teacher,
Loved to smoke his pipe—a creature
Comfort which, it may be said,
Once the day's hard load is shed,
No fair-minded person can
Hold against a dear old man.—

Max and Moritz, sly as ever,
Try to think of something clever:
How to play the man a hoax
Through the meerschaum which he
    smokes.—

Once, when Sunday morning came
(Seeing him, by duty's claim,
Hard beneath the holy ceiling,
Play the organ with much feeling),
Max and Moritz tippytoed
Up into his snug abode
Where the pipe was wont to stand;
Max has seized it in his hand,

While it falls to Moritz's task
From the blasting-powder flask
To dispense a goodly gob
And to lodge it in the knob.
Out and home then at a run!
Service must be nearly done.—

Calmly, with a gentle jolt,
Lampel shot the sacred bolt,

Toils of office well discharged,
And, with key and music, barged

Off to the domestic haven,
Driven by a joyful craving

And with decorous dispatch
Stuffed his pipe and lit the match.

"Ah! to be content," he sighs,
"Is the best of earthly joys!"—

Krroom! explodes the meerschaum head
With a crash to wake the dead.
Water glass and coffeepot,
Ink, tobacco box, the lot,
Table, stove, and chair of oak,
All goes up in flash and smoke.—

Lifting fumes show him prostrated
But, thank God, still animated
By the priceless godly spark—
Though much balder now, and dark;

Hands, facade, and apertures
Are quite like a blackamoor's,
And the hair's precarious hull
Burnt away unto the skull.—

Who is now to foster youth
And diffuse scholastic truth?
Who devote such gifts as his
To his sundry offices?
How shall Teacher have a puff
With his pipe not up to snuff?—

All in course of time is mended;
But the pipe's career is ended.

And was this their last trick? Wrong!
For the fifth comes right along.

Fifth Trick

He who in his native sphere
Has an uncle living near
Must be modest and polite
To be pleasing in his sight.—
Greet him with "Good day to you!
Is there something I can do?"
Bring him journal, pipe, and spill,
And such other wants fulfill
As when, say, some twinge or twitch
In his back should pinch or itch,
Or an insect make him nervous—
Always glad to be of service.—
Or if after snuffing gently
Uncle sneezes violently,
One cries: "Bless you, Uncle dear!
May it bring long life and cheer!"—
If he enters halt of limb:
Having pulled the boots off him,
One brings slippers, gown, and lid,
Lest he shiver, God forbid.—
In a word, one tries to ease
His existence and to please.—

Max and Moritz for their part
Do not take these rules to heart.
Uncle Fritz—the coarse offense
They commit at his expense!—

Everybody knows the May
Beetle and its crawly way.
In their hundreds they will bumble
In the trees and buzz and tumble.

Max and Moritz's stratagem
Calls for quite a lot of them.

They have brought two bags of paper,
Also needed for their caper.

These they bear with catlike tread
And insert in Uncle's bed,

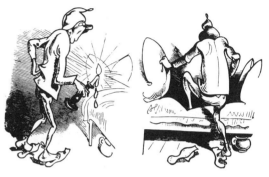

Whither he will soon repair
In his tasseled slumberwear.

In he climbs and soon is deep
In the eiderdown, asleep.

Beetles climb the featherbed
In a line for Uncle's head.

One has reached the gap and goes
Straight across to Uncle's nose.

"Fooh!" he cries, "What's up here? Ugh!"
In his hand a monster bug.

Uncle, horrified at that,
Whips out like a scalded cat.

Eek! still other beetles find
Spots above, beneath, behind;

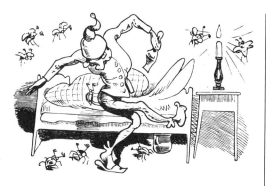

Bugs infest him, swoop, and buzz
Like some frisky, bristly fuzz.

In a frenzy Uncle Fritz
Stamps and tramples, slaps and hits.

"There! You've done, I'm telling you,
All the crawling you will do!"

Uncle, once again at rest,
Sleeps the slumber of the blest.

And was this their last trick? Wrong!
For the sixth comes right along.

Sixth Trick

Eastertime, our Savior's Passion,
Pious baker-people fashion,
Bake, adorn, and then display
Pastry work on many a tray.
Which (to see it is to love it)
Max and Moritz also covet.

But the baker, as we see,
Keeps it under lock and key,

Forcing customers to toil
Down the flue through soot and oil.

Here a pair of clients goes
Down the chimney, black as crows.

Pooff! they fall into the bin
Baker keeps the flour in.

They retrieve themselves and walk
On their way as white as chalk.

Sugared pretzels, neatly stacked,
Are the first to be attacked.

Crunch! their stairway breaks in two;

Flop! they flounder in the goo.

All encased in heavy dough,
They present a sight of woe.

Worse, the baker now discovers
And pursues the pastry lovers;

And, resourceful stratagem,
Makes two handsome loaves of them.

Good! the oven's still aglow:
Shloop! into the hole they go;

Shloop! and presently are raked
Out, for they are good and baked.—

Everyone must think they've had it;
No! they're still alive and at it!

Crisky-crusk, like mice a rusk,
They gnaw off the crispy husk.

Baker sees and hollers: Hey!!—
But they're off and clean away.—

And was this their last trick? Wrong!—
But the last comes right along!

Seventh Trick

Max and Moritz, woe is you!
For your final trick is due.—

What exactly made the two
Slit these sacks?? I wish I knew.

Here goes Farmer Klein, a sack
Full of malt-grain on his back.—

Just as he is off with it,
Grain starts leaking from the slit;

And he stops, amazed at this,
Mumbling: "Strike me! what's amiss?"

Ah! He tracks with gleeful guile
Max and Moritz in that pile.

Swoop! he scoops the worthless pack
Right into the handy sack.

Max and Moritz feel quite ill,
For this way leads to the mill.—

"Howdy, Master Miller! Hey,
Will you grind this, right away?"

"Right you are!" He dumps the lot
Down into the feeder slot.—

Rickle-rackle, rickle-rackle,
Hear the millstones grind and crackle.

Here is what the mill releases:
Still themselves, but all in pieces.

And the miller's ducks are there
To devour the loose-knit pair.

Conclusion

Those who learned this on the morrow
Gave no slightest sign of sorrow.
Widow Bolte shook her head,
Clucking: "As I always said . . ."
"Serves them right!" said Master Billy;
"Now it's they who're looking silly."
"Clearly," nodded Teacher Lampel,
"Here we have one more example!"
"Yep!" remarked the pastry cook,
"Never leap before you look."
Even Uncle Fritz said: "Hem!
Stupid jokes! For once, on them!"
This from worthy Farmer Klein:
"Ain't no business of mine . . ."
That entire place, in short,
Buzzed with joy at the report;
And they offered heartfelt thanks
For deliverance from pranks!

Jack Crook,
Bird of Evil

Here spirited young Frederick
Meets Jackie Crook, the raven chick.

Fritz would be glad (like any lad)
To have himself a raven tad.

He sidles closer, as he must;
The chick is rigid with distrust.

Now Frederick whips down his cap,
Next best thing to a raven trap.

He would have had him, right enough
Had not the tree branch broken off.

He lands in berries, but unscathed,
The raven darts aside, enswathed.

The hunter pauses, purply mottled;
The fledgling hops about, half throttled.

"Halloo!" croons Auntie, simpering.
"Why, look at him, the darling thing!"

Deep in a vessel, late of lard,
The swarthy fiend has mounted guard

Entangled in the inner works,
The captive vainly tugs and jerks.

The word has hardly left her lip
When darling nails her fingertip.

Upon a chicken leg—the same
Spitz now approaches to reclaim.

"Ha! Gotcha!" Fritz exclaims in glee.
"How happy Auntie Lou will be!"

"Alas—he is not good, I see;
For he has used his beak on me!"

They croak and growl, they wrench and
fight,
One from the left, one from the right.

Just when he thinks he has prevailed
Spitz finds his fluffy rear assailed.

While, snatching the unguarded hock,
Sly Felix darts into the crock.

Ouch! Spitz's whole coiffure is wrecked.
Jack puts the hole to good effect.

The monster mounts him like a steed
And plucks his wool like tufts of weed.

Well! There they sit and stare at puss:
This cat is armed and dangerous.

Pot rolling, tail arrested, Felix
Is made to form a partial helix.

Spitz rallies, though, and in his turn
Wreaks havoc at the monster's stern;

Amidst much discord and invective,
Jack finds the pot to be defective.

Two flee (one *courant*, one *galumphant*)—
The toughest thug remains triumphant.

No greater treat for Auntie Lou
Than purple whortleberry stew.

And hurries—terror lends him wings—
Across some freshly ironed things.

The beer jug falls. The liquid shoots
Into the tops of Auntie's boots.

But Attila prefers to squirt
And squander the superb dessert.

Still moving rapidly (O Lord!),
He passes through the china board.

Events too rapid to detail
Involve her ankle and a pail.

A brandished spoon, an anguished shriek;
Jack Crook takes off with dripping beak,

There were two dozen eggs in here
(And so expensive now—oh, dear!)

Now Jack and Auntie have a race;
Young Freddy would have joined the chase

But is detained (he should have waited:
An ear is quickly perforated).

Now, though, the vandal's in for it
(You would have thought), but wait a bit!

He whirs and staples Auntie's nose;
And evil wins, one must suppose . . .

But trouble is ahead, for sure:
For this decanter holds liqueur.

The smell is sweet. I think I will!
He dips a speculative bill;

And with an expert's pondering frown
Allows the stuff to trickle down.

He tips the glass and plants his legs;
No sense in leaving any dregs.

Not bad at all! And as before
He squats and syphons up some more.

Well, well. What fun! He feels so very
Relaxed, and . . . quite extraordinary!

He rocks, lets out a joyous yell,
And stands one-legged for a spell.

Though meant by Providence to soar,
He now prefers to use the floor.

Pure wantonness and disrespect
Run riot—all must now be wrecked!

He staggers on to snarl and jerk
Aunt Lou's artistic needlework.

The wood is slick; the yarn entangles;
The end is near . . . Look, there he dangles.

"Mischief," says Auntie, "was his joy;
Now see him hanging there, dear boy!"

Helen Who Couldn't Help It

1872

Nell Is Brought to the Country

Sadly, like the wind through ruins
Or in weeping-willow trees,
Sighs the bard of wicked doings
In the great metropoles.

Journalists!! The shameless vipers—
Do they hesitate to spread
Tales of vice among subscribers
Scarcely risen yet from bed?

Offenbach plays operettas,
Here's a concert, there a fête:
Annies, Fannies, Henriettas
Squeal and simply cannot wait.

They bedeck the sinful carcass,
Barely downing second cups,
And are off to join the larkers
In the gardens, squares, and shops.

Oh, the bowing, oh, the gazing,
Here the madly smart messeers,
There mamselles with mind-bedazing
Grandly bulging bustle rears.

And the Hebrew, sly and craven,
Round of shoulder, nose, and knee,
Slinks to the Exchange, unshaven
And intent on usury.

Let me pass in pained disquiet
Over taverns of ill fame
Where the Liberals run riot,
Blackening the Pontiff's name.

But I must not scruple naming
Concerts, where the regulars
Blithely peer about them, aiming
Insolent binoculars.

Where with bosoms plump and lustrous
One is wedged in steamy sets;
Where amid the Muses' musters
Even Lord Apollo sweats.

Then again, the pen would rather
Spare the Stage, whose thrills excite
Handsome mother, honest father,
As they amble home at night.

Couples couple and redouble
With a blithe and thoughtless air,
But the children get in trouble
If the parents do not care.

"Take to country ways and habits,"
(Said her guardian) "little Nell;
Come, dear child, where jolly rabbits
And the pious lambkins dwell.

Here we hold decorum dearest,
Virtue here and sense reside,
Aunt and Uncle, too—your nearest!"
Thus our Nell was countrified.

Uncle's Nightie

"Ah, Nell," said Uncle, "I would mention,
For the particular attention
Of Christian girls: All evil shun!
The bad may lure you when you eye it,
It is delightful when you try it,
But troublesome when it is done."

"Aye! Many (Auntie sighed) were lost
Who failed to heed this, to their cost.
From older heads a child should draw
Wise rules with gratitude and awe.
Old folk, you see, have passed that way
And sin no more, I'm glad to say.

Good night now—time for bed, I find.
And tell your beads, dear Nellie, mind!"

Dear Nell withdraws, and on her way
Finds Uncle's nightgown on display.

A needle, quick! With nimble fingers
She closes all the ports of ingress.

Her prayers said, she goes to rest,
All settled in her cozy nest.

A little later, Uncle's here;
Quite ripe for bed, it would appear.

For last relief before he goes
The bedtime pinch goes up his nose.

He then forsakes by solemn rite
The shirt of day for that of night.

But the transaction takes quite long.
There's evidently something wrong.

"There's something funny here, by
    thunder!"
Her uncle's angry, and no wonder.

Annoyance is quite useless, though.
There goes the light, I told you so.

As if this hadn't been enough,
There go the watch, the box of snuff.

The closet of nocturnal need
Succumbs to Uncle's blind stampede.

The noise brings Auntie with a light.
He has regained both air and sight.

"Oh, shameless, wicked girl, I say!
It's you I mean. Yes, snore away!"

And Nell resolves that she will never
Do this again. But never—ever!

Cousin Franz

Dear Nellie's growth is swift and steady
My word! She's in long skirts already.

With lively pleasure she looks up
One morning from the breakfast cup
On hearing Auntie Nolte say:
"Your cousin Franz has come to stay.
Be careful now how you appear:
No loud and forward ways, you hear?
Don't loll at lunch; no gaping, staring,
And think on what you should be wearing!
Be plain and proper in attire,
Is my particular desire.
That green, with neckline down to there,
I do not wish to see you wear."

Nell wonders: is he still asleep?
And bends to take a little peep.

But Franz is deep in eiderdown,
Except for sundry bits of brown.

"Ho-hum . . . howww-hummm," he yawns
at last.
"It must be nine o'clock or past."

Time to get up one's resolution
For the matutinal ablution.

One, it's the seemly thing to do;

Two, it is quite refreshing, too;

Then, three, a journey soils you so;

Four, it is simply *done*, you know.

It leaves you feeling spruce and fit;

And, lastly, there's no harm in it!

There's nothing like a change of shirt
To make a traveler fresh and pert.

He then continues, all serene,
His semi-private change of scene

And reaps the fruits of cleanliness

In full sartorial success.

Her cousin lights his pipe at last,
And Helen leaves her station—fast.

A watering can has long been standing
(Boing, clatter!) here upon the landing.

Downward the combination shoots,
And Hannchen, come for Franz's boots,

Is gathered into the mêlée.
Here's Auntie with the coffee tray.

They'll get unscrambled in a bit.
Here's Uncle, late for most of it . . .

The Frog

Young Franz endears himself apace.
He wears his scholarship with grace.
Here are some verses, grouped by four,
He has composed the night before:

Of a morning gold and blue
Through the woods I barreled;
Came a little birdie who
Gaily trilled and caroled.

Ask me no report of it
What the birdie sang:
Love's the long and short of it,
Let the rest go hang.

He dedicates it all to Nell,
Who likes the thought extremely well.

One finds in Franz so much to praise,
In this and many other ways!
You need some fixture or a nail,
Franz gets it for you without fail.
Or take that spooky cellar spot:
Franz comes along, which helps a lot.
Or in the garden, when one hunts
For beets or berries—there is Franz!

If in the corner by the wall
The butter beans have grown too tall,
There's Franz to hold the ladder taut
Lest Nell fall, or her dress be caught.

And later, when she's plucked enough,
Franz is right there to help her off.
In short, whatever might befall,
He's game, for anything at all!

What's more, he has a special bent
For witty pranks and merriment.
Thus, somewhere in the greenery
A frog may clamber: got him, see?

He shuts it, damp and in the buff,
In Uncle Nolte's box of snuff.

When Uncle next raised up the lid,
With pleasure as he always did,

Oops! in a flash the beast had sprung
Upon his nose, to which it clung.

Thence, plash! into the cup, I knew it,
Still half-full of the precious fluid.

The next bewildered little flutter
Embroils him deeply with the butter.

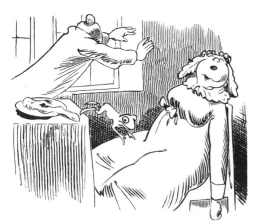

Flop! Oopla! The unnerving shock!
He's in the slack of Auntie's frock.

Poor Uncle leaps and rings alarm:
O Hannchen, Hannchen, quickly, come!

And Hannchen comes and, cool as cool,
Deports the monster with a tool.

And Auntie is at length restored
To some composure, thank the Lord.

How heartily did Helen laugh
When cousin Franz had brought this off!
There was but one unpleasing touch:
Franz was with Hannchen far too much . . .

Well, most young fellows, on and off,
Are partial to the kitchen staff;
And men are sinners, on the whole . . .
How Helen prayed for Franz's soul!

Amidst the general contentment,
One felt misgivings and resentment,
And that was Nolte—with his nose
Still out of joint, one may suppose.
He was uneasy in his mind
Till, long vacation left behind,
Young Franz, with loathing and in fear,
Had left for the scholastic year.

The Love Letter

"This would make Uncle eat his fez . . .
But do I care what Nolte says?"

And Helen writes, pert as can be,
Against her uncle's strict decree:

"My dearest Franz! We are apart,
But well you know, yours is my heart!

How heavenly a time we spent,
So full of fun and sentiment . . .

When deep in beans and watercress
A someone gave a someoness,

Let's say, an ardent cousin kiss?
O Lord, if Auntie knew of this!

Here things seem duller than before;
In fact, a soul-destroying bore!

Our uncle's daft (good thing, no doubt),
Aunt keeps on pottering about,

And both are holy as can be . . .
Oh, Franz, do come and rescue me,
My tears of longing make a well!
Ten thousand kisses from your
                              Nell."

Now for the sealing wax . . . Oh, no!

For Uncle pounces, thundering: So!!

And ouch! she has her nasal fob
Impressed into the bubbling blob.

A Restless Night

Peaceful in their nest of feather,
Aunt and Uncle sleep together.

Enter Nell with line and hook
And a surreptitious look.

Jerk! some coverment is taken.
Uncle honks but does not waken.

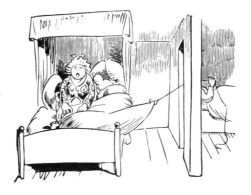

Tug! now Auntie also faces
Ventilation at her basis.

"Stop!" she hisses, driven wild.
"There's a draught! Don't be a child!"

They exchange some admonitions
And resort to new positions.

Flub! there goes the whole affair,
Further angering the pair.

Nolte is severely clouted
With the keys and promptly routed.

Nellie has no way to know
She has caught her uncle's toe.

She hauls in and does not stop.
Uncle is constrained to hop.

Now she holds the door secure;
Oh, how wicked, to be sure!

Bandaged up the wounds of war,
Peace and concord reign once more.

What nocturnal counsels yield,
In the morning is revealed,
As in chill and somber tones
Nellie's injured uncle drones:

"Ah, Helena: Our paths must clearly . . ."
"I'm truly sorry, Uncle, really . . ."

"Too late, I fear. Without ado
Pack your belongings. Then, adieu!"

Interlude

It is wise as well as human
For a virtuous young woman
In due course to choose a man
And get married if she can.
One, the force of custom merges
Two, at times with private urges;
Three, one needs to be escorted
And in every way supported:
Girls can look to spheres of action
For delight and satisfaction
Hard to enter by themselves;
Such as barrooms in hotels.—

To be sure, the Right One may
Not be handy straight away,
And one seeks, while yet alone,
Entertainment on one's own,
So one's life gains tone and varies.
Nell, for instance, keeps canaries,

Christened Cheep and Peep, who peck
Daintily with tilted neck:
What a darling little pair!

Pussy dozes, unaware.

Once a tom of brawn and gall,
Name of Eric, came to call.

Following a common vision,
By a silent, swift decision

They indulge their murderous drives.
Neither Cheep nor Peep survives.

Further, quite companionable,
They ascend the coffee table;
Puss with velvet-covered hookies
Angles for some butter cookies.

Eric worries his thick head
Down into the cream instead.
Helen enters from next door,
From some letter-writing chore,
Holding sealing wax and taper,
And observes the wicked caper.

Puss has time to get away,
But big Eric has to stay,

For the jug about his head
Cannot readily be shed.

Diving blindly down from there,
Crash! he spoils the chinaware.

By the cabinet he passes,
Sparing neither jars nor glasses;

At the same frenetic pace
See him mount the fireplace.

Ach! Poor Venus is *perdue*—
Clickety-crash! de Medici!

It's a simple leap from here
To the crystal chandelier.

Help! a whoosh, a tinkly-clinket:
Ruined is the costly trinket!

Eric races for the door,
Nearly passing through, what's more.

Now he can't see Helen handle
Paper, sealing wax, and candle.

First one adds the paper hat
To the end of pussycat.

To achieve a tighter fit,
Drop some sealing wax on it.

Set the paper hat alight,
Wait until the flame is bright,

Then release the captured vandal
As a streaking feline candle . . .

Helen Bestows Her Hand

Some mornings, when the air is cool,
In spring or autumn as a rule,
There's quite a little to be said
For lingering a bit in bed.
"Not quite the time yet," one decides,
But half awake, and changes sides.
One's thoughts meander to and fro,
How this might be if that were so . . .
But growing more alert at length,
One scrambles upright, gathers strength,
And staggers bathward, gently cursing,
To civilize the outer person.

While cleanliness is next to truth,
It is no substitute for youth;
Good grooming, one is bound to say,
Can only go a certain way.

Time leaves us somewhat flawed and
    thinned,
As ringlets vanish with the wind . . .

Invention stands us in good part,
For Beauty is enhanced by Art.—
Yet maintenance takes more and more,
Until the thing becomes a bore.

"All right," said Helen when it did;
"I'm marrying Schmuck Ltd.!"

And Schmuck, who has long since been
    buoyed
By hopes of this, is overjoyed.
He does not argue with his luck,
But makes of Helen Mme. Schmuck.

The Honeymoon Trip

'Tis Heidelberg the couple chose
As foil for hymeneal glows.

What glorious sun! A joy to lope
In tandem up the castle slope.

"Just look," cries Helen, "dearest George,
Those crumbling walls atop the gorge!"

"Quite, dearest! . . . but the heat is horrid!
Just run your hand across my forehead!"

Antiquities are lots of fun.
So is the famous giant tun.

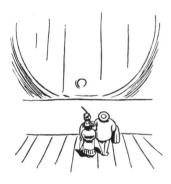

A lot of barrel, one must say!

Then gaily in a cab they sway
And let the rolling country well
Right past them to the Grand Hotel;

Asparagus and chops of lamb
Are welcome now; so is smoked ham.

"Oh, waiter! Chill us one of these!
And waiter! On the double, please!"

The waiter, instantly complying,
Is on his way, his coattails flying.

How headily fizz up and flow
The airy pearls of Veuve Clicquot!

A toast to her, and praise eternal!
Madame is leafing through a journal.

"Here, waiter! We are out of wine!"
The hands on Helen's watch show nine.

The waiter, instantly complying,
Is on his way, his coattails flying.

How headily fizz up and flow
The airy pearls of Veuve Clicquot!

"Garçon! Let's have another, then!"
The hands on Helen's watch show ten.

The waiter heeds the call and speeds
Away—but Helen intercedes.

The waiter lights them to their berth.
The gentleman is full of mirth.

One finger, pshh! the light is out.

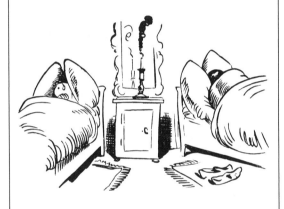

He's down and never turns about.

Good Works

Full many a wife whom fortune chances
To place in sheltered circumstances
Lets worship and religion lapse
And thinks: Another year, perhaps . . .

Not Helen, I rejoice to say;
Such laxity is not her way.
One often sees her stoutly plod
To quite a distant house of God,

Attended, with an earnest look,
By Jean complete with prayerbook.
Nor is her pious striving's summit
Her own salvation—oh, far from it!

A saintly person likes to labor
For the correction of his neighbor,
And sees, through frequent admonition,
To his improvement through contrition.

She once said: "Jean, your pockets bulge!
I wonder, Jean—do you indulge . . . ?

I thought as much! Ah, wretched knave . . .
Mock not the Judge beyond the grave!"

These words so crushed him that he swore
To mend his ways and sin no more.

But not by words alone one mellows
And benefits one's erring fellows.

Thus Helen crochets shawls and coats,
So good for scrawny chests and throats
Beleaguered now by probing gusts;
And knitted comforters are musts:
To storm-tossed torsos bringing soon
Their quite inestimable boon.
She even comforts on occasion
An officer of French persuasion,
Of those who singly or in bands
Resided then in German lands.

But her most fervid sentiment
Sustains the truly indigent.
Her doctors earnestly opine
She should take baths in tepid wine;

And so she does.— Oh, how rejoice
The needy cases of her choice

For once to have a pint or two
To heat the stomach through and through.

Spiritual Counsel

There is no need, for most at any rate,
To laud the matrimonial estate.
How thoroughly pleasing, how well-advised
Is the person who, properly authorized,
Within the conventional term, more or less
May call himself Father or Mum, God
    bless.
But once in a while one is much distressed
To find that one's union remains unblessed.
Thus, sad to tell, it became apparent
That Helen was not to become a parent.

An anchorite, perched in a rustic cell
Right close to St. Peter's-in-the Dell,
Enjoyed for his wisdom the utmost renown
With matrons and spinsters in hamlet and
    town.
(Though hardly as spry as he once had
    been.)
"My daughter," quoth he with solicitous
    mien,
"A parlous condition, not apt to know ease
Except by spiritual remedies!
Here, then, my dear lady, is what I advise:
Ascend in the steep and narrow wise
And follow the blessed pilgrims' spoor
Toward Chosemont-de-bon-secours;

For there they have sheltered from days of
    old
The Cradle of Fruitfulness, justly extolled.
Whoever it was that would thither repair
And would rock the miraculous cradle
    there,
Would feel very soon on departing thence
A change of the happiest consequence.

Ah, well I remember it coming to pass
That a God-fearing maiden, to whom, alas
Her elders had culpably been remiss
In point of instruction on things like this,
Laid hands on it inadvertently
In thoughtlessness or in childlike glee,
And though she had rocked just the least
    little bit
The least little baby was born her from it.

A saucy young pilgrim the other week
Just gave it a casual mischievous tweak;
Behold! in a matter of months or less
From his perpetrating this wickedness
It happened . . . However, this must be all!
For Vespers call me at evenfall.
Adieu—may the Lord vouchsafe thee
    surcease!
Beget thee hence in peace."

The Pilgrimage

Lo! there gleams the holy summit!
Pub and chapel beckon from it.

Up the road by rocks and canyons,
Joined in an ecstatic press
Of prospective holiness,
Pilgrims toil with bliss-companions;
Fused together for reform
By the soul's devout agenda,
Seekers of alternate gender
Breathe communion close and warm.—

In the van with solid tread,
Moisty-warm in heart and head,
Stride the trusty, merit-filled
Brethren of St. Joseph's Guild.

Further, festive but not garish,
Choiring hymns to Compostella,
March the Spinsters of the Parish,
Each equipped with an umbrella,
In a slow euphonious throng.
Brother Eustace leads the song.

Lo! upon that sacred way
Wanders Helen, sadly gay,

Unescorted, you might say,

Her sole escort and restorer
In an otherworldly aura
Being Franz, benign and stately,—
Known as Holy Francis lately.
There they fare at pious pace,
Fellow seekers after grace.

Thankfully one tops the mount,
And with joyous zeal, yet heedful
Of the hallowed spirit-fount
One accomplishes the needful.

Now one seeks the tavern out,
Reaches gladly for the stout
Which, as always, has been brewed
In his cloistered solitude
For compliance with such claims
By the expert Friar James.

Male and female devotees
Quite see eye to eye on these.

When the sultry day is passed
Soothing cool descends at last.

By the mystic lunar ray
Helen slowly makes her way,
Unescorted, you might say,
For the moon's reclining specter
Shines but on a sole protector,
Helpful, saintly cousin Franz,
As in concord they advance,
Newly blest communicants.

But the Brethren's reemergence
Is more tardy, and the Virgins
Come, a much belated throng,
Paternostering along,
In a slow euphonious lurch,
Plastered pillars of the Church.

Look, despite the vespering hour
Here appears a cruising cabby,

And this cabby, feeling crabby,
Ruled by Satan, or just sour,
Mutters "Och, to hell with that"
And neglects to tip his hat.

Pilgrims, woe! of either gender
Grimly round on the offender,
Who attempts to whip his steed
Up to more salubrious speed;

Vainly: Eustace slides the whole
Maiden-pilgrim-banner-pole
In between the hinder wheels;

The conveyance stalls and squeals.

By his legs and coat they wrench
The blasphemer from his bench.

With her crutches from on high
Elsie jolts his vertebrae.
But a certain Ethelbertha,
Hotly driving vengeance further,

Pokes the region of his hip
With her sharp umbrella tip:
Just his sturdy nether leather
Staves off ruin altogether.—

Male and female crocks of bliss
Quite see eye to eye on this.

Far afield their hymns expire;
Brother Eustace leads the choir.

But the groom who by his fault
Had provoked the just assault

Files a querulous report
At the Lord Lieutenant's Court,
Calling Sisterhood and Eustace
To his Wairship's Bar of Joostice.

There the firebrand, they ruled,
Should for twenty days be cooled;
Damages and court costs would
Fall on Broth- and Sisterhood.—

Well this broth- and sister may
Trade expressions of dismay.

Twins

Where *would* we get our babies from
If Master Stork refused to come?

'Twas he who late last night, what luck,
Brought little twins for M. Schmuck.
Mild cousin Francis, first to call,
Intones: "Congratulations, all!
What charming little tykes are here!
A double benison, my dear,

Deserves twofold felicitations:
Once more, dear Schmuck,
    congratulations!"

Schmuck dines past midnight, at the height
Of spirits, health, and appetite;

And eagerly he turns to fish
And salad for a festive dish.

Oh, bother—fishbone lodged askew . . .
Schmuck coughs a lot and turns quite blue.

He coughs—the salad reappears,
Discharged, it does seem, by his ears.

Crash! There—the flesh's no longer willing.
Jean keeps the wine at least from spilling,

And mutters: "Makes a fellow think!
Life can be over in a wink . . ."

A Fallible Friend

"Oh, Francis!" Helen sobs, bereft:
"Oh, Franz! You're all the friends I've left!"

"Yes!" Francis swears, "Your faithful pal . . .
I have been, am, and ever shall . . . !"

Good night! We'll meet (the clock is ten)
Anon, God willing. Until then!"

He halts on his way down and out:
Well, well! Here's Katie still about!

This pleases Franz. Still, on and off,
He fancies the domestic staff.

But Jean, on tiptoes, waxes wroth
To see her wrapt in sacred cloth.

Insanely jealous at this scene,
He lifts the blushful Hippocrene

And crack!! The jagged edges meet
In lofty reason's very seat.

The thread is snapped . . . this must be
   all.—
Both Helen and the candle fall.

Reform

Man is full of devilment!
Sinner, turn again! Repent!

Helen, shaken to the core,
Opens wide her closet door.

"Out, pernicious aids," she hisses,
Lotions, dyes, and artifices!

Bulging heart-shell, out you go,
Licensed lure of libido!

Out, you engines of temptation,
Shoes of pride and ostentation!

All you gear of lustful games,
I commit you to these flames!"

These, to suffer and atone,
Have a beauty all their own . . .

Pure and spare, she shuffles hence,
Fraught with naught but penitence.

Terminal Temptation

From ancient times it has been true:
He who has cares, has liquor, too.

"Oh, no!" cries Helen, "I shall never
Succumb again. No, never—ever."

She kneels afar and clears her mind.
The liquor bottle stays behind.

Without prie-dieu one still is able
To pray. The bottle's on the table.

The light is poor so far away.
The bottle glitters, here to stay.

Amazing, that was all it took!
(The bottle is no prayerbook.)

There, there, long-lost companion, there!
(Oh, Helen, stop! Beware! Beware!)

Ah . . . ! see in blessed slumber gear
Her lately sainted aunt appear!

In accents ominous and melan-
Choly she cautions:
    Helen . . . ! Helenn . . ."

In vain! The lamp begins to lean,
Still well supplied with kerosene.

And it, with less lament than stench,
Incinerates this helpless wench.

Here fume her ruins, charred and brittle.
What's left amounts to very little.

Evil Triumphs

Outside, what sudden lurid gloom!
What lightning, thunder, crack of doom?

Here by the chimney see him tarry,
Hell's longtailed, pitchforked emissary!

True, Helen's guardian leaves a mark
Upon the Spirit of the Dark.

But this does not detain him long:
He trips the genie with his prong.

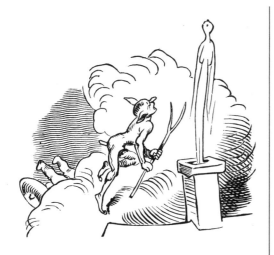

Alas! The angel falters, fails!
The Claimant from the Pit prevails.

He seizes Helen's wispy soul

And whisks it down that reeking Hole.

Flames, sulfur, torment, and perdition!
(Franz is already in position.)

Epilogue

When Uncle Nolte heard the news,
Much did it grieve him and bemuse!

Then, more composed, he took some snuff
And said: "I saw it soon enough . . . !

The good (I am convinced, for one)
Is but the bad one leaves undone.

One thing in this I don't lament:
Thank God that I am different!"

The Knopp Trilogy

I Adventures of a Bachelor

II Mr. and Mrs. Knopp

III Julie

1875–1877

I Adventures of a Bachelor

Matters Reach a Crisis

Socrates, the noted sage,
Often mourned (the insight festered):
"Ah, how much is still sequestered
From the knowledge of our age!"
One thing, though, is never hidden,
For we sense it deep inside,
And it comes to us unbidden:
That we are dissatisfied.—

That's how Knopp has come to feel,
And it pains him a good deal.

His canaries in their cage
Never worry like that sage,

While Tobias feels beset
By an ill-defined regret.
Time goes by, routine grows arid;
Think, Knopp! you are still unmarried!—

True, his linen, boots, and fare
Are in Doris's faithful care;
If he needs things done or sewn
He can't get to on his own,
She is very prompt and deft
To attend him right and left.
Still and all, he's not content.—

With a wan presentiment
He consults the looking glass
For the verdict it may pass:

Viewed in front, the place looks glazed.
But in back, the Lord be praised
(He is buoyed by joyous hopes),
There should still be wooded slopes.
Oh, the penetrating sting!
There it's worse, if anything.
East to West and South to North,
Just pure reason bulges forth.

And there is another cause
For concern to give him pause:
Somehow, growing more mature,
He has passed the curvature
Drawn by Nature and decreed
Adequate unto the need
Of the center zone in question
Both for breathing and digestion.—
Nature, though, has gentle cures
For such excess curvatures:
Sip the Karlsbad waters, stalk
Flowered path and shady walk,
Exercise in rhythmic spurts,
Shun potatoes and desserts . . .
Saying to yourself "you must"
Greatly helps you to adjust.

Knopp, who feels all this acutely,

Exercises resolutely,

Sometimes musing in a clearing,

Sometimes wholly disappearing,

But returning to the spot
To resume his faithful trot.

Two whole weeks—he never fails;
Then he climbs upon the scales;
And—what does the pointer say?
Minus twenty pounds, hooray!

Onward to his second calends,
And again he mounts the balance;
What a shock! As one can see,
All is as it used to be.

In this world, he muses sadly,
There is much that functions badly,
April, cousins, maidens, May
Irretrievably decay;

And I also, soon enough,
Shall be cancelled and crossed off.
Of me too it will be read:
Knopp existed—and is dead.
Worse: will any tears be dripping
From the eye that reads the clipping?
Not a single soul will grieve
Or much notice when I leave . . .
Heads will not be sadly shaken
Where no interest is taken:
"Knopp? Who was he, anyone?"
You will hear when I am gone.
Knopp's own eyes are blinking,
   smarting . . .
At the thought of such a parting,
Of a grave untended, sere,
He himself extrudes a tear.
See it lie (commensurate
With his sorrow) where he sat.

Is this really necessary?
Shake a leg, old man, and marry!
Air yourself, get up and out,
Travel, wander, look about,
Pay some calls, you can't go wrong;
Just you see—it won't be long.

Minimal encumberments
Will be best for his intents.
Worthy Doris wipes her eyes
As she waves her fond good-byes.

An Old Flame

First, and with the least delay,
Knopp has thought to make his way
To that far idyllic vale
Which has sheltered his Adèle:
Her whose charms would so delight him
(But who did not then requite him,
Though he loved her with the whole
Of his lyrical young soul.)

He survived, as people will,
But her likeness haunts him still.
Timid, moist with perspiration,
He beholds her habitation;
Pulses pound him, tie to socks,
But at last he also knocks.

"Toby! Joy! you here at last!"
(Knopp stands riveted, aghast.)

"Here, you naughty, wayward loafer,
Sit beside me on this sofa.

You alone, my dear delight,
I have thought of day and night!
Down restraint, decorum, fashion . . .
Love me, as I love, with passion!!"
Knopp, from lack of proper feeling,
Finds his eager sweat congealing.

At this crisis in the center,
From the flank three mongrels enter.

"Help!" Adèle is heard to shout,
"Help, beloved, drive them out!"

Knopp, though, cannot see what for,
As he tiptoes to the door.—
At a run he exits there
And betakes himself elsewhere.

Clerical Help

Forward now his travels carry
Knopp on his itinerary.
To old Knarrtje (thus his name)
Warden of the local game.

As he strides along with vigor,
He observes a subfusc figure,

Which, as he is walking by,
Takes a shortcut through the rye.

Well—here comes old Knarrtje, too!
"Good old Knopp, that's nice of you!"

Chatting happily, they trudge
To the nearby keeper's lodge.

"Here—don't wait to be invited!
Why, my wife will be delighted."

But there's something to upset him.
"What the . . . Sic him, Rover, get him!

"Wait, you slut . . . I never knew . . .
Let me get my hands on you!!"

Knopp's remonstrance with his host
Has no more success than most.

Hurriedly he exits there
And removes himself elsewhere.

Eggbert Nebischitz, M.A.

Now his travels carry Knopp
To the next appointed stop,
Where he hopes to spend the day
With friend Nebischitz, M.A.

Nebischitz, though not quite done
With a lesson to his son,

On perceiving his old friend
Gladly brings it to an end,

And prepares to do his best
For the comfort of his guest:
"Mark, my Kuno! Swiftly flit
Where I order you, to wit
(Listen well): Betake yourself
Cellarwards, where on a shelf
Wrapped in straw upon a trestle
Some Bordeaux is found to nestle.
This Bordeaux, I charge you, fetch
And deliver with dispatch."

Kuno, suitably equipped,
Gladly hurries to the crypt,

Where he quietly diverts
Some invigorating squirts
Down his esophageal chasm;
And a world of good it does him.

The resulting short supply
He replenishes nearby.

"From its shape one might infer
Pigeon droppings . . . as it were.

And his friend responds . . . In vain:
Foreign matter, once again.

Claret is for men of wits
One of life's prime benefits.

Kuno, tell me if you can
What has caused this—man to man!"

"Well, now—this, I would have sworn,
Is a sparrow, newly born.

Seldom is a glass declined.
Knopp, however, makes a find.

Having probed to Kuno's core,
He desists and pours some more.

Kuno!! Tell me if you can
What has caused this—man to man!!
Your transgressions' inky maze
Lies transparent to my gaze.

Go! my trust has been abused.
Leave my sight. You are . . . excused!"
Eggbert's rule has ever been:
Caning merely skims the skin;
Only reason's scalpel can
Penetrate the inner man.

Knopp decides to exit there
And remove himself elsewhere.

Bucolic Entertainment

Now his travels carry Knopp
On to yet another stop.
To a dear old friend he came
In the country, Ruff by name.
Ruff has always thought a skinful
Salutary for the sinful.
And a sterling medicine
In advance of any sin.
Prior to the village dance
He applies it to his Franz.

Knopp can hear while still remote
The familiar plaintive note.

Then all four proceed in state
To the local marksmen's fête.

Francis has discreetly snatched
A curvaceous tail, detached,
As he has been well aware,
From a pig just slaughtered there.

Soon the guest's bipartite stern
Takes a most amusing turn.

Presently the French horn brays
For the opening Française.

None, the company agrees,
Match our Knopp in grace and ease,

Or contrives like him to sway
To the tune and swoop away.

But a magic all his own
Works when he performs alone.

Everyone is quite uplifted,
Finding Knopp so greatly gifted.
Soon, alas, the tunes subside,
And with pardonable pride

Here the star returns to base

For a drink and change of pace.

Oops! there is no base at all.
Knopp sustains a grievous fall.

His recovery is fleet
But, he senses, incomplete.

For, aghast, he feels abaft
An unseasonable draft.

Rapidly he exits there
And betakes himself elsewhere.

Pastorale

Knopp's sartorial default
Brings his progress to a halt.

For this lonesome, flowery mead
Answers his undoubted need

Of a dry dock, as it were,
For inspection and repair;

Just the haven, it would seem,
To restore one's self-esteem
After recent bare escapes.
Just a baby rabbit gapes.

Here comes farmer Reuben. Rightly
Knopp conceals himself, but lightly.

But with Reuben's consort, Susie,
He becomes a lot more choosy.

Now they vanish up the lea,
And directly Knopp is free
To devote his full concern
To his lacerated stern.—
He attends to it, becalmed,
When once more he is alarmed

By an imminent—oh, Hades!
Troop of promenading ladies.
Here they are! Of Knopp, though, phew!

Just the top remains in view.

First a gasp of petrifaction,
Then the governess takes action,

Pealing loudly: "O mon Dieu!
C'est un homme! Fermez les yeux!!"

Flustered by his near escape,
Knopp resumes his social shape

And forsakes this Central Station
For another destination.

Bubbelmann

On again his travels carry
Knopp on his itinerary;

To another friend he came
(Bubbelmann his charming name),
Whom he knew as bright and hearty,
Life and soul of any party.

He emerges. "Happy day!"
Burbles Knopp, "I've come to stay!"

Bubbelmann, benign but pale,
Answers: "Worthy brother, hail!

Firstly: lodgement for the night
Would not seem to be in sight,
For a churchman of renown
Has arrived from out of town.

Second, as to boarding here,
There is little hope, I fear:
First day, we are born afresh,
Second day, we kill the flesh,
Third day, purge the soul of dross,
Fourth day, walk beneath the Cross.

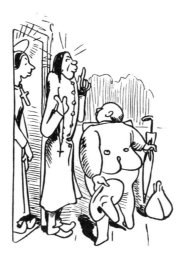

On the last and saddest score . . .
Hush! my wife is at the door!"

Disconcerted by all this,
Knopp, while wishing loads of bliss,
Turns his back upon these two,
Bidding them a cool adieu.

Swiftly exiting from there,
He betakes himself elsewhere.

Enough Is Less Than a Feast

Knopp on his peregrination
Reached the next appointed station;
To a worthy friend he came,
Sexton Plünne was his name.

Coming through the gate, he sees
Shirts aflutter in the breeze;
Whence he gathers right away:
It's the Plünnes' washing day.

And for added confirmation,
There's old Plünne's occupation.

Gladly, though, he frees his lap,
Crying: "Welcome, Knopp, old chap!

Hold the baby while I find
Dinner for us—would you mind?"

This is something new to Knopp.
Plünne clears the tabletop.

Knopp feels more and more unable,
While the sexton sets the table.

Now he dives into a pouch
In the matrimonial couch,
And it opens to the sheen
Of a handsome soup tureen.

Insulators of renown—
None compare with eiderdown.—
Now, if dinner, for example,
Has been relatively ample,
And the children, duly cautioned,
Had their seconds strictly portioned,
Leaving loads of tripe, or oodles
(As the case may be) of noodles,
It is plainly for the best
That one should conserve the rest
As a hot and wholesome saving
In the parents' downy haven,
So when shades of evening climb
Supper's ready in no time.

Plünne, here, has all along
Kept this custom, right or wrong.

"Now," says Plünne, "if you will,
Sit with us and eat your fill!"
Knopp has lost his appetite
And resorts to sudden flight.

Hastily he exits there
And betakes himself elsewhere.

Friend Klaeppi

On his further travels Knopp
Came to yet another stop,
Where he called upon a chappie
By the merry name of Klaeppi.

Anyone can see how happy
Klaeppi is with Mrs. Klaeppi.

With a tenderness which pleases
He embraces her and breezes:
"Well, dear, for the nonce, good-bye!
We're invited, Knopp and I,

To the Antiquaries' Club
For a lecture and some grub."

It appears the learned gathering's
Round the corner from St. Catherine's
In a cozy little place
Called the Merry Boniface.

Klaeppi seems no stranger there.
He bespeaks some wholesome fare.

Cockerels and breaded fishes
Both are admirable dishes;

With it? Excellent proposal!
Quite! A lively little Mosel.

After which, a sparkling Rhône . . . ?
Sine qua . . . ? Precisely—*non!*

Good! They're joined by Resi, who
Will accept a glass or two.

"Well, now—all good things must end!
Would you mind . . . the bill, old friend?"

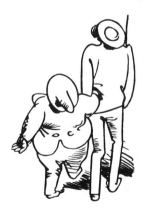

Presently, the two are swaying
To the inn where Knopp is staying.

True, it's late, but—how absurd!
They can't make their presence heard.

Klaeppi waves: "Who cares?" says he.
Come and stay the night with me."

What with one thing and another,
Finding keyholes is a bother.

"There, it's open . . . After you!
Enter, friend, and pass right through."

Knopp complies. But canny Klaeppi
Temporizes, looking happy.

Then, with no alert at all,
Knopp is pinned against the wall.

"Got you!" Mrs. Klaeppi cries.
"Antiquaries . . . stuff and lies!"

All in darkness, and unhappy,
She's confusing him with Klaeppi.

Wheee! how Knopp is brought to grips
As the besom pokes and whips!

Shlop! he shelters, more or less,
In some tub of nastiness.

Ouch! the broom's no longer whole,
And the center is all pole.

In a damp, amorphous clutter
Knopp is swept into the gutter.

Hurriedly he exits there
And betakes himself elsewhere.

Happy Event

Onward his migrations carry
Knopp on his itinerary;
To a valued friend he came,
Sourdough was his curious name.

Sourdough, full of bouncy cheer,
Has just spiked and mulled some beer.

"Yoicks!" he yodels, "Step inside!
Hip hurray! My wife just died!"

Look: beneath the candles here
She reposes on a bier.

Now she can't butt in on us . . .
Come, sit down and have a glass;

Down the hatch, and take the pledge:
Never tumble off that edge!
Marriage squeezes, let me own,
Tears and money from a stone:

Pay for curlers, girdles, bras,
Novels, fashion journals, spas,
Buy new dresses, silk-lined capes,
Concert tickets, window drapes—
Chatter, natter, nag and pout . . .
Bottoms up! She's down . . . I'm out!"

"Be not downhearted,
Morning dawns bright;
Troubles departed
Count for delight."

There, a creak, the door uncloses—
And who issues? Holy Moses!
His lamented, who had suffered
From some seizure, has recovered!!

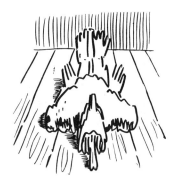

Salted, like the wife of Lot,
He is dead now, she is not.

Knopp is leaving, *ventre-à-terre*,
To betake himself elsewhere.

Oh, No . . .

Knopp once more has come to rest
On his self-appointed quest;
To an older friend he came,
Pippo was his handy name.

Laughter, bell-like voices tolling:
Pippo with his daughters, strolling . . .

"This dear fellow, is my Hilda.
Here the elder is Clotilda.
Hilda's bridal party's due
In the morning, twelve to two.
But Clotilda, I may state,
Still is fancy-free to date.

Ah—the balmy eventide . . .
Knopp and Tilda, side by side . . .
Tilda plucks a rose for him;
And he senses, deep within:
"Knopp, this moment you were blessed
With the answer to your quest!"

Soon by Pippo he is guided
Where his couch has been provided.
"This big dining room we borrow
For the big affair tomorrow.

Over here you find the spot
Set apart for you-know-what.

And your room is opposite.
Have a restful night in it!"

Knopp's sweet fancies, all awhirl,
Dance about that slender girl,
And he presses, lips apart,
Her dear rose against his heart.
"Oh, Clotilda, you alone
Shall and must become my own."—

Then he feels an inner pleading
For a little quiet reading.—
And why not? He takes the paper
And proceeds with rose and taper
Straight across the empty hall
To obey the harmless call.
Sitting, reading, like enough
You get drowsy and nod off.

It's next morning, rather late
After sunrise, seven or eight—
Peals of merry girlish laughter
Echoing from wall and rafter:
It's the bridesmaids' busy throng,
Who have been astir quite long
Decorating and adorning
Doors and walls this festive morning.—
"I can't spend all day in here!"
Quavers Knopp in stark despair,

And, well camouflaged, he streams
From the locus of his dreams
Like a rushing wind on legs;

But the threshold rudely pegs
All advance—his fall is fated.
Gosh . . . ! He is defoliated.

Secretly he exits there
And betakes himself elsewhere.

Warning from on High

Knopp ascends in headlong flight
Up a rugged mountain height.

In a stark and craggy glen
He detects a hermit's den.

Now the hermit, hoar and sere,
Issues from the crevice here
And from the old gladstone's wattle
Gravely lifts the brandy bottle.

"I am Krökel," he intones,
And I loathe all worldly drones.

All below is dross and swill.
Many thanks, I think I will.

Oh, you sponges, brushes, combs,
Body lotions, shaving foams,
Grooming aids and eyebrow tweezers,
Eyelash teasers, pimple squeezers,
Shirt-and-tie and breeches, pooh!
Krökel scorns the lot of you.

All is dross to me and swill.
Many thanks—I think I will.

Phew, you women! Pshaw, you girls!
Legs and torsos, bumps and curls,
Glances luring, bottoms inching,
Fingers amorously pinching,
All your frills and folderol,
Krökel execrates it all.

All is stench to me and swill.
Many thanks, I think I will.

But to Her, in halos golden,
Only Her, I feel beholden,
Thee alone I worship, love,
Unattainable above,
Thee, my lovely, ever far
Blessèd Emerentia.

All the rest is rot and swill.
Many thanks, I think I will.

Here the holy hermit yaws
Over backwards. Knopp withdraws.—
Knopp reflects: this anchorite
Was a pretty loathsome sight,
And long-distance mooning, roundly
Said, depresses me profoundly.

And he leaves this cheerless spot
At a dogged homeward trot.

Return and Conclusion

Knopp's return is swift and steady.
Here he is, at home already.

Heaving to behind the billows
Of his Doris, smoothing pillows,

"Wench," he stammers, "if I were . . ."
And she smiles: "With pleasure, Sir!"

Soon a modest printed head
Frames the two as duly wed:

*Tobias Knopp
Dorothea Lickyfat*

First by dry official motion
Then with fervor and devotion.

There—at peace at last and certain . . .
Whoosh! Young Cupid draws the curtain.

II Mr. and Mrs. Knopp

Admonitions and Hints

Oh, how fine, example-forming,
So to speak, heart-cockles-warming,
Is the spectacle of two
Reasonably well-to-do
People rather like each other,
Female one and male the other
(I.e., not alike in sex),
Managing to clear their decks,
Regulate their civil state,
Find that birth certificate,

And before things go too far
Step before the Registrar,
As decreed by those in charge
For young couples still at large.
Then the world exclaims, delighted,
"Thank the Lord, they are united."
Such an outcome is foregone,
This we all agree upon.—
Surely, games of forfeit fail
To appease the adult male;
Dancing? Token satisfactions
From symbolic interactions?
Spooning under rambling roses
In uncomfortable poses?
True, the last is not unwanted,
But is apt to be confronted
With parental prohibitions
Prompted by inane suspicions,
Which to lift, one must (that aged
Chestnut!) call oneself "engaged."
And that's dandy, if you will;
Yet it has its drawbacks still.
There one sits, and so does she,
Warm and snugly *en famille*,
Whispers tender nothings, squeezes
What is handy, Father wheezes,
Mother knits, the clock strikes ten,
Suddenly, you can't tell when,
It's "good night" and "soon, we hope . . ."
With your collar up, you lope,
All let down and disconcerted,
Down the sidewalks, now deserted,
Of the dark and drizzling town
To your digs; you wriggle down
Chilly blankets, cower beneath,
Chitter-chatter go your teeth;
It strikes one before your feet
Thaw within the polar sheet.
Thus, both reason and affection
Urge a marital connection.—
Then your heart is really in it:
Any day, or hour, or minute
Now you may, approved and calm,
Issue strolling arm in arm;
More—whatever is delicious,
Customary, and propitious
To embellish life and flavor,
You now sample, have, and savor.

Conjugal Delectations

Much heartening proof of the truth of this
We find in the Knopps' connubial bliss.

How uxoriously here they lie abed
On the broadbeamed couch of the happily
    wed.
Lids open early, and, all affection,

They trade sweet simpers of recollection.

The prelude, this, and fond preparation
For a long-drawn oscular salutation.

Soon Knopp, as is often the case with him,
Gives in to a mischievous vein or whim.

Quite unexpectedly he goes "eeks!"—
Producing delectable squeals and squeaks.
But Doris, who for some time has known
Knopp's own most vulnerable zone,

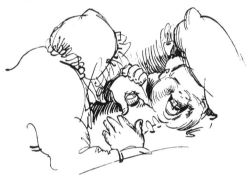

Pokes under his chin, much though he
    wriggles,
Reducing him, too, to the bleating giggles.
Attempting to rise and gain his feet
By way of a tactical retreat,
He finds himself spirally restrained

By the slack of his garment and so detained.
But faster than eye can make it out,

He performs a masterly turnabout,
Attacking deep under the featherbed,

Where then a hilarious chase is led.
Eventually, after much fun and play,
It's time to get dressed and begin the day.

Then Doris is fond of directing her gaze
At Knopp's pantaloons in their morning
    phase,
Which fascinate and divert her so
By their physiognomic variety show:

Now scowling in outraged disbelief;

Now wrenched by a paroxysm of grief.

At times the accomplished mime will pass

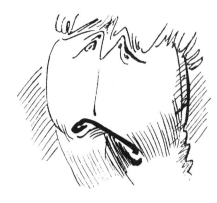

To a haughty mask of the butler class,
But presently, downing its pride, express

Most selfless and prayerful kindliness;
And, just as abruptly, reappear,

Beaming with what-can-I-do-for-you
    cheer . . .
Dorette much treasures this morning view;
Others, though, find entertainment too:
There oftentimes beckons to be seen
With dazzlingly white and glistening sheen,
At bottom quite narrow but wider on top,
A spectacle interesting to Knopp.

A stoop will develop it without fail;

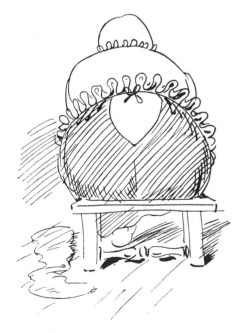

In feminine jargon they call it "white tail."
"White tail, Madame," cries Knopp with a
    laugh;

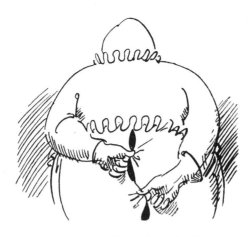

And instantly it is curtained off.

Good Times for the Old Boy

Of late his breakfast hour has meant
To Knopp the acme of content.

When Liz has brought the coffee up,

Dorette in person pours his cup.

Today a special gift of love
Is superadded from above.

Dorette presents him with a hat
On which, in braid and beads and that,
A fine embroidered pattern twines
To simulate a wreath of vines.

Knopp loves this reticule of reason,
For after Michaelmas the season
Is apt to turn from brisk to grim;
Moreover, it enhances him.

There he is seated, justly proud,
His headgear dapper but not loud,

And Doris holding spills for him
Makes his contentment overbrim.

Time passes pleasantly and fast;
Elsewhere they cook the noon repast.—
Here too, it cannot be denied,
Knopp's needs are nobly satisfied.
You might look far afield to sample
Such perfect pancakes, for example.
This is Frau Doris's shining hour:
When she takes milk, a scoop of flour,
As many eggs as will suffice,
Say, four (unless too high in price),
And bakes the subtly blended whole
With shrewd address but peace of soul,

Each time a beaming Knopp must own:
"Your pancakes, Doris, stand alone!"

How cozily he now may rest
Against dear Dorrie's ample chest;
Which times he has enjoyed of late
A light, loose tickling of his pate;
And dozing off, has blessed his fate
And the connubial estate.

Off on the Wrong Leg

There's something about Saturday
That rubs a husband the wrong way.
Much dust is raised, damp mops are used,
One errs about and gets confused . . .

Here on the sill, where Knopp must pass,
Stands Lizzie, polishing the glass;

And Knopp, whose pipe has gone to ground
And absolutely can't be found,
In that abstracted mood of his
Applies a casual tweak to Liz.

It was administered quite far down,
But Doris has noted it with a frown.
And cries: "No, I won't stand for it!

You impudent hussy, go pack your kit!"

For a while, then, the Knopps must face
their chores
Unassisted by feminine servitors,
And the morning watches, formerly void,

Now find Knopp bracingly employed.

In "Positions Vacant" it was relayed
That the Knopps required a general maid.
There soon responded, benign of mien,

A godfearing spinster by name of Kathleen,
Who firmly and faithfully undertook
To launder and clean, pray, bake, and cook.

This she does, as efficiently as Liz,
But for several idiosyncrasies.

Where at the spout of the syrup pot
A glutinous overflow tends to clot,

Shlip-slurp! its glistening neck is wrung
By a vigorous upsweep of her tongue.
Or if she feels at the baking trough
A lengthening dribble which might fall off,

Her remedy is to free her nose
By a brisk twin stroke like a violin bow's.—
The action, though graceful and rapid-
    paced,
Is noted by Doris with strong distaste.
She cries: "No, I refuse to stand for it;
You ill-mannered hussy, go pack your kit!"

Once more, then, the Knopps confront their
    chores
Unassisted by feminine servitors;
And Knopp, at the flush of the morningtide

Finds himself usefully occupied.

Once more, due advertisement was made
That the Knopps were in need of domestic
    aid;
In response to which there appeared at the
    door

A substantial maiden named Ellinor,
Who firmly and faithfully undertook
To launder and clean, pray, bake, and cook.
She clearly knows how; and in person and
    dress
Gives proof of immaculate cleanliness.

She tidies with promptitude and care
The marital boudoir of the pair;

And favors, for hair and underarm,
The lotions and toiletries of Madame;
For the care of the teeth, the tools of the
  Master

Strike her as sturdier and faster.
These choices subserve a most laudable aim,
But Doris finds fault with them all the
  same.
She cries: "No, I refuse to stand for it;
Go, ill-mannered hussy, and pack your kit!

And Knopp at the pink of the morningtide

Finds himself earthily occupied.

Knopp's Little Outing

We all, it goes without saying, aspire
To wrest from life what we most desire.
And yet, when the just man is vouchsafed
The boon for which he has begged and
  chafed,
And in the fullness of time succeeds
In grasping what he so sorely needs,
He stands, crestfallen, and hems and haws:
"Dear Lord, it's not what I thought it
  was . . ."
So Knopp, in a petulant mood of late,
Has felt at odds with the marital state.

For dinner are meatballs with barley grits—
Far from unanimous favorites.

He declines with thanks, and all suasion
  fails;

He makes for his suit of swallowtails
And, wearing a most independent air,

Stalks off straightway to the Golden Bear.

"Why, look who's here now, can it be true?
Cry out with a flattering view-halloo
Both Pelikan, skilled in the medical arts,
And Bellow, the gamekeeper of these parts.

But Knopp is not sociably inclined;

They would cut him in, but are paid no mind.

A lonely and ruminating sitter,
He drains an abstracted pint of bitter,

Pays up at ten o'clock on the dot

And makes for home at an easy trot.

A Coolness

Doris—trouble lies ahead—

Has just smoldered off to bed.

Knopp approaches on his toes . . .

The reception is morose.

"Doris!" lisps his loving plea;
"Turn around, dear—look at me . . ."

Foof! her elbow lands, quite hard,
In the bulge of his façade.
This he takes extremely ill.

Deeply hurt, but firm of will,
Back he stalks in proud chagrin

To his cronies at the inn.
Now the house may count on Knopp:
Set them up, pull every stop!

Tempers are gregarious,
Brews are multifarious,

Three o'clock is heard to sound
Ere the final stein is downed.

Homecoming

Knopp, who feels a little low,
Paddles homeward under tow.

And an entry-port is struck,
Left unfastened by good luck.

In they launch him like a raft
By a gentle shove abaft.

In the dark a helpful tray

Holds him up, but then gives way.

Light is needed, but the catch is
How to find the safety matches.

Crack! The nose-bone comes to rest
At an open kitchen chest.

Anguish thrills his very soul,

But he rallies to his goal.

By this box here . . . wait a minute . . .
No; there's milk or something in it.

Here, amidst a lot of clutter . . .
Droops a pliant lump of butter.

Wait—within this farthest nook
Is, I bet you, where we hook . . .

This (oh, hush, you'll rouse the house!)
Was intended for a mouse.

Lastly it occurs to Knopp
To investigate on top.

Yechhh!—a slide of plum preserves
Both disfigures and unnerves.

Still, along with jam he catches
Candlestick and box of matches.

This entails more frequent tries
Than are common otherwise.

All the more he feels relieved
When it is at last achieved.

To be ridda alla thish

Is his dim but fervent wish.

There, the bedroom door at last.
What? Yes. Locked and bolted fast—

Leaving but a boneless flop
To the threshold for poor Knopp.

There, he's out, just like the light;
Quite secure if somewhat tight.

Thunder and Lightning

Here Knopp scowls in the seat of power,

Dread to behold, at the breakfast hour,
Vengeful Jehovah from fez to toe
(And sore thumb throbbing like billy-o).

Look who's back! But the smile from Liz
Kindles no answering glow of his.

Whoosh-clang! with a roar and a single,
vicious
Swipe he accounts for the breakfast dishes.

A tearful Doris moves very near
And whispers a tiny word in his ear;

Which word, like a flash-fire, seems to tear
Through his head, heart, rump, and the
easy-chair.

Here's Doris, rueful and gentle-miened;
But Knopp turns into a raging fiend:

And the rubble, with terrible unconcern,
He seeds with ash from his meerschaum
urn.

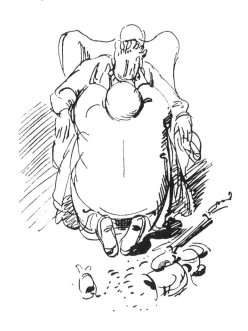

And straightway, magically improved,
He shows himself contrite and deeply
moved.

Worrisome Transition and Happy End

With a bellpull at her gate,

Name and calling on a plate,
Lives the estimable, steady,
Much demanded, ever ready

Mrs. Angst, the midwife, whose
Favor everybody woos.
Should it drizzle, pour, or snow,
Should the wind blow ever so,
Or herself be taken poorly
(Which at times must happen, surely)

Still: just let that never-single
Nervous tinkle-tinkle jingle,
And Frau Angst wakes up at once
And pursues her sustenance.
Quietly today she drops
Over to assist the Knopps.

Faintly redolent of kippers,
Mildly shod in carpet slippers,
First she warms her clammy fingers,
For the summer barely lingers;
Then she is observed to glide
To that door and slip inside.
Dr. Pelikan's long face
Helps to aggravate the case,

Signalling by frown and pout
That the outcome is in doubt.

What suspense, remorse, despair

Knopp now suffers, waiting there!
Smoking palls, he is so shaken;

His old meerschaum dies, forsaken.

Nothing shields him, it appears,
From tormenting thoughts and fears.

Be it to the loftiest casement,

Or to dungeons of the basement
That his demons drive him now,
Fever beads bedew his brow . . .

Why, he even turns to prayer,

Which with him is rather rare.—

There! The door gives way at last:
Handshakes, chuckles, pats are passed;
As in countless earlier hallways,
Smiles Frau Angst, as meek as always.
There beams Dr. Pelikan
With the glow of duty done.

Father Knopp for his part lauds
Providence with loud Thank Gods.—

There! At peace at last and certain . . .

And Frau Angst can draw the curtain.

III Julie

Prefatory Note

Being Father is a thing
Tougher far than fathering.

Lawful or iniquitous—
Fathering's ubiquitous;
Both the fit and quite unfit
Seem to take delight in it.
But the wicked sow their surplus
For no higher social purpose;
When unplanned expenses loom
They recoil in fear and gloom

And with singular discretion
Shun the clerical profession:
These, they sense with secret dread,
Are the ruthless men who wed.—

This type may well live out his life
By preference without a wife.
Without a virtuous commander
To whom to yield, defer, and pander,
He potters vaguely here and there,
Has not a decent shirt to wear,
By stages turns uncouth and gloomy,
Neglected, rumpled, coarse, and rheumy,
Till in the end by day or night
No likely girl could stand his sight.
While he may be an uncle, true—
That's all he can look forward to.

Ah, not so the man of worth!
Resolute if not with mirth,
He pays up and walks the aisle
Duly spliced in solemn style,
Does in private with elation
What befits the situation
And one day emerges, glad,
A progenitor and Dad,
And can never talk enough
Of how well he brought this off.

Julie Swaddled

Madame Knopp, as we have said,
Happily was brought abed,
And Frau Angst, who *ex officio*
Saw the baby *ab initio*,
Tutted as she swung it high:
"Just a girl, oh, my, oh, my!"
(Mrs. A.'s a downy crow,
There's not much she doesn't know.)

Knopp indeed is somewhat slow
To believe that this is so,

But, persuaded in a while,
Summons up a complex smile
And declares, inspecting her:
"Pretty thing—à la bonne heure . . . !"

Baby Knopp, for worse or better,
Has an aunt called Julietta,
And the child, the two concur,
Shall be "Julie" after her.

Julie, swaddled yet and new,
Does as babies mostly do.

Long she will be snuggled deep
In her downy nest, asleep,

Other times, lie comatose
In a pleasurable doze.

Then some whim of nature calls
For a bout of rending squalls,
Purpling countenance and gums,
Till the pacifier comes.—

All that pleases is legit
Seems the principle of it,
For the bent of natural man
Is to hog the most he can.
Parents of a son or daughter,
Never spare the soap-and-water!
Here Frau Knopp has truly earned
Grateful praise from all concerned.

At the morning's very crack
She undoes the baby's pack,

Not unlike a parcel top
(Unattended soon by Knopp).
Hygiene's brisker onward drive
Sees his interest revive.

Flushing baby's nasal track
Takes him painfully aback.

As remarkable, but welcome
Is the soothing dust of talcum.

All are glad and full of fun
Once the cleaning job is done.

Even Knopp by then feels fit
To take Julie for a bit.

Piping pretty melodies,
He will ride her on his knees

And enjoy a father's smack
On her rosy lower back.

A Restless Night

Onward in its breathless race
Rushes Time—and we keep pace.

Between diapers and pot
Julie's grown and filled a lot.

Doris slumbers; Father keeps
Rocking Julie till she sleeps.

Julie, though, for reasons best
Known to her declines to rest.
Knopp recalls that many a child
Quiets down when camomiled.

But the bland decoction fails:
She emits still louder wails.

Goodness me, what can it be?
Other end, then? Let us see . . .

Oh, how glad Knopp is to proffer
Any help he has to offer.

Not a bit of good, alack!
Burping? . . . Patting on the back?

Grant her, in the cradle's stead,
Refuge in the double bed,
With both parents warm and near?
No—she bellows even here . . .

There—a smile! It worked, at that!—
Leaping like a scalded cat,
Father marvels in mid flight:
"Drat the girl—so I was right . . ."

A Sabbath Morning

Onward in its ceaseless race
Hurries Time—and we keep pace.

Julie's smart now, and quite steady
On her own two feet already.—

Sunday morning; Daddy's up,
Splashing in his shaving cup,
Slapping airy sudsy stuff
On his whiskers' bristle-fluff.

He will go to Mass today,
For the pretty tunes they play.
Faithful Doris brings to Knopp
Swallowtails and beaver top.

Julie watches, all agape,
Daddy pinch himself and scrape.

Soon his cheek is fit to kiss;
Practice made him good at this.

Daddy goes away to dress.
Julie looks for business.

Daddy's desk first; up she wriggles.
Daddy's pen makes funny squiggles.

Look, his tick-tock watch and string.
What a pretty shiny thing.

Oops! as Julie leans and rises,
Mercy me! the stool capsizes.

What impairment Julie suffers
Is but to her rearward buffers,
But the watch is badly tossed,
And the ink as good as lost.—

Huddly, cuddly, soft and full
Is a sock, for it is wool.

Wiping ugly messes off
Wants a sock, for wool's the stuff.—

Job all done, no fuss and bother.
Julie's ready for another.

Nothing makes a better chopper
Than big Daddy's whisker-lopper.
Daddy's outfit: to what profit
Are those pigtails dangling off it?
Here a slash and there a slit,
Slice across and off with it.—

Job all done, no fuss and bother.
Julie's ready for another.

Daddy's pipe: a tarry blob
Often clogs the smoking knob;
Worse, within the hole as well
Grows a nasty, crusty shell,

And the smoker will be cheered
When the bowl's all scraped and cleared.
Job all done, no fuss and bother.
Julie's ready for another.

Here's the lid of beaver fur.
Handsome, but too large for her.

And, for heaven's sake, unfit
For a thoughtful little sit!

Stricken Pop, all washed and dressed,
Ready for his Sunday best,

Sadly noting all of this,
Has to give the Mass a miss.

Bad Boys

Onward in its breathless race
Hurries Time, and we keep pace.—

Julie—chubby, saucy, cool—
For some time has been in school,

And in her regard for boys
Tempers interest with poise.

Derek, with his shirttail out,
Isn't much to moon about.

Nor does Freddy, dim at best,
Light a flame in her young breast.

As to stumpy "Porker" Farrel,
He's the bottom of the barrel.

Fritz, so fair and crisp of curl—
He's more comfort to a girl.

No one else can do a tree
On his head as straight as he.

Julie comments with a giggle:
"All you others do is wriggle . . ."

Wounding is such loss of face.
Julie has to flee apace,

But is rammed amidships, which
Topples her into the ditch,

Upside down before those three,
Who're beside themselves with glee.

Just you wait, for Fritz is coming!
Nemesis is swift and numbing.

Fritz, dear Fritz, so kind and wise,
Helps poor Julie dry her eyes.

Julie's dress, of course, is lost.
Knopp is conscious of the cost.

Paternal Cares

Onward in its heedless race
Rushes Time, and we keep pace.—

Julie's practically "out":
Cute and plump and sound throughout.

Father marvels: where's my head?
This young miss is fit to wed!

Pondering the matter then—
There's no dearth of nice young men.

Farrel, certainly; and yet,
He's in practice as a vet.

Then there's Fred; he is apprenticed
To some pharmacist or dentist.

This is Derek, who is next on
Father's roster; he's a sexton.

Lastly, Fritz, the keeper's heir—
Not a lot to build on there . . .
Simply as a person, mind,
He's as nice as you could find,

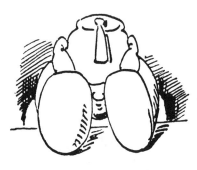

But as son-in-law he'd be
Quite a costly luxury . . .
Scanning all the coast, in short,
On whatever ready port
The paternal spyglass seizes,
Not a single prospect pleases.—

Fathers would be less unnerved
If decorum were preserved.
But, absorbed in dark affairs,
Dreadfully in love, who cares,
Who will even feign to please
Elders' sensibilities?
Your young fool but seldom asks
What goes on behind their masks;
Dads to them are paying phantoms . . .
Louts cut up and strut like bantams
For young Julie's benefit;
And she doesn't mind one bit . . .
Knopp can turn quite fierce and grim
When this is brought home to him.—

Here's the kind of thing: he might
Saunter home one moonlit night
And observe to his chagrin
A young threesome, masculine,

Joined in longing self-abasement,
Cluster at young Julie's casement.

He may poke them from the pane
With the ferrule of his cane,
Managing to scare and maim—
But it irks him all the same.

Winsome Arts

Everyone's admiring stare
Follows horsemen everywhere;

Farrel, too, who clearly shows
To advantage in this pose.
But the hornets at the bend
Misconstrue his harmless end;
Their response to equitation
Is pursuit and perforation.

Whoa! both quarters rear and buck,
And the top part comes unstuck.

Rearranged, they barrel on;
Knopp is happy, Farrel wan.—

Derek, now, promotes his suit
To the twanging of the lute.
Julie's heart thereby the better
To enchant, disarm, and fetter.
To this end he has been wringing
From his soul (and scored for singing)

An appealing slumber song;
Hear it purl, so sweet and strong:

Serenade

The eventide is mild and fair.
What chords bestir the balmy air?
    Fear naught, oh, dearest, it is I—
    A lullaby
    Your Derek offers on the sly!
Now you prepare for rest, mayhap,
Drop this and that external wrap,
Releasing now those extra locks,
Confining garments, shoes and socks,
Then clothe your limbs in silken gown
Of purest white and bed them down . . .
Ah, as your bosom softly swells,
Know where it is my spirit dwells . . .
And should there be
        A little flea
            That makes so free—
    Fear naught, my darling, it is I—
    The lullaby
Your Derek warbles on the sly!!"

Slosh! The higher powers mute
Lilting lullaby and lute;

And the singer streams away.
He is downcast; Knopp is gay.

A Visiting Aunt

Unexpectedly (as often)
Auntie Julia comes. They soften
Her with speeches warm and honeyed,

For this relative is moneyed.

Julie, too, who holds her dear,
Welcomes her with artless cheer,
Seems to find this quite exciting,
And goes up to do some writing.—

Farrel, doctoring his blues
With a restful little snooze,
Rises galvanized and swallows
When apostrophized as follows:

"Gather roses while they bloom . . . !
Come—tonight—to someone's room . . . !"

Farrel stirs himself, abeam;
And to share his self-esteem,
At Fred's pharmacy he pauses,

Reckless of the pain he causes.
Envy falls on Freddy's heart
Like a millstone on a cart;
But he doesn't let it show.
In a hospitable glow
He compounds an elixir

To his friend's success and cheer
With "good-lucks" and "cheerios";

And old Porker likes the dose.
Gay, expansive, warmly willing,
He continues guggling, swilling,

Then one sees him by degrees
Register concern, unease,

Rise from table at a bend . . .
"Come, what's up?" inquires his friend.
"Can't you stay a little more?"

But he's bolted through the door.—

Fred, the traitor, does not hover
Waiting for him to recover,
But departs for where he reckons

Sweet reward of cunning beckons.—

There—he enters, heart at throat
Straining like a tethered goat,

And encounters fingertips,
Which he raises to his lips.

Next, he clasps with desperate vigor
A complete nocturnal figure.—
You're in trouble, Fred, you chump!
Auntie's long beyond the hump!—

And with yells of shock and dread
Rings a bell to wake the dead.

Here's a posse, roughly armed.
Fred is mortally alarmed;

Shame and terror send the lover
Diving for the nearest cover.
Ouch! the sabre pricks the joint,
For it tapers to a point.

Pain, constriction, hue-and-cry
Lead to panic by-and-by.

Crash! the captive bucks and wrestles,
Emptying a set of vessels.

Everyone is stunned and damp:
Fred is able to decamp,

With a rosebush from the shelf
Needlessly attached to self.

The Garden Shed

Love is—as is rightly stressed—
Full of human interest.
If one's own respective rating
In itself is fascinating,
One's concern is hardly less
With one's neighbor's business.—

Murmuring, mumbling, rumbling, rumors
Run the rounds among consumers
(Wide perhaps or near the mark)
That not seldom after dark
Julie Knopp and Fritz are lolling
On a garden bench, or strolling.—

This report or rumor bothers
Three young persons more than others,
Who, alas, have grown apart
Over matters of the heart.

Each has privately resolved
That this problem must be solved.

Farrel leaves a flower-bed
For the open garden shed,
Wherein the incumbents store
Garden implements galore.

Shush! he slips into the shed,
Just a jump ahead of Fred.

Freddy follows quickly, whoosh!
There are Dereks in the bush.

Derek squeezes in as well:
In the moonlight's wavering spell
There approach in close formation
Subjects of investigation.

What a misery it is
When three bosom enemies
In enforced togetherness
Sweat with hatred and distress!

There was bound to be a falling
Out, volcanic and appalling.
All the horticultural kit
Gets into the thick of it.

Boom!! the rumpus is enlarged
As the shotgun gets discharged.

In the shed, now cleared of welter,
The upset young pair seek shelter,
In confusion and some fright:
Here comes Father with a light.

Nip keeps scratching at the door.
Knopp starts wondering what for.

"What the . . ." He stands petrified;
So does the young pair inside.
Then he rumbles with a grin:
"Have it your way—I give in . . ."
Mum and Julia lumber near
In peculiar slumber-gear.

What a touching, clutching, warm
Family tableau they form!!—

Conclusion

Cards are written, banns are read,
And the couple duly wed.—
Derek, as his terms require,
Pumps the pipes and leads the choir
(Freely though his tears may flow),
Glum but *ex officio*;
While, ensconced behind a barrel,
Fred the Pill and Porker Farrell
To the sound of gulps and clinks
Re-cement the broken links.

Life by now has left for Knopp
Little really worth the stop.—
Nature's plan for him is met.—
Wrinkled grows his silhouette.—

Fez and meerschaum, coat and bags,
All his aspect shrinks and sags.
People whisper with concern:
"Saw him—gave me quite a turn . . ."

Lurking in her rain-cloud, swart
Atropos of the nasal wart,
Lifts the fateful shears and, pop!
Snips the vital thread of Knopp.

Peace is his, well-earned and certain.
Zip! they draw the final curtain.

Eight Sheets
in the Wind

1878

Introduction

The thinker in his deep settee,
Sunk in profoundest reverie
And gravely relishing the yield
Of misty verities revealed,
Now drains his ruminant carafe,
Sniffs up a pensive pinch of snuff,
Exclaims ha-chooh! and wipes his phiz
And rumbles: "Laddy—here it is:

"Before arriving on this earth
You take the place for what it's worth;
At large and uncommitted yet,
You drift about, are free of debt,
You own no timepiece, feel unhurried,
Are seldom bored and never worried.
But then you fail to take due care
And shlop! are given birth to. There!

"At first the life is easy, true;
But just you wait, they'll get at you.

The title of this collection of eight vignettes on the havoc wrought by the Demon Rum is *Die Haarbeutel* ("hair bags"). This term refers to the black taffeta bags worn in the wig era to hold the fringe or pigtail of one's powdered peruque to protect the overcoat. It would bob up and down and swing back and forth like a seismograph indicating the degree of inebriety reached. In Low German, Busch's biographer Friedrich Bohne claims, "Haarbüdel" may be called to this day in the wake of persons "under the influence" or other staggerers. The English title adopted here alludes to the English saying "three sheets in the wind" for sozzlement.

"Your parents start off nice enough,
But soon turn querulous and rough.
They bring a stick and brandish it
And hurt you with it where you sit.
Whap! Wham! soon it's a double faceful,
And you exclaim: 'But how disgraceful!'

"Then you grow up, and off you go.
The world is crammed with people, though,
Most often wenches, Christians, Jews,
Who would much sooner see you lose
Your shirt than do you any good,
As you naively thought they would.
You cop it, jawful after jawful,
And you exclaim: 'But this is awful!'

"But then, behold in shady booths
Grown men, spry grandsires, tender youths
In jovial companionship
By puckered and prehensile lip
Bestir themselves to siphon up
A fluid from a bulbous cup
And send it down esophagi
With joyous zeal and upturned eye.
The zest with which the thing is done
Is proof that it is good for one.
You go to try their regimen,
You cultivate these merry men,
You do it often, do it well;
The nose expands, the bulges swell,
Until one day you start in terror
At your reflection in the mirror,
And once again you strike your forehead
And you exclaim: 'But this is horrid!'

"I feel for you; it makes me sad.
You lack self-abnegation, lad.
Self-abnegation is believing
In the rewards of not receiving.
Live frugally, on wisdom feed:
He has enough who conquers need."

Thus closes Nestor, hoar of hair,
With candor, pith, and savoir faire
To match profundity of thought.
He has a dozen oysters brought,
He lubricates their smooth disposal
With a concluding jug of Mosel,
Draws up a pinch, exclaims ha-chuie!
Collects his hat and parapluie

And homeward weaves with measured tread
To settle down and rest his head.

Silenus

Lo! Silenus at ease with the nymph, the
  pleasingly fashioned.

Gladly he drains the jar, not for the first
  time today.
Finally, though, it is time to mount the
  dependable jackass,

Though it does not come about but with a
  measure of toil.
There! he almost forgets the thyrsus,
  lifelong companion;

Were it to be mislaid, it would disturb him
  no end.—
Thus he departs at a walk, with no concern
  to be stylish;

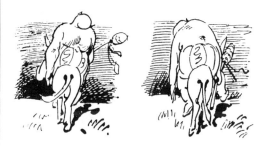

Sometimes seated like *this*, other times
  rather like *that*.
Hark! Who plays on the reed-flute?
  Doubtless young Eros, the rascal;

Up go the donkey's ears, roused by the
  gravest unease.
Worse than the notes of the flute is the
  soundless way of the blowpipe;

Given a puff at the back, pricks will fly out
  at the front.

Justly the pain incenses the laudable bearer
  of burdens;
But the unsaddled, too, feels that a line
  must be drawn.

Haply the bird may be caught by stealth
  and dissimulation;

But if he notices, he changes his place as a
rule.
Many have gained their end by ruse and
clever deception:

Body aslumber conceals vigilant spirit
within.
Whap! he has caught him. The squalls of
the winged offender are piercing,

As the convenient staff tunefully touches the
cheek.
Great is the bird's chagrin who is rudely
deprived of his pinions;

One, they are pretty to see, two, he can put
them to use.

Homeward jogs Silenus and plays on the
sonorous reed pipe;
Various airs, to be sure; oftenest, though,
toodle-oo!

The Ingrate

Here old Oscar, mildly puzzled,
Is abruptly shoved outside
On the ground that he is sozzled
(A report he has denied).

Down the roadway see him travel
At a loose and shambling stroll,
Ploughing through the jagged gravel
Saggy-kneed, but in control.

Presently his eye surprises
In the road a sudden hump,
And accordingly he rises
To negotiate the bump.

A mirage! he notes with loathing;
His façade sustains a jar,
Wreaking havoc on his clothing,
Not to mention the cigar.

All the poplars get excited
Even Oscar is sucked in.

Ragged, jagged, and in danger
There he sits in glass and soot,
But a charitable stranger
Notices what is afoot.

Hardly is he up and righted
When the road begins to spin;

Crunch! he falls upon his pockets,
Which (a prey to weakened nerves)
He has shrewdly made the sockets
Of his yet untapped reserves.

Filled with pity and compassion
For a brother sunk so far,
He restores him in some fashion
To the perpendicular.

Poof!! an unexpected whopper
From behind him finds its mark
On the stranger's silken topper
And consigns him to the dark.

Now the crumpled cover sunders
Him from sights and sounds without;
And he stands bemused and wonders
How—and why—this came about . . .

A Bland Affair

Farmer Bumpkin, blithe with schnapps,
Coasted homeward in his cups.

He encountered where he went
Some obscure impediment,

With no way to overcome it
But to climb across its summit.

All at once he has succeeded—
More abruptly than was needed.

He forsakes the foundered pipe,

Homing with a sideward swipe,

And by wayward feet is led
First into the storage shed,
Where a vessel long and low
Holds a load of rising dough.

Feeling rather faint and worn,
He maneuvers to be borne

To his couch—and for a rest
This accommodates him best.

Ah, how tenderly the bread
Pampers torso, limbs, and head!

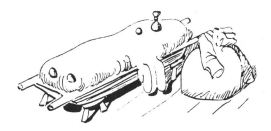

But it plugs the breathing hole,

Shattering his peace of soul.

Quickly, with a stifled moan,
He would change supine to prone.

Now he rests on waving paws,
Like the turtle of far shores.

But the novelty grows stale.
He is anxious to inhale.

The inexplicable sight
Strikes Frau Bumpkin numb with fright.
Then, bemused, she wields the broom

In perplexity and gloom.
One thing it is safe to say:
She will bake no bread today.

Fritzy

Fritzy was a shop assistant,
Also honest parents' son;
Grocer Ehrlichmann's apprenticed
Helper now a twelvemonth gone.

"Fritz!" his master once instructed,
"There is something I must do.
See you don't get into mischief
While I leave the shop to you."

But she cannot help confiding
That her pain is on again,
Calling for a gill of brandy
As a tonic there and then.

There! One shudders to report it:
Where is Fritz's upright stance?
What portends the wan expression
On Eliza's countenance?

With this caveat he exits.
Fritz, with an indulgent smile,
Lifts the demijohn of brandy,
Tilting back his head the while.

Fritz, all courteous attention,
In a warm and woozy trance
Seizes, not the brandy bottle
But the vitriol by chance.

Fritz's limbs are flailing wildly,
But the soap receives his soul;
While Eliza has her maiden
Form dissolved by vitriol.

Presently Eliza enters,
Spinster decorous and grey,
And applies for yellow soft-soap
For tomorrow's washing day.

As the suffering Eliza
Tilts the glass with eager hope,
Fritz, attending to her order,
Leans into the keg of soap.

Brandy wine is not for youngsters,
For it hinders them to grow;
And a staid and worthy spinster
Should no longer crave it so.

Hush!

Young Bumbel, undergraduate,
Kept meeting modest Widow Kate
As she came down the common stairs
To go about the day's affairs.
Since she was the proprietress,
Young Bumbel soon resolved to press
His suit, declared his warm affection,
And sought a marital connection.
"Dear Sir," her cautious answer went,
"I must esteem your sentiment,
But late at night that rough-and-tumble
Upon my stairs is bad, Herr Bumbel."
Young Bumbel swore an oath to her
That such a thing would not recur.

No use; for late that night the swain
Is half-seas-over once again.
He makes his landfall from the road
With poodle, pipe, and quite a load.

Belowstairs, prudently enough,
He pulls those heavy jackboots off,
So that he might with catlike tread

Creep up the stairs and so to bed.
By now he nears the upper end
And feels the final stair impend.
In this he takes too much for granted:

The pipestem has become implanted

Behind his gums. The staircase trembles,
The meerschaum loudly disassembles;

Like thunder tumbles boot on boot,
A rumbling Bumbel follows suit.

The poodle wails a piercing wail,
For Bumbel occupies his tail.
Here's Widow Kate. Her light impinges

On most of Bumbel, though he cringes.
From Kate is heard a dwindling mumble,
Which sounds like "How disgusting,
Bumbel . . ."

Fourhanded

The person seen relaxing here

Has not drunk up his rum-and-beer.
His pet, attracted by the brew,

Investigates the residue.

The potion seems in wondrous wise

To quicken and revitalize.
He earnestly gets down to it;

But sections of his tail are lit.

The breath is soothing, to be sure;

But dipping is the better cure.

He happily scoops up the dregs

And dances on alternate legs.

The vessel in its empty state

Has plainly ceased to fascinate.

When boredom threatens, it is wise
To vary fields of exercise.

He demonstrates a thorough grip

On elements of scholarship;

Then, for a realistic stroke,

Elects the after-dinner smoke.

He lights it expertly enough

And settles to a happy puff.
But this, like many dissipations,

Does not come up to expectations.

Both rum and seegars cheat you so:
First set you up, then lay you low.

Here rest the revelers, as one,
Till wakened by the morning sun.

The noggin heaves like molten lead;
We humans say: a morning head.

A Chilly Affair

The night is cool; the wind is keen;

And homeward wanders Master Twien.
Farsighted, as he likes to be,

He has made certain of his key.

The keyhole is a bore to spot

If it is sought where it is not.
It starts to snow to some degree;

The chilly fingers drop the key.
In bending double fore and aft

One tilts one's hat and risks a draft.

The hat feels very cold and wet;

It may get down to freezing yet.
And once again the Master bends;

The key eludes him past amends.
The water in the barrel here

Is close to zero Réaumur.

At this point, scientists advise,

The substance tends to "crystallize."
The watchman drones: "Good night to all!"

The chilly figure spurns the call.
It sits unfeeling, stark, and still;

The snow envelops it at will.

The morning dawns so grey and drear;

The milkmaid, Madam Heyndt, is here.
Frau Twien receives her at the door

And notes the singular décor.
"Well, well," she calls in agony,
"He's had one for the road, I see!

Henceforward, worthy Madam Heyndt,
I'll trouble you for just a pint!"

Night-Crawlers

The Master's out again quite late.

His furnishings sedately wait.
There. Made it back, as good as ever.

The furniture has doubled. Clever!
Now look at this! The jackboot-tree

Has made him fork below the knee.

The hatstand, too, so staid before,

Has lost its former solid core.
One's strength is clearly overtaxed.

High time one—easy! . . . aah—relaxed.
No point in taking off more clothes.

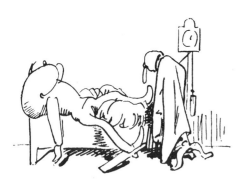

All that is wanted is repose.

Ouch!! Dammit! In the interim

Some bug or crab has got at him.
It tweaks however one may dodge;

The very devil to dislodge.

There—shaken off. No, it is not!
It's got him in another spot.

He whirls to face what he may find.

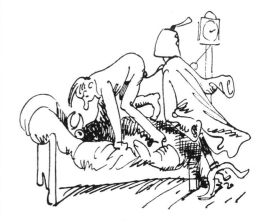

Then someone jabs him from behind.
Eek!! Yipes! He feels him, hard and jolting;

A shape unearthly and revolting.

Ha! Strike and parry, rise or fall!

A fight to win or lose it all.

They roll and writhe, up flies a limb;

A fresh assailant falls on him.
But there! the foe succumbs, undone.

The fight is over; he has won.

At last! Exhausted, he retires;

To rest is all he now requires.
But something's happened to his face.

His nose moves outward into space.
His head expands. It hums a lot.

It's metal now. Gone all to pot!

A watering can. But sore, and numb . . .

Oh, devil take it! It's a drum!
Next morning, strange anomaly:

A corkscrew where each hair should be . . .

Fips the Monkey

1879

Pegasus, my noble charger,
Carry me to Africa!
Man is black there, fruit is larger,
Birds are gaudy, life is raw.

Dress in Africa is simple:
All one needs is, say, a hat,
Or a G-string, or a dimple.
One is black and that is that.

True, it leaves the spirit lower,
Even father apes will blanch,
When the never-ending Boa
Slithers hissing down a branch.

Capsized Turtles gesture tensely,
Panic hastens every leg,
And the Ostrich toils immensely
To depose her mighty egg.

Marabous are short on culture,
Tearful is the Crocodile,
And around the screeching Vulture
Hover the Hyenas vile.

But the Monkeys, eyeballs roaming,
Cunning hands both fore and aft,
Hunt for vermin in the gloaming,
Full of clannishness and craft.

Uncle scratches with abstraction,
Papa scours his rump with care,
Auntie uses brisker action;
Ma inspects her son and heir.

"Fips" shall be his appellation.
As for conduct—ah, we fear
That the course of this narration
Will disclose a sad career.

Constancy is not his talent.
Once he earns abiding trust.
First he is alive and gallant.
In the end he bites the dust.

Chapter One

This Fips, except to biased eyes,
Could hardly win a beauty prize.
Instead, the source of his appeal
Are nerve, vivacity, and zeal.

No goings-on go on without him.
He mimicks everyone about him.
His mind is ever set on loot,
And mischief is his strongest suit.

A Blackamoor did there abide,

Who captured monkeys (and then fried).

He much prefers to catch them young:
"They fairly melt upon the tongue!
The old are hardly worth the baiting,"
He often said, expectorating.

To set his trap, he goes and culls
Three plump and tempting melon hulls.

For on his head the jumbo prize,
For on his hands the smaller size.

He dons a sheaf of straw and hay

And waits in hiding for his prey.—
This still life looks indeed delicious
To anybody unsuspicious.
The melons' size and luscious green

Bring Fips in haste upon the scene.
Of course it would not be the least

He chooses for his morning feast.
But as he lifts the topmost treat,
Some underneathness lifts his feet.

He turns and is appalled to find
His limbs enclosed in melon rind.
The wicked man picks up his prize

To push it home wheelbarrow-wise.
This huntsman wears a nasal ring
(For smartness more than anything).

Fips coils his tail around this charm.
The huntsman stiffens with alarm.

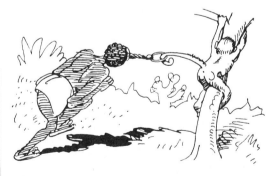

The nose revolves in pain and stress
And forms a spiral of distress.
A branch is bent in its direction.

The ring is hooked to make connection.
The captive captor curls his hands,

His soul contracts, his nose expands.
A sudden jerk relieves the tension.

The ornament stays in suspension.

The hunter, after this event,
Pursued a vegetarian bent.

Chapter Two

Fips, need I mention, leaves chores and
    bothers,
With no twinge of possessiveness, to others.
But when he observes something being done
Which appears either profitable or fun,
He tends to approach with indecorous haste
To examine the thing and attempt a taste.

One sunny day he chanced to be
On top of a palm overlooking the sea.

A ship lies at anchor in the bay,
Whence a boat just now is pulling away.

A man is seated on the thwart
Without boots or footgear of any sort.

Yet before him, quite visible to all,
Stand two pairs of boots, one large, one
    small.

The smaller pair, we may confide,
Is coated with glutinous pitch inside;

And here, having shipped the second oar,

He carries both pairs of boots ashore.
He bears them carefully under his arms

While raising most pitiful wails and alarms.

But the very moment this man of woes
Feels one of the boots about his toes,

He displays most evident signs of relief
From his recent paroxysm of grief.

And with both boots on, as one can see,
He beams with the jolliest bonhommie.
And soon, at a carefree and jovial trot,

He makes for the steep-to shoreline—not
Without leaving, unthinkingly as can be,
The small pair of boots underneath the tree.
Fips shins expectantly down the trunk,

And when he, prompted by greed and
    spunk,
Has pulled the boots up just so far,

Who would come back but the jolly tar!

Alas! with his shanks so smartly decked,
He cannot move fast, and his flight is
    checked,
His frantic squirms are of no avail;

The sailor embarks him by means of his
    tail.

They make for the schooner with undulant
    motion;
The schooner sails up the Atlantic Ocean,
And the sailorman (whose name is Schmidt)
Takes Fips to Bremen—no help for it.

Chapter Three

At Bremen here, a Master Krüll

Lived by the barber's quiet skill,
And every burgher of the town
Possessed of whiskers, hair, or down
Resorts to Krüll's tonsorial arts
And issues as a man of parts.

Schmidt, too, receives a trim and set,
And Krüll, much taken with his pet,

Reflects what such a treat might do
To entertain his clients too.
Since Schmidt can be prevailed upon,
Krüll buys and owns him from then on.

It came about and happened so
That Krüll, when business was slow,
With rapid strides, as was his way,

Withdrew into his atelier,
Where shimmering pomades are blended,
Toupées are woven, pigtails mended,
In short, where dedicated skill
Accomplishes the spirit's will.

On Krüll's departure, Fips is joined
By Farmer Dümmel (stoutly loined

If thin of head) who takes the pose,
Emits a strong bouquet, and shows
A speechless need for being barbered
(Of which no doubt could well be
    harbored).

Hop! Fips has mounted him and snip!
Embarked on his apprenticeship.

The scissors scamper, missing badly;
The client bears it, but not gladly.

Oops! quite a painful blunder here,
Injurious to the outer ear.

"Whoa!" Dümmel shouts, alarmed and
    vexed.
Fips gets the curling irons next.

The iron glows and heats the tissues;
A plume of smoke and vapor issues;

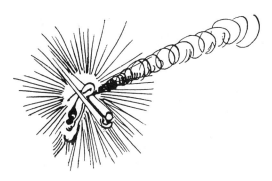

At once the world's delights have dwindled
In throbbing blazes, ever kindled
Afresh at one live source or pole,

Which Dümmel douses in a bowl.

The Master's back, a heavy twist
Of horsehair whistling in his fist.

The mirror rings, the arm goes lame,
Krüll's face appears within the frame.

"I soon may be unwanted here,"
Thinks Fips, about to disappear.

Chapter Four

Dusk had fallen when, sedately,
With a friend she valued greatly,
Long her suet-pudding mate,
Maud was dining tête-à-tête.

"Pudding smoothes," he said, "my inner
Man"; so past the little dinner
See a shapely, plump, caressing
Pudding with madeira dressing,
Brown and subtly fragrant, rise
To the friend's ecstatic eyes.

But they haven't started eating
When—Good Lord! their hearts stop
    beating!—

Aromatic vapors tracking,
Here is Fips—at once attacking,
Covetous of hands and mind
To abstract the precious find
(For himself as like as not)—

Ouch! the thing is much too hot!

Much too hot to hold, in fact.
Shlop! the friend is capped and sacked,
With the pudding still unflawed.

Glubba! down the neck of Maud
Deep into her bodice course
Waves of red madeira sauce.

Thus sweet peace is shattered often,

Just when souls and manners soften
On some warm congenial pleasance,
By a rude and alien presence,
Leaving naught astir within
But a croak of choked chagrin.

Chapter Five

Fips feels a clamorous urge to feed.—
His native agility spurred by need,
He darts by secluded alleys and nooks
Into the back of a pastrycook's.

There delicious creations of cream and
   paste
For every conceivable want or taste
Abound—sweet cornets and puffs in droves,
And artfully braided pretzels and loaves;
Nearby, for the taster's more manifold
   pleasure,
Lie almonds, nuts, raisins in heaping
   measure.—

"Hark!" cries Master Köck with an anxious
   look,

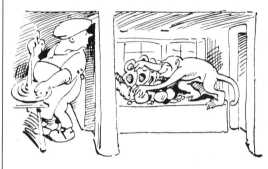

"What's rummaging in my storage nook?!"

Anxiety turns into shocked dismay:
There's Fips like an animate pastry tray,
Four pretzels, like so many peas in a pod,
Are strung on his tail by way of a rod,
And chocolate puffs, as if on pegs,
Adorn the four thumbs on arms and legs.
Köck seeks to arrest him, to be sure,
By his handy posterior annexure,

But having just mixed the batter for crêpes
He loses his grip, and the thief escapes.

He raises a desperate hue and cry;
Mamselle Clothilda just happens by.
With a piercing squeal the dear old thing
Keels over, pot, bag, and everything.

Fips charges beneath, between, and out.
But here comes a boisterous cobbler's lout,

Who, scoring a bull's-eye on his hip,
Jars all the fine cream puffs from his grip.

A beggar man next bars his advance

With crutches and an expectant stance.

This hunchback clearly would like very
  much

To snag a nice pretzel by means of his
  crutch.
Success, though, is only partly won:
Fips leaves him no leg to stand upon.—

Like a foundered beetle he weaves his
  limbs.—
But Fips, unstrung and exhausted, skims
Hastily over the bridge and down
With the last of the pretzels, and out of
  town.—

It is dark by now and not cozy a bit;

He clambers over a parapet
In hopes of a well-earned night's repose

When zap! the jaws of the fox-trap close.—

At once there steps from the mansion's side
A gentleman, looking gratified.

"Ah," he cries, "you, it seems quite clear,
Are the chicken thief! Well, well, well, come
  here!"

With this and a shove of bonhommous fun

He decants Fips into a sack, whereupon
Without any further inspection rains

Chastisement over all it contains.

Then, just in case, he locks his catch

In a recently vacant poultry hatch,
So after a calm night's interim
He may turn a more searching gaze on him.

Chapter Six

He who is inclined to stray
From the straight and narrow way
Finds the cure of cane and fasting
Chastening (though rarely lasting).—

Fips endured his cell of lumber
Till, upon refreshing slumber,
Dr. Fink (such was his name)
Eager to inspect his game,
Gingerly untied the sack . . .
He is taken quite aback
When, much sobered, weak, and dim,
Meek of spirit, limp of limb,

Fips, reordering his frame,
Greets him, courteous if lame.

Mrs. Fink with a kind smile
Proffers him an apple, while
Farther back the pudgy, chubby,
Plump and kindly nursemaid Nubbie
And Eliza at her breast
Get the giggles at this guest.—

Only two dissent from that:
Snips the dog and Grips the cat,

For this uninvited boarder
Augurs discord and disorder.

Fips disarms his watchful forum
By observing strict decorum.

In the morning, quick as quick,
He brings wood and lights a stick
For Fink's pipe; he even will
Grind up coffee in the mill,
And keep silent when they play
At a musical soirée.
But he quite incontinently
Loves to rock Eliza gently,
Or if she is cross or sick,
Cheer her with a merry trick.
He is happiest, one can see,
In Eliza's company.

His deserts are not forgotten:
Out of gaily flowered cotton
He receives for graceful boons
Subtly tailored pantaloons,
And a pea-green (charming taste!)
Dress-coat with a tapered waist;

Which combine to make a trim,
Finely turned-out lad of him.

Chapter Seven

Here in her crib Eliza lies.

Fips watches patiently for flies.
Meanwhile, as Nubbie idly wonders
What she might do, a hornet blunders
With buzzing up and down, in vain
Belaboring the windowpane.

She wafts the lost excursionist
Into a handy paper twist,

Then proffers it, a smile of guile
Suggesting hidden treats the while.

Fips deftly pulls the bag apart;
Mistrust is alien to his heart.

A buzz, a stabbing pang—the stinger
Is driven home into his finger.

The odious thing is brought to book;

And he regains his tranquil look,

Returns to where Eliza lies
And watches patiently for flies.

One proves a quite uncommon pest
By its tenacity and zest,
Now crawling low, now whizzing high,
Now farther off, now closer by,

Now climbing slopes to Nubbie's peak,

Now basking on her bulbous cheek.
The worthy girl has nodded off;
The shock is therefore rude enough

When—shlop! the swatter interferes,

And it deceases and adheres.

Fips settles back upon his stern
With almost instant unconcern,

His visage bathed, as one can see,
In impious serenity.

Chapter Eight

Let a person get lucky the least little bit,
And someone will give him green looks for
    it.
Fips has abstracted a turkey bone
With quite something left to work upon,

While in the background moisten their lips
The cat called Grips and the dog called
    Snips.

Mee-arf! They are jumping him, catch and
    snatch,

Rrr-clamp! goes the dog, and the cat
    scritch-scratch!
Fips hastily scrambles, hands over hocks,
On top of some sort of a pantry box,
Where, it would seem, his hosts and friends

Store sundry domestic odds and ends.

The twosome, before this godlike feat
Beats an undignified retreat.

To an end of string Fips found inside
The bone is attached and adroitly tied.

Now he snakes it, unholy joy on his face,
Through a basket with an imperfect base.

Grips promptly chases the drumstick bait

Deep into the open wicker gate.

Oops! he's constrained in it, while Fips
With a pair of pincers that grabs and clips
Takes care to remove those dangerous
claws.

As it happens, just at the tips of his paws
Is where he most exquisitely feels,
And heavenward rise the poor footpad's
squeals.

The tail, bent aback and upward headed,
Is passed through the handle and fully
threaded

Then neatly secured with a laundry-pin,
Lest nervousness make it slip out again.
Snips finds himself left with the bone, and
thus
Elects to take leave without undue fuss.

This modest design, though, was bound to
fail

When Fips laid hold of him by his tail,

Imparting to him such centrifugal vim
As to drive cerebration right out of him.

Not unlike a sleigh he is dragged or jarred
Outdoors to the middle part of the yard.

And there, like a clapper for some great
bell,
Fips dangles him over the well for a spell,
Where persons of delicate nerves must
frown
Upon being suspended and looking down.

He then, looking anything but aloof,
Is helped by the drainpipe onto the roof,

And rested across the chimney flue,
Now far from smoke-free, it is true.

Such smoke to the eye is tart enough,
And it makes you sneeze, too, and even
  cough
Until it drives out any other idea
But: "This is enough, let me out of here."

Snips, smoked now, and having reached this
  stage,
Drops backward and over a mansard cage,

And Grips, on an exit route of his own,
Discerns that he is no longer alone.

They pour off the roof at confusing speed,

But come to a stop, temporarily treed.

Here's where they separate, not without
  pain,

And each carries on

By himself again
Henceforward Fips is acknowledged lord

By these two creatures, if not adored.

Chapter Nine

A grand or upright, one must own,
Well polished, lends a parlor *tone*.
In terms of music, it affords
Less incontestable rewards.

Yet Fips is tempted, for his part,
To try the keyboard's subtle art.

Right at the start his left hind limb
Proclaims the talent lodged in him;

And with both right and left employed,
An apple still may be enjoyed.

Four-handed play takes two, of course;
Fips is his own complete resource.

Piano sounds, thus executed,
Uncommon tender, soft, and muted.

Here join, like tugboats in a fog,
The tomcat Grips and Snips the dog.

Like all duets, this too presents
A pair of open oral vents.

Loud bursts of music and good will
Are often taken fiercely ill;

While artists yield in haste and pique
To gusts of uninformed critique.

Chapter Ten

After their wont engrossed in fragrant port
  and in converse,

Here sat Professor Klöhn and Fink, the
  worthy physician;
Roundly the former concluded his lucid
  discourse as follows:
"O most reverenced friend! Nay, nothing
  surpasses the lofty

Wisdom of Nature's resource.—Most
  manifold herbs she created,
Tough ones as well as soft (though the last
  in the main for the table).

Animals, too, she devised, delectable,
  harmless, and utile,
Wrapped them about in skins, whence
  boots are then manufactured,
Filled their insides with meat of substantial
  nutritive value;
But at the last she shaped, as grateful heir to
  her bounty,
Man's high form, and bestowed the port of
  the mouth for an inlet:

Upright, behold! he stands, and in dignity
  bears what is sent him!"

Thus the Professor spake, rose up and
prepared to be covered.

Woe! by the slopes of the nose, ink trickles
and enters the mouth-port;

Glutinous—woe!—with gum, adheres the
commodious kerchief.

Wroth, with an ominous flourish he raises
the willowy knobstick.

Ouch! a loop on the thumb brings pain and
instant tumescence.

Hastily then he withdraws, with dignity
scarcely apparent.

Chapter Eleven

Comfortably tucked in bed,
Flannel nightcap on her head,

Here is Nubbie, all engrossed
In the *Ladies' Weekly Post*.
Soothed by this, she soon enough

Blinks, and nods, and dozes off,
Ceasing thus to be aware
Of the candle burning there.—

First the taper burns obliquely

And consumes the hapless weekly,
Then the drapes, the walls, the lot!

People issue at a trot.—

Running limberly, the Master
Saved his bootjack from disaster;

Mme. Fink, though much alarmed,
Brought her mousetraps out unharmed.

Here comes floating from a ledge
Nubbie, smoldering at one edge.

Luckily she hits a bin

Cool and damp to settle in.

Three are now in safety there.

Where's Eliza, though? Oh, where?

Look! With baby cradled tight,
See the gallant Fips alight,

By a graceful swing and reach,
Nimbly on a nearby beech,

With restrained agility
Slither gently down the tree,

And depose her, safe and sound,
By her parents on the ground;
Setting down the bottle first,
Lest Eliza suffer thirst.—

Chapter Twelve

Fink was insured, praise be to the Lord,
With the Aachen Fire Insurance Board,
And after a year or two, no more,
Lives far more grandly than before.

Fips's life since then, one need hardly say,

Has been pleasurable in every way.—

He soon finds it tedious, though, or more:
A complete and unutterable bore.
For, sadly, the slave to a life of crime
Must hanker for novelty all the time
And evinces, as well, a most infamous trend
To remain what he is to the bitter end.

It came about that the Finks one day
Set out together in full array
To do some shopping along the mall
And pay old Professor Klöhn a call.—
Fips, who is dying for deviltry,

Makes up his mind: he will break free.

He is at large. The bunnies quail.
Downfield a wanderer plods the trail.

His heart stops beating, more or less.
Before him marches a potteress.

Now, earthenware is quite fragile matter,
And, falling, creates an unearthly clatter.
Just down this lane (thus Heaven has
    aimed)
Lives farmer Dümmel, whom we saw
    maimed.

Fips helps his halfgrown chicks escape,
Regardless of their gauge and shape.

Here's junior, swaddled and besnotted,
A sandwich in his . . . Fips has got it.

Her young one's ululating squawk
Brings out his dam, as white as chalk.

With the terrified cry: "It's Beelzebub!"
She lands in a neighboring laundry tub.

Dümmel knows him at once, though, and
    hollers out:
"It's that devilish murdering barber's lout!"

He seizes the rifle, last tried and found true
In an earlier crisis at Waterloo.

A posse of neighbors in battle trim,
Hastily gathered, fall in with him.

And as they advance with deliberate speed,

One suddenly cries: "You've got him
    treed!"
All freeze with a shrinking sense of doom.

Dümmel gets in position;—takes aim;
—and—Wooom!!

An almighty bang and kick to the rear:
This gun has not fired in many a year.

The End

Lackaday! too stoutly aimed, I fear.
Fips must die as befits a rogue's career.—
And all those he has offended once
Arrive on the scene, as if by chance.
There's the black with the bipartite nose,
Now Adele's groom, one must suppose;
Mieke, Krüll, the bellied Köck we knew,
Beggar, wayfarer, that pottress too
Are met; yet of all assembled here,
Is there even one to shed a tear?
You would surely look for one in vain
In the rheumy eyes of Professor Klöhn
As he lifts them from the bleeding chest,
Standing with the Doctor and the rest.
But Liza seeks Fips's hand as she nears
And, alone, her eyes abrim with tears:
"Fips, poor Fips . . ." she whispers to her
    friend.
Thus he dies. And all is at an end.

He was buried at the garden's edge,
In that corner by the leafy hedge
Where the banks of white hydrangea
    bloom.
There, they say, you still can see his tomb.
Grips's and Snips's bereavement knows no
    bounds,
It is said on very slender grounds.

Clement Dove,
THE POET THWARTED

1883

First Chapter

I envy people who can pen
A pretty poem now and then.

Congenitally shrewd and clever,
Man recognizes, now as ever,
That much contrariness and woe
Besets him daily here below.
Joy is capricious and elusive,
Annoyance blatant and obtrusive.
One goes about all glum and dank,
His buttonhole so void and blank;
Another feels that life is blighted
Because his love is unrequited.
Perplexities dog every stride;
And one that cannot be denied,
The worry how to make ends meet,
Keeps us forever on our feet.
A hearty "How are you" will quickly
Make most of us feel somewhat sickly;
We manage but a feeble glow
And mumble "Oh, so-so, you know . . ."
Avoid the lying hypocrite
Who yodels "Splendid! Very fit!"
For by and large, we spend our days
In vague discomfort and malaise.

Not so the bard. For hardly palls
The dreary sight of his four walls,
When, presto, he has struck and furled
The moldy backdrops of our world,
And issues from its gloom and tension
Into the poets' fifth dimension.
(The fourth is full of cosmic mists
And rank with ghosts and physicists.)
Here is the realm of light and buoyance,
Here he is rid of all annoyance,
Here from the boundless-bosomed Muses
The priceless stuff forever oozes
For him to gather and decant
To his hygienic dairy plant.
The honest dairywife each day
Creates fresh butter just this way.
The first to rise, the last to drowse,
She tugs between the legs of cows
With cunning wrists, astride a stool;

And what comes out, she sets to cool
On shelves, where soon with finger bent
She skims the fatty element,
Collects it in a mighty urn,
Rolls up her sleeves and starts to churn.
Long with the perforated brass
She worries the elusive mass.
It squelches, squooshes, gulps and goops,
Leaps up and down in tortured loops,
Until the substance, tickled sick,
Disintegrates in thin and thick.
And now she reaps the rich return:
She lifts the thick stuff from the churn,
She works and plies it, kneads and tucks;
At last she reverently plucks
With tender fingers from the mold
The cake of butter, plump and gold.

Just so the poet. All devout,
He's squeezed and sweated something out
And eyes with pleasure and respect
The product of his intellect.
But an unselfish man desires
To share the things that he admires.
The author with his precious freight
Is not at ease, he cannot wait,
He savors neither work nor leisure
Until he can display his treasure

To kindred souls. He goes to look,
He finds a friend, by hook or crook,
And him, although he gently strains,
He unavoidably detains
And steers, as for a quiet harbor,
To some secluded bench or arbor
By one lapel or button vital
To offer him a free recital.
And there we are: Like magic issues
With crackles of unfolding tissues
From the recesses of his dress
A most voluminous MS.
His eyes grow bright, his gestures rampant,
The listener gets a little dampened,
For close and hot like pipes of Pan
He feels the impact of the man.
"Superb!" the poet's friend may say;
(The author's view, in every way.)
To credit what is clear as light
Is surely everybody's right.
What sweet fulfilment, when the find
By him discovered, shaped, and mined,
His sparkling spirit's graceful caper,
Is printed in the morning paper
And early at the dewy dawn
Delivered to the porch or lawn!
The hiss of steaming kettles rouses
The sleepyheads in all the houses,
Grandma and parents, youths and girls
With shining teeth and glistening curls
Sit down to coffee, eggs, and toast
And one by one peruse the *Post*;
And each in turn has panegyrics
For our poet's charming lyrics.
Up soars the verse and forthwith passes
Through their pince-nez or other glasses;
Past lense and retina it darts
Into the readers' brains and hearts.
Its vagrant lilt, its sinuous vowels,
They liquefy the very bowels,
They percolate to every cell
Of persons subject to the spell.
Thenceforward, deep in their insides,
Encompassed snugly by their hides
And by the divers outer covers,
The poet wafts his balm and hovers,
Until at last he is depleted,
Absorbed, exuded, or excreted.

A happy fate! But should it bore him,
A happier yet is still before him.
For Beatrice, his lady fair,
His *femme fatale*, his sweet despair,
Who tortured him with distant charms,
Now nestles glowing in his arms
And breathes: "It's me! Like, your admirer!
D'you do that pome in the *Enquirer*?
I really was RELATING to it!
It beats me, honest, how you do it!"

I envy people with this brand
Of poetry at their command.

Second Chapter

A gentle clerk named Clement Dove
Was well aware of the above.
Not that he feels deprived or harried.
He has a job, and he is married.

Four healthy children, too, all told,
Are his to cherish and to hold.
And yet he feels, for all his bliss,
That deep down something is amiss.
He yearns to write, to speak with tongues,
He wants to blossom forth in songs
That strike a chord in every man.
He feels he must, and therefore can.
Seized by the drive, his mind a hive,
He leaves his office after five

And seeks the Park, to woo the Muse
In those congenial purlieus.

One who, like him, is darkly fraught
With images, and great with thought,
Needs for his consecrated labors
A place to sit, away from neighbors.

But all the benches are encumbered
With parties odd- or even-numbered.

One might do better to repair
Where beer is served in open air.

Among the seats set out for drinking
He picks one suitable for thinking.

The waiting girl's proximity
Disturbs his equanimity,

But soon a noble draft of grain
Uplifts him to a higher plane.
A genial glow warms head and rear . . .
By Jove! A marvellous idea!

Quick for the phrase to bring it out!
Alas, it does not come about.

Just as the pen begins to fly,
Dove's hat descends on ear and eye.
A friend who has this type of mind
Thought thus to greet him from behind.

Dove leaves enraged and out of trim.
The friend drinks up his beer for him.

Arrived, he hangs his coat and hat
Upon the tree on hand for that

And gets down from another bracket
His soft beret and smoking jacket,
Which grace the poet when at home
As rhyme and meter grace the po'm.

He paces with a somber frown,
Now looking up, now looking down.

There slowly ripens in his brain
The rhythm of the first quatrain.

The doorbell shrill dispels the thrill.
Here comes his lady with a bill.
She warbles to him: "Clement dear,
I have to bother you, I fear.
The cobbler's boy is at the door.
He says we owe ten-twenty-four."
With special venom one resents
Pecuniary botherments.

Now let us hope he beats the jinx.
He stands by his *prie-dieu* and thinks

"O vision graceful and appealing!"
Enraptured he adjures the ceiling.

This time the door bursts even wider:

"Dad, you're the horse and we're the rider!
Come on, we're carrying the mail,
And Indians are on our trail!
Whoa, let me get up on his rump.
Now jump, you lazy pony, jump!

Oh giddyup! Hey, little Jim,
You'd better lay the whip on him!"

No loosely anchored compositions
Can gain a hold in such conditions.—
A man so circumstanced who might
Conjecture that the dead of night
Should be conducive, inter alia,
To lucid thought, is in for failure.
Papa has just gone on to bed.
His feet grow warm, and in his head
There starts that incandescent glow . . .
Someone goes Waah!, at first quite low,
But one Waah always wakes another.
Soon the whole room is in a pother.
From Mama's mouth a strident hissing
Supplies a part that has been missing;
And last, beneath the overtones
Chimes in the bass of Papa's groans.
A father's feelings at this stage
No bachelor can ever gauge.

Third Chapter

An intellectual in a pinch
Acts, while a lesser man would flinch.

Dove realizes that his power
Needs but the quiet place and hour
To catalyze in calm seclusion
The tranquil growth, the final fusion.
Thus diagnosticates his mind:
Leave this environment behind!
Retire to a rustic scene,
Where life is pleasant and serene,
Where Nature stills all haste and passion,
And Virtue is not out of fashion!

Poets are apt to travel light:
A Gladstone bag, embroidered bright,
Is trim and does not take much packing.
A little hat should not be lacking.
A campstool, notebook, bow-tie spruce,
Soft-collared shirt a little loose,
A Faber pencil sharp and yellow,
And last not least, the old umbrello.

Seen off by all the family,

He cries: "Good-bye, dear Emily!
I'll think of you among the peasants
And bring you back some lovely presents!"
With this he makes on wingèd feet
For a bohemian's third-class seat.

With hoot and hiss, with clank and cough
The little engine potters off.

First slow, then swiftly flitted past,
By wires interknitted fast,
The dour and dull fraternal souls
Of countless telegraphic poles.

Those fanning fields and whirling fences
Are apt to stupefy the senses
And turn the spirit back inside.
The undulations of the ride,
The gentle sway and rhythmic tremble
Help thoughts to waken and assemble;

And some that might have meant to hover
Just out of range, are flushed from cover.

At length to Clement's mind appears
A brace of exquisite ideas.—

Here is his stop! The whistle toots.
A countryman in hobnailed boots

Now enters like a buffalo
And throws his weight on Clement's toe.

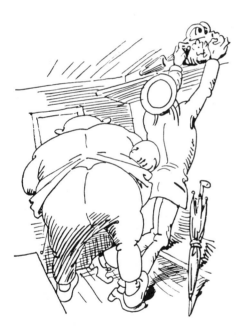

The bloom of youth, it fades and wanes.
A corn remains.
We know the symptoms well enough:
The lips are pursed, as though to puff;
The limbs grow stiff, the eyes are closed,
Some curled-up nerve ends are exposed.

The subject as a whole is glued
In an eccentric attitude.

This ritual posture of distress
Does not afford the least redress.
But any witness of one's plight
Seems much the better for the sight.

Fourth Chapter

How blithely in the noonday haze
The little hamlet meets the gaze!

The poet, bothered by a blister,
Welcomes the unpretentious vista.

Here on his horsie little Art
Rides through a puddle, bless his heart.

There in the barnyard, blunt and young,
Stands Ebenezer in the dung.
His mood serene, his stance superb,
He scents the air with homely herb.

The honest churl admires Pearl,
The pert and buxom hired girl.
She keeps the goatshed nice and clean;
And peace enfolds the rustic scene.

In modest quarters of his choice
Dove listens for Apollo's voice.
Inhaling deeply, he admires
The placid view, the sunset's fires;
He listens to the pensive knells

Of vesper and of cattle bells;
And presently the Delphic lyre
Strikes up and touches him with fire.

Kerplunk! Above the pink geranium
Intrudes a huge and hornèd cranium.

With evil breath and muzzle spread,
It trumpets fit to wake the dead.
The poem's graceful counterpoint
Is jarred and shattered out of joint.

Let poets hide when Nature sings!
The singer exits through the wings.

Fifth Chapter

The morning dawned; the sun arose.
Is Dove restored by sweet repose?
Dost know the tiny fiend with wings
That flits about the nose and sings?
Dost also know that other batch,
Quite wingless, but as hard to catch?

Take a good look at Clement's map.
Don't ask, just pity the poor chap.

Beneath the flowering lilac here,
Clement has settled with his gear.

Behind him, where the fence is rent,
Young Arthur loiters with intent.

He arms his horsie with a stinger
And evidently means to linger.
He starts committing hostile acts
His victim misconstrues the facts.

Suspecting a mosquito bite,
He claps his hand upon the site.

This makes the poet somewhat warier.
More strength is needed in this area.

The stool is snatched away. He settles
Into a thicket full of nettles.

He pauses to inspect the haul.
Perhaps it wasn't one at all.

So down again, and that was that.
Now let us—Oops! there goes his hat.

"A breeze," he mutters with a frown,
Retrieves his hat and pulls it down.

This is conclusive evidence!
A joker lurks behind this fence
The thing to do with such a chap
Is to play dumb and lay a trap.

But hardly has he found it so,
When he is punctured from below.

Still unsuspecting, he resumes
His seat, or rather, he assumes
The stance, and takes the seat for granted.
No wonder he is disenchanted.

He stoops again and sits in wait,
A tempting overhang for bait.

The stick is quick, but he is quicker;
His timing could not have been slicker.

The reasoner was not misled.
He hit the nail upon the head.

Dove skips about and sheds some blood.

Young Art regains his native mud.

Sixth Chapter

Most men of letters like a date
With Nature in her virgin state.
The gentle folds of flowering heaths
Invite to saunter, braiding wreaths
Of buttercups and dandelions.
One wanders through the scented pines,
Glad to renounce for Nature's essence
All architectural excrescence.

Here Clement dallies in a trance,
Devoutly raising limbs and glance.
He feels the world is vast and blue
Especially in upward view.

But isolationist and shrinking
Remains the earwig's way of thinking.
Deaf to creation's joyous chord,
It clambers meanly through the sward.
To feel protected, snug, and smug
Is all that matters to the bug.

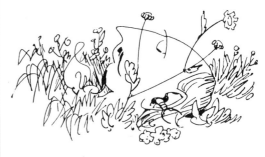

Seen from the viewpoint of a boarder,
The poet's ear looks made to order;
That close and gloomy shelter seems
Ideal for sleep, perchance for dreams . . .

But if it thinks a long career
Is yet vouchsafed to it down here,
It errs.—A swipe of Clement's shoe
With energetic follow-through

Destroys, but for a scrambled rest,
The shape peculiar to this pest;
And as an independent agent,
It disappears from Nature's pageant,
Thus proving it no pass to bliss
To crawl and mind one's business.
Forthwith, and at a lively pace,
Our friend relinquishes this place

For a more elevated perch
Atop a knoll, beneath a birch.

A bird skips overhead and trills.
The poet's soul expands and thrills.
Fresh glories swim into his ken.
His genius crackles in the pen.

Whiz-ping! Oh ding! A shocking thing.
Relieved, the little bird takes wing.

And likewise the terrestrial singer
Has just decided not to linger.

The sky, at first but lightly clouded,
Now lowers ominously shrouded.
A little rain is safely shed
By an umbrella fully spread.

Ungainly and of little use
Is an umbrella with a sluice.

Across the meadow, fast and lithe,
Strides Ebenezer with a scythe.
The gust and rain obscure his view.
Dove's canopy is slit in two.

But this will not cause Dove to flinch,
Who kept his head by half an inch.
What's more, the rain-cloud has receded,
And shelter is no longer needed.

Dove strolls downhill a little while
And meets young Pearl atop a stile.

He stops in passing, half in jest,
And tries to fasten at her breast
A playful flowery caress—
(The Poet and The Shepherdess).

A slap strikes home like thunderclap.

A fall compounds the sad mishap.

What fools men be! They stand perplexed,
Look sheepish or a little vexed,

Instead of calling upon Science
To solve the thing by ergs or ions.
There swells a cheek, all lush and free.
Here hangs a hand. Add Energy.
Now, by the secret operation
Of extra-physical causation,
This Energy, at first but latent,
Becomes kinetically patent.
It yanks the hand up like a streak
And turns to Heat along the cheek.
This heat is carried by the nerves
Through many complex twists and curves
To a compartment in the brain,
Where the effect is felt as Pain.

(Thermodynamics, ch. 3.)
A clouted ear to you and me.

Seventh Chapter

The Moon. O name so apt and round,
Of soft, insinuating sound!
Who could be so invidious,
So callous, cold, and hideous
As not to have his heartstrings stirred
To gentle tremors at the word?

The hamlet in the moonlight gleams;
The peasants dream their hoggish dreams;
In slumber wrapped are man and brute,
Alone the watchman has to toot,
Because his office brooks no dozing;
But Clement, moonstruck, is composing . . .

What signal is this from the stable?
It's Pearl who beckons from the gable!

She evidently feels remorse
For having been so rude and coarse.
The poet, who is not a boor,
Accepts the tender overture.

He climbs, by way of some manure,
Through a restricted aperture.

Hullo? A harsh and scornful bleating
Is a most unexpected greeting.

The charge comes with a single grunt.
The author's pelvis bears the brunt.

A two-pronged thrust that hurts and vexes
Strikes home about the solar plexus.

A hamper offers welcome shelter.
The poet takes it, helter-skelter.

The wickerwork is sound and tough.
The point is, is it deep enough?
All of a sudden, Pearl is here
With her devoted cavalier;

She carries mischief in her soul,
And he a sturdy wooden pole.

He threads it through the hamper's eyes
Between the inmate's weaving thighs;
And thus uncomfortably grooved,
Dove feels himself picked up and moved.

He struggles hotly, for profound
Yawns the dark query: Whither bound?

A well-spring, moonlit, deep and cool
Awaits the swaying reticule.

Here they proceed to dunk the basket
More frequently than Dove would ask it.

Their hamper tipped and shaken clean,

The rustic lovers leave the scene.

Eighth Chapter

What boots it to defy the tide,
If just one's feet remain outside?

To Dove, besides chagrin and choler,
It booted a neuralgic molar.

A toothache, not to be perverse,
Is an unmitigated curse,
Except for one redeeming feature:
That it compels the stricken creature
To marshal all those vital forces
It used to spend on drink and horses
And bring them into proper focus
Upon a single inner locus.
The pain is hardly on the job
With that premonitory throb,
And fare ye well, embattled nations,
Forgotten are those stock quotations,
Deadlines, deductions, yearly giving;
The pattern of accustomed living
That once was palpable and plain
Seems insubstantial now and vain.

One does not like one's coffee hot,
All auld acquaintance is forgot,
For in one tooth a paltry hole
Comprises the immortal soul,
And with each purgatory bout
Grows the resolve: Let's have it out!

Before we write another date,
The poet has attained this state.

Shot through with anguish to the core,
He fumes at Dr. Pocket's door.

Projected from his cozy nest,
The doctor heeds the bell's behest.
He does not mind Dove's urgencies.
In fact, he likes emergencies.

He cries: "How do you do, dear Sir?
Won't you be seated? In this chair!

Now let us see—what have we here?"
(The finger tastes a little queer.)

"Ah yes. Quite so. Looks pretty black.
Now just relax and settle back!

Heave-ho!!
How was it? Did you feel it shift?"
"I certainly felt something lift."

"In that case there is nothing to it!
Another little tug will do it!

Heeaa—ve-ho!!!"
He prises with a hamlike paw.

The tooth stays rooted in the jaw.

"I thought as much," says Dr. Pocket.

"The obstacle is in the socket.
Five dollars net is all you owe.

I hope it passes. Let me know!"

Ninth Chapter

True, lyric bards must pay their toll
In noble anguish of the soul;

But Clement's proletarian hurt
Contributes little to convert
A singer without rank or name
Into a laureate of fame.
Above, a scowl; below, a growl;
A kerchief frames the swollen jowl.
He now detests rusticity,
With little Art's duplicity,
With Pearl's insidious perjury,
And Dr. Pocket's surgery,
The cows, the bugs, the yokels' smirks,
The whole insipid footling works,
And hears his martyred molar nag:

Oh, let's go home! (First pack your bag.)
He would have liked to reach the station
Without a noisy demonstration.

As it turns out, he must endure
A final small discomfiture.

Crude imitations of a bleat
Accompany him down the street;
The very goat behind her door
Remembers that they met before.
A guileless city man who read it
Would probably refuse to credit
How fast such information flows.
The countryman will nod. He knows.

When Dove at last has caught the train,
He feels some respite from the strain.

A mother and a wicker bag
With baby's bottle and a rag
Companion the exhausted tripper.
The infant is alert and chipper.
It waves and kicks its chubby limbs,
Its rosy muzzle overbrims,
It's such a precious little nugget,
A bachelor might want to hug it.
Oh-oh! The sunny mood departs.
Mama solicitously starts
To pipe to him his travel ration.

But he rejects it in a passion,
And with no civilized restraints

He trumpets long and strident plaints.
The milk is cold! It's not his fault.
Oh good! The train comes to a halt.

"Could you just hold him on your arm?
I'll run and get his bottle warm!"
She races to the restaurant place.
The train, one fears, will win the race.

Tooot . . . All aboard! They spring the trap.
The wailing baby on his lap,
With throbbing tooth and swollen cheek,
Dove sways along in soot and reek
Toward his own, his native station.
At five they reach his destination.
The tot, worn out by his alarms,
Rests warm and still in Clement's arms;
And yet the hope swells very large
To place him in official charge.

The guard to whom the find is brought
Declines to entertain the thought.

So does the master of the station.

So does the man at Information.

To take the foundling home to stay
Seems for the nonce the only way.

Homeward the weary wanderer fares.
Four happy children line the stairs.
"Come, children," Mother says, "let's see,
What can that great big present be?"

But when the burden meets her eyes,
She does not relish the surprise.

"Clement!!" she falters, "take it back!!"
Then everything around goes black.

The infant's mother intervenes,
Forestalling more distressing scenes.
The bottle once again is cold,
But he is in no mood to scold.

With hasty thanks the guests depart.
Dove does not take it much to heart.
Most men are gladly separated
From infants who are not related.

Conclusion

Now Dove lays down his aching head.
His loving wife tucks him in bed.

His bulbousness begins to wane.
Soft waves of sleep assuage the pain
And bring a dream of joyous calm.
His soul is soothed as with a balm
Of indescribable delight.
There shimmers in his dazzled sight
A lady, snowy-draped and winged,
Her feet by rosy vapors ringed.
She smiles and beckons to enfold
Her hand, be wafted off . . . Behold—
Most natural of wondrous things—
He too has grown a pair of wings

And starts aloft with outspread hands
To soar with her to other lands.

His lady's voice at ten past eight:
"Wake up, my pet! It's getting late!"
At nine he passes through his door
Bound for the office as before.

Thus fades all glamorous illusion
Before the obvious conclusion:
The obstacles are always small;
One mustn't get involved, that's all.

But oh! A thrill of nameless dread;
With viselike clutch and tons of lead
Reality and all her minions
Encumber his unfolding pinions
And halt the rapturous ascent.
By demon bleats the air is rent.
The sweet celestial vision wanes,
And only one stark fact remains—

Painter Squirtle

1884

First Chapter

Free Speech is what we all commend,
While we are at the speaking end.

The proud flotilla of ideas,
How bravely it sets sail and clears
The speaker's oral floodgates, bound
With favoring breeze on waves of sound
For earports, and the neural deeps
Of man, including man-who-sleeps.

Above all others, politicians
Indulge in powerful renditions,
And when they say a thing is so,
One may be certain that they know.

To those more backward in this field
Such verities are not revealed.
Their gentler and more wayward hearts
Drift to the gracious realm of arts.
Where as the mind becomes a blank,
The tongue grows voluble and frank.

I would not dream to look askance
At any man who likes a chance
To drink free sherry and be courtly
To matrons sensitive if portly,
Discuss the ballet, grace salons
With poetesses and bonbons,
Or otherwise to train his soul
To see life steadily and whole.

Nor do I blame the man who shuns
All literary teas and buns,
Hates ladies' clubs and would refuse
Pale sherry proffered by a muse.
His spirit thrives, his cab will call
At opera and concert hall;
And these, at least in theory,
Are just the thing for colloquy.
One feels right sociable and cozy
In serried ranks, all warm and rosy
With fellowship and genial frowst . . .
Until, confound it, one is doused
With grunts and buzzes, blares and whines,
Those orchestrated monkeyshines
Of gadgets which tail-coated freaks,
With restless hands and bulging cheeks,

Chased by a spastic with a rod,
Unmercifully blow or prod.
A really satisfying chat
Can't prosper in a place like that.

That's why I flee the crash-and-whine
For the still realm of turpentine.
I know of no more poignant boons
Than those bemusing afternoons
I spend in raptures of a sort
Viewing Emancipated "Ort"—
(Most of the time, of course, with dames.)
Here is the world of tasteful frames,
Creation free from nature's taint.
Here is the pleasant smell of paint.
No crowded wall offends the eyes:
Stark artifacts of modest size,
Discreetly hung, await in patience
The expert's trained interpretations.
For just a minute comment lags,
While secretly I note the tags.
(I emulate the trade's elect:
High price engenders high respect.)
I form a spyglass with my hand,
I squint, I nod, I back-step: "Grand!
What feeling, both naive and deep!
What broad authoritative sweep!
The thrill transmitted as one traces
That lattice-work of patterned spaces!
Those economical designs
Of trailing asymptotic lines!
Look, Genevieve, this you will *lurve*!"
Miss Genevieve adjusts the curve
Of tilted eyebrows, looks astute,
And says at length: "Why, that *is* cute!"

Praise to the Artist, who contrives
To spice and variegate our lives.

The Architect's deserts are great,
(However high his estimate),
Because he conjures from the dust
Of our old Earth's unsightly crust
Neat edifices, stalks and flowers
Of churches, dorms, and office towers.

The Sculptor also let us name,
Who turned to stone our men of fame.
In greyish, greenish, beige or buff
He fashioned profile, wig, and cuff.

When he was done, the likeness fair
Was mounted in the courthouse square
Affording special consolation
To strangers coming from the station,
Unmet by anyone they know:
At least old Schiller says hello.

But higher fame rewards the man
Whose art wells forth from tube or can.

Who gives to capitols and such
That handsome allegoric touch
With fresco murals, made to last,
In colors very nearly fast?
Who paints that genre stuff with zest,
Replete with Human Interest?
Or landscapes with their wholesome
  greens?
Or covers gay for magazines?
Who did your ancestors of fame
(of old or very recent name),
In mellow oils and varnish brown?
Who is the coolest man in town?
The picture painter! Willy-nilly
We love the man who gilds the lily.

Therefore I say: Young man, take hort
Let sideburns grow and study Ort.
See that you learn the current style:
Who knows—perhaps you'll make a pile!

With this inspiriting annotation
Let us embark on our narration.

Second Chapter

Our Earth for many a year and day
Had lumbered on its ancient way,
When suddenly the word was bruited:

At midnight, when the watchman tooted,
A baby boy had come to stay
At Squirtle's house across the way.
The parish book records the news.
For all new citizens who choose
To start on life and take up stations
With hitherto unknown relations
Must thus be entered and recorded
As permanently lodged and boarded.
As Georgie Squirtle they have booked him:
Scritch-scratch! A happy pair have hooked
  him.

He is robust, as one can tell
By his all-penetrating yell;
Experience led him to conclude:
Persistent yells result in food.
Then he imbibes, intent and deft,
Until there is no liquid left.

Most fascinating is the sight
Of someone bringing in a light.
He marvels, rolls his eyeballs, beams,
And relishing the candle's gleams

Pursues the image in and out.
He will go far, without a doubt.

He gains much weight and grows apace
In bodily and mental grace,
And evidences from the start

A striking aptitude for Art.
With slate and stylus, he is deft
At drawing faces looking left;

Both eyes are always plain in view:
He knows that people come with two.
Experience instructs his pen:
Soon he can do entire men;
And with especial skill and pleasure
He draws a gentleman of leisure;

And not alone his outer shell:
He shows the inner works as well,
Revealing for our introspection
A longitudinal cross-section.

This man is sitting on his seat,
Consuming, say, some cream of wheat.
Observe the spoon bring up its catch;
It spills and slithers down the hatch,
And further down the wholesome ration
Accumulates in tidy fashion.

Thus we are granted, phase by phase,
Rare insight into Nature's ways.

But oh! my friends, how soon we lose
The bounties of our infant Muse!
How soon is mother's lap exchanged
For classroom benches tightly ranged!

To teacher Beadle (for his part
No connoisseur of graphic art,

But strictly practical of taste)
All works of fancy are sheer waste.

One day our friend portrays this teacher
Lifelike in every salient feature.
But he, who has not ordered it
And thinks the image less than spit,

Approaches stiff with rage and cunning.
The sequel is confused and stunning.
Old Beadle swoops and starts erasing.

The artist's face does the effacing.

This treatment wakes in Georgie's breast
A sense of grievance and unrest.

A church key, long and reverend,
Is stuffed with powder at one end.
A breech is opened in the stem;
A spray gun joins the stratagem.
He fills the trusty squirting-rig
With blood from someone's fresh-killed pig.

Old Beadle reads at eventide,

When boom!! a shot goes off outside.
He thinks: "What can the matter be?

Perhaps I ought to look and see."

A jet of blood leaves Georgie's gun.

Old Beadle cries: "I am undone!"
And shaken to the very core,
He flounders prostrate in the gore.

Ma Beadle, summoned by his groans,
Appeals to him in tearful tones:
"Oh speak! Are you alive or dead?"

"Don't know," he answers. "Wipe my
head."

But soon they ascertain the fact:
Old Beadle lives and is intact.
He vows in outrage and distress:
"George will pay dearly for this mess!"

When it is plain a chap has erred,
One counsels that he be transferred
Into a new environment,
To counteract his lawless bent.
The place is fresh, the setup new,
The same old crook is right there, too.

With this not unwarranted observation
Let us continue with our narration.

Third Chapter

Soon after this spray-gun affair
Our Georgie finds himself in care
Of honest master painter Paste:

A paperhanging pro of taste,
A toucher-up of window sills,
A man of multifarious skills
Whose *Longa Ars* and lofty feeling
Brings within range the highest ceiling.
The artist's life is rough in spots:
This one must carry lots of pots.

Quite gladly, though, he lugs the box
Of victuals for their five-o'clocks.

He soon observes that every pup
Stops at this box and glances up.

This impulse should be put to use.

Let's leave the lid a little loose.

A dachshund, first to find the gap,
And too naive to sense a trap,

Is pounced upon and swiftly dosed.
He seems a leopard cub, almost.
Another, more the racing type,
Looks better with a transverse stripe:

This greyhound presently comes out
Quite zebralike, though not so stout.

A bulldog next comes up for paint.
Here Georgie uses more restraint:

In sober green and yellow tweed
Milord looks very well indeed.
This is great fun. But Master Paste
Views the diversion with distaste.

He hates the fanciful and quaint
And all misuse of time and paint.
He keeps his peace. But after five,
When one needs something to revive,
He chuckles in a mellow mood:

"For hearty workers, hearty food!"

He cuts some bread for his collation.
Georgie receives no invitation.

Salami next. He slits the skin.
The 'prentice watches with chagrin,

Keenly aware of his disgrace.
The sausage disappears apace.

At length the boss discards the peelings,
Insensitive to Georgie's feelings.

He gives his paunch a playful pat:
"I'll want no supper after that.
Cook will enjoy an evening out!"

That night our friend must do without.
Paste enters at his bedroom door
And murmurs cozily before:

"I bid you welcome, restful doze!
Clear conscience earns me sweet repose."

George is not ready yet for bed.
He has a job to do instead.

He longs for action, but before
He sets his satchel by the door.
Then he assembles in the hall
Of pots and stools and broomstick tall
A nicely poised memorial pile,
Vaguely pyramidal in style.

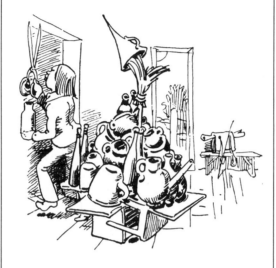

A paint jar in his hand appears
Along with paperhanger's shears.

The boss, like everyone in town,
Sleeps in a nest of eiderdown.

A stealthy cut, prolonged and slow
Bisects the tightly stuffed *plumeau*.

There goes a jarful of white lead
Upon that unsuspecting head.

Paste, roused, and fooling like a clown,
Gets much involved with eiderdown.

He blunders forth, confused and stirred,
In aspect not unlike a bird,

And crashingly puts on the skids
The latest of the pyramids.

How gaily flap the traveler's jeans
If he has independent means.

With this elliptical observation
Let us continue with our narration.

Fourth Chapter

Few alma maters will say no
To undergraduates with dough . . .
George has arrived. In thoughtful vein
He pens this letter blunt and plain:

"Beloved Father: With Master Paste
I felt my talent was going to waste.
So I decided to make a fresh start
At the Academy of Art.

Please send some cash with the utmost
   speed
To cover the dire and urgent need
For clothes on the back and food in the
   gorge
Of your ragged and harassed specter—
                              George.
His father, much against his will,
Scraped twenty guineas from his till.
Protesting that this was no pittance,
He glumly sent the fat remittance.

Now Georgie has the stuff en masse.
He proudly joins the drawing class.

He has a way with art utensils:
Not only can he sharpen pencils,
But he erases with such vim
That few can hold their own with him,
At stippling plain and fancy shades,
He also earns the highest grades.
Only at night, at the White Stag,
He shows some tendency to lag.

He sips, before the evening's out,
Some two or three great mugs of stout.

No wonder, with his kind of talent,
That coming Easter finds our gallant
In the great Hall of Classic Sculpture,
The seedbed of all art and culpture.

The ancients' ever youthful gods—
Who in the face of crippling odds
Braved time and tide and many a blow
And only lost a limb or so—
Are George's joy, his spirit's kin,
Especially when feminine.

He draws in charcoal his impressions
And greatly profits from these sessions.

At times, though, he forgoes this pleasure
To spend some time in outdoor leisure,
And hurries with a lit Havana
To the White Stag and his Susanna.

With her he lowers without fail
Some three or four great mugs of ale.

And word soon spreads among her buddies
That George is good at portrait studies.

Palette in hand, he'd stand and toil
With many-colored blobs of oil,
And paint this shriveled baccy-chewer
That almost everybody knew her.
Of course, before the vesper bell
He visits Susie for a spell.

Five or six mugs, to mutual profit,
He empties, thinking nothing of it.
But one fine night, this pleasant wench
Draws herself up at George's bench,
Announcing with a nasty sneer:
"Now pay up, lad, or no more beer!"

They show a dank and clouded brow
Who are to pay and know not how.

With this lugubrious observation
Let us continue with our narration.

Fifth Chapter

A young patrician Georgie knew
Came strolling down the Avenue.

With frank address and cordial clutch
A hopeful George performs the touch.
The baron's countenance turns sad.

He speaks with feeling: "Oh, too bad!
I came away without a shilling!

Some other time I'll be most willing!"

From that time on, it was a shame
How hard to meet this friend became.

Some chance would conjure up his shape
Apparently beyond escape;

A moment later, it was strange
How fast he flickered out of range.

Whenever Georgie has in mind
To stalk his patron from behind,

Some unexplained posterior sense
Appears to come to his defense,

And aided by a cruising cab
He nonchalantly beats the nab.
Another time, when George with glee
Has trapped him on a private spree,

Eel-like, he wriggles off in flight
And once again eludes the bite.

With Fortune looking thus askance,
George sees but one remaining chance
Of foiling death from inanition:

To sell his recent composition.

It shows how Friar Berthold Schwarz
Has just combined the proper parts
Of sulfur, coal, and caustic nitre
To render warfare so much brighter.
This work shall save him from perdition:
He sends it to the Exhibition.

The painter, keen and self-reliant,
Pursues the rich, elusive client,
But meets instead the parasitic
And only too forthcoming critic.

With this cantankerous observation
Let us continue with our narration.

Sixth Chapter

In this metropolis resides
One Dr. Stykker who provides
The leading papers of the town
With art reviews of high renown;

A walk of life which tends to spoil
The sales of those who paint in oil.
George used to read with interest
The views this arbiter expressed.
Today he looks with keen attention
For Stykker's honorific mention.

But soon his eager look turns grim.
How Stykker has lambasted him!

His eyes aflare with baleful glare
He beards the critic in his lair,

And offers the obnoxious fella
A thrashing with his stout umbrella.

But he, with wrath-inspired skill,
Sticks Georgie's nostril with his quill,

The foe takes a defensive stance.

Now Stykker summons to his aid
An inkpot for a handgrenade;
The damage, though, is not severe,
Thanks to the sheltering hemisphere.

And savors with a vicious wink
The anguish caused by caustic ink.

A brace of fast and furious lunges

But then the fiend employs a ruse

George rides a charge with leveled lance;

Is foiled by faster skips and plunges.

And drags him through the inky ooze.

The barrier falls. Fine blotting sand

The naked eye finds hard to stand.

Now Georgie makes a vengeful dive
For his sharp Faber No. 5.

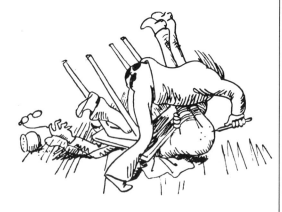

The outmaneuvered foe's defense
Is probed and pierced in every sense.

His markings only half concealed,
George proudly leaves the battlefield.

Perhaps a painter's key utensil
Is after all a sharpened pencil.

With this provocative observation
Let us continue with our narration.

Seventh Chapter

One may be pardoned the suspicion
That the pictorial rendition
Of universal history
May not be Georgie's specialty.
Instead, who knows but it might prove
That Landscape is his proper groove,
Which yields to him who knows to choose
A rich array of pleasing views.

For instance yonder rock formation
Affords one a commanding station.

A stroller on the bridge? Ah, yes:
It is the maiden baroness,
A dame of wealth, though somewhat dated,
Half worldly still, half sublimated,
She airs her dog and peace of soul,
And yonder convent is her goal.

Two hounds that someone leashed together
Come bounding up across the heather.

Spitz goes to ground in headlong flight;

The noble miss is trussed up tight.

A sudden sally: Spitz breaks clear;

The baroness brings up the rear.

Now Georgie leaps into the fray;
He deftly cuts the leash away.

And in the sequel also shows
Address: she asks before she goes:

"May one inquire your studio?"
"Holzgasse 5." "Thanks! A bientôt!"

Who knows where Georgie's gallant deed
Might not eventually lead?

With this restorative observation
Let us continue with our narration.

Eighth Chapter

She did not fail. She came, alone,
And spoke in dulcet, private tone:
"My worthy friend! Long before now
I have been minded to endow
With an appropriate *tableau*
The chapel of the old chateau.
Let me commission it with you.
Some pretty legend theme will do.
Here's an advance!" He feels, like balm,
Two largish banknotes in his palm.

The sphere of legend seems occult,
So George determines to consult
An antiquary wise and frail,
Who knows this interesting tale:

The Bold Knight
and
the Horrendous Dragon

The dragon crawled a-slaverin'
From out his rocky caverin
    With loud and hideous sound;
One noble maid he claimed p.a.
Or he would snort and roar away
    Devouring all he found.

What train 'neath yonder awning
Comes forth in drapes of mourning
   With sad and halting gait?
Behold, the king's fair daughter
Is carried to the slaughter;
   The monster lies in wait.

Halt! From the forest shadow
Comes charging down the meadow
   A knight-in-armor bold;
One-two, the scaly whopper
Is punctured good and proper;
   He flops there limp and cold.

The king with joyful bustle
Cried: "Gallant knight and vassal,
   I have a place for you.
If it be your opinion,
Take half of my dominion
   And this my daughter too!"

"Egad!" The knight stood quaking,
His shining armor shaking,
   His golden locks on end.
"I've married one too many,
And I'm not having any!"
   And galloped round the bend.

Oddsbodikins! I wager
We're pluckier and sager
   Than that benighted flop.
We'd tip our shiny bowlers
And grin with all our molars
   And sing: Come hither, Pop!

This lay of chivalry (omitting
The latter part) appears most fitting
To be roughed out in charcoal faint
And later boldly done in paint.

The baroness with pleasure views
Her painter's sweeping curlicues;

Though often no more confident
Than he precisely what they meant.
The maiden's figure seems to bother
The artist more than any other.
"Imagination flags," he sighs,
"Without a shape to guide our eyes!"

"Shall I be model?" whispers she.
"Good! Wednesday morning let it be!"
And when at dusk the vespers toll,
He heeds the stirring of his soul:
To the White Horse Inn as of yore!
And Sue is gentler than before.
For love revives, as good as new,
If it be profitable too.
Here it revives to a degree
One could not readily foresee.

If it is ill to serve two masters,
Two mistresses portend disasters.

With this Cassandrian observation
Let us continue with our narration.

Ninth Chapter

It's Carnival, the season when,
Like any other season, men
Incontinently scheme and plot
To seem to be what they are not.

This time our Georgie deemed it right
To don the costume of a knight,

While Sue looks fetching in the dress
Of a naive young shepherdess.

Skirts fly, plump thighs cut graceful capers,
Halos of dust surround the tapers,

As drum and fiddle skirl and pound,
And happy pairs whirl round and round.

Alas! Soon ends King Carnival's rule.
The morning dawns; the wind is cool.

Two people wander through the snow
Toward young George's studio.

And here these two seal with a kiss
Vows of eternal love and bliss.
Love soars above the commonplace,
Oblivious of time and space . . .
And so our hero has no warning
That this is really Wednesday morning.
Next door, the rustle of a dress:
Ye gods, it is the baroness!

"Beloved, you must not be seen!
Quick, use this easel as a screen!"

"Fair patroness, at your command!
Will you be good enough to stand
Right here?" Now on with the routine.

Spitz takes a look behind the screen.

The artist is quite busy now.
But Spitz, suspicious, goes "bow-wow!"

Next there is heard a piercing squeal,
As he makes contact with a heel.

And now he charges, all abristle;
The canvas bulges, and the trestle,

Collapsing with the sudden stress,
Unveils a bashful shepherdess.

This crisis, permit us the observation,
Augurs the close of our narration.

Conclusion

Time trickles steadily and fast,
And future changes into past;
Year follows fleeting year to pass
Through the eternal hourglass,
And up from Lethe's stream they scoop
Of men a brief and motley troupe,
Who bob about, with grin or frown,
Their transient span and then go down
To drift, well chilled, for quite a time
Far from the current pantomime.

How anxiously one's glances wander,
How one is pleased if here and yonder
Some Tom or Harry one may note
Chin up and cheerfully afloat!

Mine Host of the White Horse is dead.
A younger man reigns in his stead.
It is this landlord who has just
Informed the public, as he must:

"Be it now published and duly noted
"That Mistress Susanna, my spouse
    devoted,
"Was brought abed of another boy,
"The fifth to date; of which we have joy.
"The turning years prove kind and fertile
"To the White Horse Landlord—George B.
    Squirtle."

Thus Time, malign him ever so,
Does have some comforts to bestow,
And sometimes, bless him, he unites
Men set at odds by ancient spites.

The outraged miss and her trousseau
Have joined the convent long ago.
But Beadle, here on his vacations
To see the town and his relations,
And Master Paste, who always buys
In town his sundry art supplies,
As well as Georgie's noble friend,
Now covered with a hairpiece, and
Old Stykker, Art's severest judge,
Unmindful of the timeworn grudge,

They all imbibe, year after year,
At the White Horse their evening beer.
And as Mine Host hands round the snuff,
They tease him pleasantly enough:
"Without sound schooling, Landlord, say,
Where would we be? Eh, Georgie? Eh?"

With this pedagogical observation,
We are pleased to terminate our narration.

SHORT GRAPHICS
AND VIGNETTES

Diddle-Boom!

1874

Idiosyncrasy

The day is dull. The clouds sail over
The old mill's clackings and wheelings.
I shuffle through the sodden clover
And wonder about my feelings.

I put on it what face I can,
But wrangle with the old Adam.
The miller is such a dear, good man,
And still I prefer his madam.

The Village Dance

Here slumbers the parental pair
The evening of the village fair.

Dad still maintains, as one can see,
Firm hold of the essential key;
This, he is confident, will keep
Young daughter home and safe asleep.—

Ah me! Is it not always so?
Show me the girl who doesn't know!
The moment there's some chance of fun
There's the old man to frustrate one!

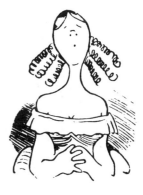

Mathilda sighs—
then smiles once more:
Whatever is a window for?

Her exit is adroitly gained;

Now down by where the vines are trained,

Then outward at an eager bounce
In fuchsia pink with triple flounce.—

Bass, tootle-horn, and fiddles sound
All ready for the second round.

Ta-oompa-tiddley-oompapa,
Boom-fiddley-tiddley-tralala!

What heaven on earth to heave and whirl
One's bulging armful of a girl
And in that interplay of splendid
Anatomies all meshed and blended

To practice the foreboding arts
So meaningful to feeling hearts!

Here sways Mathilda like a lily;
Her partner is the trim young gillie.

This pair shows grace and harmony;
The gent's behavior seems quite free.

Here is some elegance of motion,
But little genuine devotion;

While these, desiring close communion,
Have entered a more perfect union.

Our Hansel, fond and very fetching,
Has got a handle on his Gretchen;

Sweet urges stir in either breast,
As cheek to glowing cheek is pressed.

Then, masterfully swift and gay,
He executes a deft chassé.

Here bashful Konrad watches, awed;
Detached, perhaps, but far from bored.

Gyrations, turmoil, lots to see—
This thing wants closer scrutiny.

He has another, seventh, shot;
This lessens diffidence a lot:

He asks his (mutely, but no less
For that) long-venerated Bess.

His bosom swells, his spirits grow,
And Konrad charges, tally-ho!

And bold are his extravaganzas,
Until his orbit touches Hans's;

For with a frightful crash and clank
They topple the orchestral plank,

And hurt the tonal gear not least . . .
With this, the memorable feast
Concludes, to everyone's distress.—

Mathilda, gathering up her dress,
Now hurries homeward, confident
Of getting back the way she went.

But something snaps—and leaves the fair
In limbo, neither here nor there.

The dawn wind blows; she gently rocks.
Her kindly Mum just then unlocks
The window by her wont, about
To pour the morning fluids out,

And sees Mathilda in a stupor
Suspended like a giant pupa;
Some passing youths are overjoyed
To see a lady thus employed.

But presently her father issues
And severs the obstructing tissues.

With smothered wails she soon reposes,
Well centered, in a bed of roses.

Romance

A slender tailor lad was there
With needle and with shears,
Who loved a maiden pert and fair
Devoutly and for years.

Quite late one night he came to call,
And hemmed and hawed, and said:
Could he not be of help at all
With needle and with thread?

The maiden turned with wicked glee:
"Oh, dear, oh, dear, how so?
Your needle is all crooked, see?
Go, little tailor, go!"

The tailor raised a frantic fist
And cried: "You heartless chit."
He bought himself a yard of twist

And hanged himself with it.

The Virtuoso

1865

Silentium

Adagio

Introduzione

Adagio con sentimento

Scherzo

Piano

Smorzando

Passagio chromatico

Fortissimo vivacissimo

Maestoso

Fuga del diavolo

Finale furioso

Capriccioso

Forte vivace

Bravo, Bravissimo

The Flying Frog

1894

The one who barely, heave and lurch,
Has reached an elevated perch

W.B.

W.B.

And fancies now he is a bird

Has erred.

Insouciance

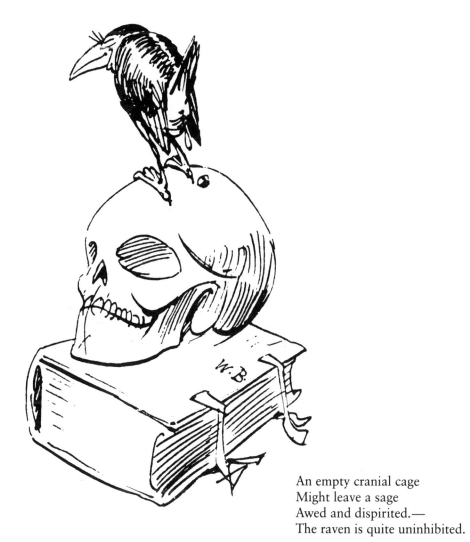

An empty cranial cage
Might leave a sage
Awed and dispirited.—
The raven is quite uninhibited.

1890s

SELECTED POETRY
AND PROSE

Poems

1874–

Who would be brave enough to dwell
On earth and walk his rut
If all of us resolved to tell
The truth and nothing but?

Then names would swarm on busy wings
Like scoundrel, hoodlum, skunk,
We'd tell each other awful things
Before we're even drunk.

The length and breadth of every land,
By every tree or shrub,
The ineffective human hand
Would sprout a trusty club.

I value graceful falsehood more,
The courtesy that eases;
I know the score, you know the score,
And every contact pleases.

Their love was ever unsated,
They all but wasted away;
A thousand things they debated
And always had more to say.

Long years they were baulked and harried,
But time provided release;
They had their way and were married,
And now at last are at peace.

She sits there, loosely appareled,
Creating some bedroom shoes;
He studies the Morning Herald
And gives her the gist of the news.

Sad to say, there's not a virtue
I can ever have much fun with;
Always I am at my easiest
When that business is done with.

Quite conversely, it is vices
That agree with me, I find:
Pleasant little jobs I'd rather
See before me than behind.

She was a blossom dear and bright,
Full-opened to the morning light;
He a young butterfly who clung
To her, by ecstasy unstrung.
A bee with busy appetite
Might buzz and sip in bumbling flight;
A scrambling, scrabbling bug might walk
Right up and down the blossom's stalk.
How such events would tear apart
The quivering butterfly's wee heart!
But that which left him quite aghast,
The most appalling thing, came last:
A wandering ass ate the entire
Perennial of his heart's desire.

Curriculum Vitae

My life? There isn't much to tell.
In still eternity forlorn
I slumbered, all at ease and well,
Till rendered visible and born.
What followed? Down a knobbly track,
A flimsy bundle on my back,
I lightly marched through field and wood,
Now on the crook, now on the straight;
At last I settled on the grass
To catch my breath. I scratched my pate,
I scrutinized the neighborhood:
I'd come full circle—yes, alas!
Back to the place where I had stood,
And far and wide in front of me
There ranged, as then, eternity.

Self-Critique

Much may be said for self-critique.
Say I point out where I am weak,

And right away I earn the credit
For modesty at having said it.

Next, people note what is so true:
This man is honest through and through.

Thirdly, I snatch a tasty morsel
From critics by my first endorsal.

Fourth, I may hope the accusation
Will spur a welcome refutation.

The final verdict: all in all,
There's nothing wrong with me at all.

The Butterfly

(DER SCHMETTERLING)

1895

Children in their simplicity keep asking why. The person of understanding has given this up; every why, he has long found out, is merely the end of a thread that vanishes into the thick snarl of infinity, which no one can truly unravel, let him tug and worry at it as much as he likes.

Years ago, to be sure, when I was engaged in the little excursion reported below, I was still in the habit of wondering why all this had to happen to me, such a fine, sterling fellow. Now I sit back serenely and gently whistling, on the simple assumption that what has been decreed in the congress of all things surely must be salutary and purposeful.

My name is Peter. I was born in the good old days, when young misses were called *ma'm'selle* and geese were called Gwendolyn, on a lonesome peasant holding, down the first left of the world and over by the next sharp right, not far from the honest town of Geckelbeck, where they always know better.

Another feature of that neighborhood is the bottomless Grummel Mere, in which everyone knows the "Muddy Butt" with its long tail is up to its wicked tricks. Frau Paddeke, the dependable old delivery woman, once actually saw it stick its head out of the water; it looked at her keenly and slyly, with all the calm superiority and sangfroid of a multimillennial fiend.

My mother died early. Father and good handyman Gottlieb kept busy in the fields. My pretty young cousin Katharina looked after the household.

Since I, for my part, even though grown into a sturdy young lout by and by, showed not the least inclination for either ploughing or cutting chaff, my father sent me to town to Herr Damisch, the learned schoolmaster; who, however, after a very few years returned me with thanks as not quite fit material.

Then, after dallying away a mere year or so, I was apprenticed to the celebrated master tailor Knippipp; board and lodging found.

"A pretty superior trade, that, too!" said my father. "Your tailor earns his bread dry-shod like the finest schoolmaster, rain or snow."

After no more than nine months, the fat tailor lady's lean water soups washed me back home.

I had put on finery: straw hat, sky-blue neckband, tight yellow nankeen trousers, red cotton handkerchief. This time, though, Father really flew off the handle. He reached for the oxtail whip and would certainly have executed his fell design, had not dear Gottlieb and good little Katharina, he from the front, she from the rear, imposed effectual restraints.

That winter I spent at home. While I did not overly care for food, I did like to hang about the kitchen on account of my pretty little cousin. Sometimes I would snatch one of her pins and calmly run it through my ear. Or I might try a foolhardy dance on the rim of the well and couldn't be better pleased but to have little Katharina watch me and shudder mightily. Other times I might just stand there, completely benumbed like an old heron in a carp pond. But what

I particularly enjoyed was to lie on the stove bench of an evening and watch little Katharina shell beans and Gottlieb weave baskets. Watching this finegauged, twisty, crispy job, I was always seized by a kind of faint, delicate, cozy shudder. It started at the very top of my hair, went rippling down my back and spread all over my skin, while my soul most daintily drifted forth from my eyes in order to miss nothing, and my body lay there like a blissful clod. One evening I went so far as to climb into the linden tree on the sly, having taken a notion to watch little Katharina get ready for bed. There she was, telling her beads. But when she started undressing and matters became awkward, I cleared my throat and phut! out went the lamp. The following afternoon there was some busy sewing at a green curtain.

My little room was high up in the gable. Late into the night I would read a fat volume of legends; and when the wind roared and snow whispered at the window I used to feel wonderfully private and comfortable as a gentleman of leisure.

A witches' passage ran right by there; at times they reined in their broomsticks and peeped through the panes; for the most part shriveled old faces, as if dried at hell's fire. On one occasion, though, there was a young, pretty one. She wore a string of gold coins woven through her hair; she winked and laughed, her white teeth gleaming against the dark background as the light shone on her face.

When summer came and the world grew dense with foliage and blossom, I made a net and went hunting for butterflies. To rove about in reckless freedom, or to lie down to rest as the spirit moved me was my real forte; and as for skipping like the most active of grasshoppers, I was good at that too.

One Sunday morning, while the others were at Mass, I put on my Sunday best and went out by the back door, the butterfly net in my hand and my coattails full of plums. The sun shone brightly. Through the garden and into the field, from the field into the meadows I happily went sauntering along. There was no dearth of butterflies on the wing. Now and then I caught one, inspected it, and let it go, for I had long ago filled all my boxes with the common kinds. But there now, at some distance, one rose that I hadn't seen before. I was up and after it, over hedges and fences, as much as two or three hours at one go, until at length I tired of the chase. I flung myself into the grass in a sulk. High up in the air a kite hovered. My eyes caught in its gentle swoops, I soon dropped off. When I woke up, the sun was about to set; and since it was high time to be hurrying home, I climbed a tree at the edge of the forest to get my bearings. Nothing but unknown countryside the length and breadth of the view. Taken aback at first, then serenely indifferent, I resigned myself to my fate. I climbed down, looked for a comfortable spot, sat down and started eating plums. Suddenly—I caught my breath with the joyful shock of it—it came fluttering up, that charming butterfly, adorned with the loveliest colors in the world, and impudently settled on the tip of my foot. Soundlessly I raised the net; cautiously I took aim. Whoosh! off it went. But my aim had been true, anyway, for the iron hoop of the net had hit my little toe a glancing blow right at its most sensitive spot. I leapt up and danced on one leg, to the accompaniment of whistling.

"Ho-ho!" somebody laughed behind me. "Right on target!"

A goodlooking, pale lad, dressed like a huntsman, was sitting under a beech tree.

"I'm Peter!" I said and sat down next to him.

"And I am Tony," said he.

A snake, all silvery glitter, was coiled around his left arm, a little golden crown on its head; on his knees he had a bird's nest with small blue-green eggs in it.

"Not to be trusted, that creature!" I said suspiciously. "Bites, too, doesn't it?"

"Not me she doesn't. Isn't that right, Cindy!" he said, offering her an egg.

On my bare chest I was wearing a medallion, a gold coin, the present of a godfather. The snake stretched out for it.

"She scents the gold," said the hunter.

"Down, vixen!" I called out and gave her a smart flick across the nose with the pole of my net.

She recoiled with an angry hiss, unwound herself and slipped off into the brush with a rustle. The hunter paused only to give me a swift kick in the stomach, causing me to turn up my legs, before he ran after her.

By degrees the forest turned as black as the inside of a tar barrel full of coal. The air was mild. I leaned back against the tree trunk and fell asleep on the instant; I might even say faster.

In general I never had the least difficulty with sleeping; and I slept fast, almost as soundly as the woman with the easy conscience who had her big toe nibbled off overnight by the rats and never noticed.

It was only the noon sun which opened my eyes next day. And to be sure! There it was again, three paces away, my butterfly of many colors, sitting on a purple thistletop, fanning its wings and letting them shimmer in the sun at their full alluring spread. With artful guile I crept closer. . . . No good. The exact second before I could reach it, it took off like lightning, and then it did it once more, and yet again, and finally, whee! off it was in an elegant zigzag swoop across a hawthorn hedge as tall as a house.

What a bore! I thought out loud, for I was much heated: "Such a tiny little beggar and won't let me catch it; created on purpose for man's benefit, it persists in just wasting its fine talents on its own selfish ends. Revolting!"

In the heat of pursuit I had left one of my boots stuck in the morass, deeply too, so that it took me quite a time to grope and grapple for it in the black soup before I found it again. I shook out the frog spawn, rinsed myself off and then, having cooled down and regained my composure, made off at an easy saunter toward a faraway hill which had the road running across it as a bright ribbon. There I hoped to run into people of the neighborhood who might tell me how to get home.

Upon a milestone sat a man of middle age wearing an uncommonly broad-rimmed hat. Between his knees he held a woolly dog.

"Dear Dad," I addressed him. "I would like to get to the town of Geckelbeck."

"No objection!" he replied.

"Could you point out the way to it?"

"No go. I'm blind, all the way around."

"Has it been a long time?" I asked compassionately.

"Going on for fifty-nine years; next Thursday is my fifty-third birthday."

"What? It began six years before you were born?"

"Seven actually, by strict count. Eager even then to go out into the world, I groped for the door in the dark, fell face first on the horns of the bootjack, and that did it."

"Then let me give you some advice, old man!" said I. "Don't ogle the pretty girls too much, for that has been many a young buck's downfall."

"Sic him!" the blind man cried and let his dog loose.

I tucked my coattails under my arm, stuck my butterfly net back out between my legs, and thus, bent down and wagging it, made off; a phenomenon which struck the cur as so bizarre and uncanny that it turned tail, tucking the same between its legs.

In front of me strode a farmer, looking neither right nor left; and since he made a serious, thoughtful, and trustworthy impression, I decided to address my question to him.

"Hey!" I called. He paid no attention. "Hey!" I called out more loudly. He would not be disturbed in his reflections. So, when I was close behind him, I clapped my net over his head. Oh, how this startled him! I could distinctly hear his heart drop into his boots.

"Could you not tell me, good friend, where Geckelbeck is?" I inquired and raised the net.

He had turned around. His eyes closed tightly, and gaping so cavernously as to show all of his thick, coated tongue, he stuck his thumbs into his ears, fingers spread, and shook his head sadly.

"Blockhead!" I exclaimed in the first shock of disappointment, but took care to do so with an uncommonly affable mien.

The deaf-mute, who must have taken this for a polite parting expression, devoutly pulled off his tasseled cap, heedless of his considerable pate.

Dusk fell. I pulled half a dozen turnips in somebody's field and, since a heavy dew was wetting the ground, climbed into a spruce, tied myself fast with my coattails and fell upon the juicy fruits of the field with much crunching and slurping. I dozed off over the last one, half of which was still hanging out of my mouth, greens and all, when I woke up the next afternoon. I quickly climbed down, refreshed myself at a spring, and returned to the highway. I found myself in the serenest of good humors. I knew, for an inner voice was telling me, that something uncommonly pleasant lay ahead of me today.

In this pleasant premonition I was disturbed by the plaintive sounds of a beggar who was approaching me, hat in hand.

"Young sir!" he pleaded. "Let me have a gift, do. I have seven wives—sorry! seven children and a wife, and my parents are dead and my grandparents are dead, and my uncles and aunts are dead, and I have no one in this hard, cruel wide world to turn to except your very self, handsome sir."

These words fired my innate generosity. I had seventeen single groats in my pocket. With a cozy sense of grandeur I tossed ten of them into the beggar's felt hat.

This was hardly done when he took one groat out again and laid it at my feet.

"Here, my good man," he said, "I am making you a present of the tenth part of my fortune. Be grateful and do not forget the highminded donor, who is now modestly withdrawing."

After a moment of petrifaction I ran after the lout in order to land a kick on his wind-and-weather side. But he had his pocket full of stones and his aim was so accurate with them that despite my taking cover behind the net the very second stone knocked a perfectly sound front tooth straight down my throat into my windpipe, causing me to cough for about an hour before I could dislodge it.

I gathered some field peas into my net and let the green, pleasantly cool pills roll down my inflamed gullet, thus filling my covetous stomach with tender young vegetables at the same time. I then withdrew into a thicket and quite simply lay down to rest, face up.

I would probably have snored through the entire following day, had not a cockchafer dropped into my wide-open mouth toward noon. The moment he proceeded to crawl down into the depth of my being, I woke up. The wind was shaking the treetops. Besides, my stomach was growling on account of indifferent nourishment. I therefore got on my way and did not rest until I reached an inn, where I was just about to order something sustaining for my last groats, when a very merry-looking and well-nourished farmer entered the taproom and sat down at my table.

"You look happy!" I said.

"Every reason to!" said he. "Sold the grey one at market."

"Fine beast, I suppose."

"Well, yes and no. Once a week or so, or whenever the fancy takes him, he kicks the stars out of the sky and the plaster off the wall."

"You warned the buyer of this, I take it."

"What next!" replied the farmer, seeming quite sad and depressed of a sudden. "May the Lord preserve an honest Christian from losing his reason. Do I really look so stupid?"

"No, but listen!" said I. "If you didn't you certainly are one of the worst scoundrels that walk on their hindlegs between heaven and hell."

"That's what I like to hear!" cried the farmer, his face lighting up. "Am I not, just? I'm a devil of a fellow. Hey, innkeeper! Give this fine gentleman a sandwich and a glass of beer; my treat."

While I was eating it struck me that the man kept looking sidelong at the window. Suddenly he seemed to recall something. He paid his bill, remarking that he had to go out for just a minute and would be back presently. He was hardly gone when a hurried patter of hoofbeats sounded from the road. I stepped out.

A hatless man on a grey had arrived and was asking, quite out of breath: "Didn't a farmer come through here? Heavy paunch, heavy stick, heavy watchchain?"

"That is so!" I said. "He just had to step out by the back door for a moment."

"The blackguard!" shouted the horseman. "The chiseler! Didn't that hound sing me the praises of a grey which has the devil and his grandmother in his barrel!"

"Yes!" I said calmly. "Idiocy is expensive."

Lobster-red with fury, the man on the grey mount raised his whip. I gave a flourish with my butterfly net.

This turned out to be the kind of signal the grey had been waiting for. He rolled his eyeballs back, pricked up his ears, sidled, backed, pressed a window in with a good deal of clatter, whinnied both front and back, and with a prodigious, legendary leap, sailed clean over the board fence.

I ran out into the yard to keep abreast. The grey by this time was an indistinct dot in the far distance; the rider was in plain view in a plum tree, quite close by.

[The central portion of the story, about one-half of its length, is summarized below:]

The butterfly reappears and is pursued into a pond which proves full of leeches. Peter witnesses a cock fight, meddles in a quarrel between the cocks' owners, and takes refuge in a hollow tree in the forest, where he is inextricably wedged in by a trick of his pursuers, who want to give him the full benefit of his position, for the tree trunk is full of furious ants. Two ruffians happen up and tie a donkey to the tree, stolen from one "rich old Schlumann." They run off in panic at Peter's frantic shouts, which bring the sleek, somberly attired owner upon the scene. He recovers his donkey and frees Peter, who seeks shelter from a violent thunderstorm in a leaf hut, falling straight into the arms of a girl who hugs and kisses him with abandon, "so that I, who was unaccustomed to such things, was seized by the most acute anxiety." A bolt of lightning sets a nearby haystack afire; the girl, a wild gypsy beauty with gold coins braided in her hair, darts out dancing and taunts the sky for "missing her." Peter now finds her "extremely well worth noticing, after all." She eats from a lapful of fine pears, which at Peter's touch turn into scampering mice who bite him severely. She eludes his pursuit—("I meant to talk to her very earnestly about the error of her witching ways, and after that, I decided, I would give her some hearty kisses to punish her for her wickedness")—and is lost also to Tony, the huntsman, who had seemed to own her earlier in her serpent's guise. Peter is dismayed to realize that his medallion, so carefully guarded hitherto, is missing.

Throughout further bizarre or farcical adventures and run-ins—in the sluggard village of Drowsington, "where they don't bother to close their mouths between yawns"; in Jokesham, the prosperous hamlet of tricksters, where he spots the gypsy witch Lucinda again and in amorous pursuit comes to agonizing public grief at the hands of her and her sinister hunchback swain; in new involvements with his treacherous rival, Tony, with the mysterious Schlumann's ass, which discharges jackpots of ducats, and with Lucinda-Circe in a variety of disguises—Peter keeps asking for directions back to Geckelbeck from a succession of ill-qualified or ill-intentioned informants. He is trapped by Lucinda, whom he has rediscovered and robbed of her gold fillet, is turned into a poodle (the fillet of coins, which had been in his coattail pocket, thus ending up inside his poodle tail, where it rattles at every movement), and is kept in humiliating but devoted slavery.

[Translation is resumed at this point.]

I had gradually become quite canine in my manners. I would yawn without restraint in the presence of my mistress, scratch myself, roll shamelessly on my back; I would always turn around three times before lying down to sleep, bark for no reason, just to show off, and whenever I found an old sock or shoe I would chew on it.

My treatment, regardless of the fact that I practiced the utmost humility and unfailingly kept my eye upon my beautiful despot, did not improve. I had to be content to wag my tail from afar and smile, dog-fashion, every time she happened to look at me. I did not dare to come close, for my ribs were in constant danger from the pointed heels of her graceful slippers. At last, driven to despair by hunger and distress, I flew the coop.

I ran as far as the nearest little town, where an old maid lured me into her house with lumps of sugar and tender clucking. Here I lived in luxury. She used to wash and comb me, she tied a pink ribbon around me, she crocheted me a sky-blue overcoat, she called me her sweet, her one-and-only darling, amid a thousand kisses. All day I used to lie on the couch, and at night I even enjoyed the privilege of lying at her maidenly feet in place of a hot-water-bottle. Soon I grew so lazy and fat that my digestion failed. Instead of showing myself happy and grateful, I turned sulky and disgruntled; not to make a long story of it, when my benefactress, whose affection did not seem to suit me, was next off to attend early Mass as was her custom, I slunk away, keeping close to the houses, and finally sidled through the first door I found open. I had happened into the apothecary's.

"Hoy," cried the pharmacist. "Delicious! Here comes dog tallow to give the farmers a rub with. Very profitable over-the-counter stuff."

He offered me a pill. It had a suspect smell; my instinct warned me against accepting it. I bared my teeth, growled, turned tail, and ran flat out all the way through the city gate; for I preferred to get rid of my lard, cumbersome though I found it, some other way.

Not far from the town I was caught by a milkman who happened to be in need of a dog to pull his cart. This proved the right cure for me; after only a few days I felt lighter. But there was one unpleasant thing about the job: when I pulled the cart, the other dogs, having taken a sniff of me, used to bark at me and bite me horribly. I bit them back, but the conduct of business would suffer considerable interruption. His mind stimulated by these setbacks, my master devised an ingenious remedy. He fitted the underside of the cart with a box open at the bottom, wherein I was harnessed and did my pulling; all he had to do was to steer the pole.

Thus I was, on one hand, protected against any temptations and trials posed by the outside world; on the other hand, the more leisure I had to inspect my inner self, the more distinctly the image of the mistress I had first left, wicked though she was, began to form before my servile, slavishly devoted soul.

In the evening I used to get tied up in the yard by the dog-house. I gnawed through the rope and hurried to the forest as fast as I could in order to be close again to her who had treated me so cruelly; I scratched at the door, and it was opened at once. I was received with unwonted graciousness; I offered my paw; she scratched my head and back. I had never felt so blithe and contented.

"You're just in time!" she said coaxingly. "The full moon is about to rise. Then we'll have a cozy time!"

She kindled a merry flame and stoked it with the tongs, leaving them in the fire, as I happened to notice. She then fetched a little roast bird from the cupboard, which had reached exactly the right degree of ripeness to suit my current taste, held it under my nose, tossed it into the open chest next to the hearth, and challenged me to look for it. Joyfully wagging my rattle tail, to the noise of which I had long grown accustomed, I plunged head and forelegs into the depth of the chest in order to enjoy the tasty morsel.

One of the most painful moments of my life had arrived.

In a flash the witch slammed the lid. A sudden squeezing pain, about the spot where at one time the coattails had taken their common origin, an unspeakable searing agony, a desperate scraping with all four legs, a horrible wail which reverberated hollowly in the cavern of the chest, a spasmodic jerk—I free myself, I rise. Unbelievably, I stand upright again on my human hind legs.

My first movement was to touch my back: the tailcoat had become a jacket. A smell of singing filled the kitchen; the fire-tongs still lay on the floor, steaming, one coattail next to them. The other one was in the witch's hand, and she was shaking her golden fillet out of it with a laugh.

"Satan ride you out on the poker, you accursed sorceress!" I cried in a rage. "You'll never see me again, not me!"

I reached for the door handle; but before I could get away, the wicked creature had seized the bellows from the hearth and sent an ice-cold blast at the nape of my neck. From this witch's bullet* my head is awry to this day, to the point that strangers have taken me for a dreadful hypocrite and sanctimonious fraud.

In great leaps, heedless of the stabbing pain in my neck which every jar caused me, I left the forest, only slowing down after a long time to collect myself and adjust my tie; at which point I made a surprising discovery. My medallion was back; it must have somehow wrapped itself around my neck during all that kicking and commotion in the witch's chest. At once my home rose to my mind: the quiet farmstead, my worthy father, pretty little Katharina, honest Gottlieb, all of whom I had recklessly abandoned and not given a thought to for so long. What had I encountered out here in this alluring world but pain and disappointment? How low I had been brought by my restless cravings! I had become a tramp, a wastrel, all but a blackguard, and finally a poodle, a fawning cur with a pelt full of fleas, the contemptible slave of a ruthless and grasping witch.

Clouds shrouded the sky; I stood there at a loss, in complete darkness. Just then something seemed to brush about my nose and ears as with unseen wings, and suddenly it began to glow. It was he! Sparkling like a green jewel in the homemade halo of his hindquarters, he was borne close before me, my old butterfly, whom I would never have credited with such a beautiful night light. My hunting instinct revived. I snatched off my hat and had a go at it, but in vain. I had to step up my pace more and more; I stumbled over rough spots underfoot; I had a fall. The light went out.

When I had picked myself up, the moon was breaking through the clouds; it briefly lighted up a church with a pointed steeple and hid again. I was sitting on one end of a grave mound; on the opposite end sat a ghost, nebulously white, nothing but a bedsheet, as it were, with its folds falling into near-human shape.

He wore an uncommonly dolorous look and spoke in hollow ghastly accents, looking all about him:

"No monument! Still no monument! Five hundred guilders

---

* Popular term to denote the sudden onset of lumbago, or lumbago itself.

allotted for the purpose, and still no monument! When, oh when, will I get a monument?"

"I see," I said, "You must be Tony's cousin! I know that Tony. You may put "paid" to that business, the money is down a rathole, and your monument you may wait for, if you please, until you are black in the face."

The ghost on hearing this developed some deep transverse folds and gave a horrible groan.

"I am surprised at you, I must say!" I continued. "Dead for ages and still full of vanity. You should be ashamed of yourself, old sport. Go back and lie on your ear, there's a good ghost."

This wellmeaning admonition of mine seemed to have torn it, as they say; I should never have supposed that a ghost could get so annoyed.

The phantom elongated itself, floated over to me at great speed, swooped on my back, took me by the collar, dragged me three times around the church and soared into the air with me as high as the steeple.

Boom! The clock struck one; the ghost let go of me. I fell and fell—and kept falling—

It took no more than three seconds for me to reach a state of most profound ignorance.

A foolish state, let me tell you! When there is no more how-come or I-see, when florin and groat, kinsman and kinswoman, uncle and aunt, butter and cheese equal sausage and each other and are one and the same thing; when nobody cares about a few thousand years one way or the other; when—but that's enough of that! The sanest thing to do is to imitate the experts, those to whom it is happening: they sit, lie, or hang there in sensible silence.

All I care to say at the moment (although that, too, is superfluous) is this: I woke up again; I bethought myself again of my existence as a live part of this so-called universe, which after all is a tricky business to take in as a whole.

I assumed a sitting position, rubbed my eyes and stretched long and luxuriously, as though I had had a sound refreshing sleep after a long walking tour; only then did I notice that I was in a spacious garden surrounded by a high wall.

Close ahead lay a field of cabbages, nothing but cabbage heads of considerable caliber. On the leaves sat countless cater-pillars, eating and spinning cocoons with great rapidity; and chrysalises were breaking open every moment and helping to fill the air with a colorful cloud of butterflies.

But there was also a tree of astonishing height, thickly dotted with nests, from which swarms of birds came fluttering without pause, as black as ravens and as swift as flycatchers.

And the thing that astonished me most was that the cabbages kept growing as I watched and instantly turned into all kinds of people. Each of these cabbage men had a net in his hand, and the butterflies flew across the wall, followed by the birds and the men.

The field at my left was still fallow. Two men were busy digging it up. They paused, leaning on their spades and looking around; and now I noticed that they weren't a regular human sort but two enormous beetles, one in a black-and-yellow piebald coat, a gravedigger; the other bluish black, of the sort which when among ourselves we call dungbeetles.

The sun was already setting. Nonetheless the gravedigger said to me:

"Good morning! We were just going to put you under!"

"Is that so!" I exclaimed.

"Why, yes!" he said. "Seven years flat down should be long enough!"

I smiled like one who can take a joke.

"We are sowing idiots," he continued. "A whole field full of them, while we are about it, so that we won't run out."

"Manure is needed, you see!" added the dungbeetle.

To change the subject I said:

"You have more blackbirds here than bright butterflies, I see."

"Quite right!" replied the dungbeetle. "It is only over there, beyond the wall, that you really notice it. For each pleasant expectation there are at least three unpleasant possibilities."

"Now see that you lie down and don't hold up the work!" admonished the gravedigger impatiently.

"A pity for the beautiful beard, though!" remarked the other.

I felt my chin. He was right. I had grown a beard an ell long.

Should it really be true, I thought . . . but before I could pursue the idea, my butterfly fluttered out of the cabbage field in rejuvenated splendor, more nimble and colorful than I had ever seen him before.

"A net!" I shouted. "I want to get out!"

"Anyone may who wants to!" buzzed the beetles.

One gave me a net, the other a whack with the flat of the spade from behind to help me on; and there I was, skipping off and over the wall with supernatural ease in high bounds, bouncing off again as soon as the tip of my foot had touched the ground, as sometimes happens in dreams where gravity is suspended and one's soles are as elastic as if they were on springs. And I would certainly have caught the butterfly, too, for I could almost outjump it, if one of the black birds had not snapped it up just when I was going to make my decisive pounce. Angrily I threw the net down, skipped on indifferently and only resumed those higher jumps when it had long become night and I saw something bright in the distance. Soon I found myself in a park, close to the windows of a brightly lit palace, in which there was a merry to-do to the sounds of the most magnificent band music.

This was an aristocratic party. Gambling was going on in all the large rooms. My first glance fell on Lucinda, who was sitting at the gambling table and laughing. A silver-embroidered train five ells long was coiled next to her on the carpet like a glittering snake. She had a pile of gold lying before her. Her partner was a jovial gentleman of mature years, whose hands and face looked quite black. His nails were very long, his ears very pointed, his nose very hooked, and two fetching little gilt goat horns adorned his forehead. Old Schlumann was there too. He glittered with diamonds but was not in the game, merely walking from table to table, looking benign. He seemed to be the host.

I would gladly have gone on watching if a black dog with fiery eyes had not come round the corner with a horrific bark, which caused me to jump all the way out and beyond the palace gate in a single leap.

Here the coaches were already drawn up to take the people of quality home. The footmen who were standing about made a solid trustworthy impression. They were powdered white, clean-shaven, portly, and sleek, and each bore a fine device in large golden letters on his livery, one saying "Good," another

"Beautiful," a third "True," a fourth "Ora," a fifth "Labora," and so on.

"It is a treat," I said, "to see such sterling people!"

"Just so!" said the fattest of all, who bore the device "Loyal and Honest" on his back. "We are the high principles." I was touched and wanted to press his hand, but it was softer than butter, and when I patted him on the shoulder, the whole chap sagged like an expiring balloon, the air escaping noisily through all his buttonholes.

"Why, a puffball!" I exclaimed. "Are you all like this, then?"

Before I could look into the matter more closely, servants with torches came up from the palace.

"Make way for His Grace, the prince of this world," calls resounded. "On your way, tramp!"

I hurriedly skipped off down the highway. A state coach, glowing brightly like fiery gold, came scurrying up behind me. Within, leaning back into the yielding upholstery, sat the black gentleman and the witch Lucinda in intimate flirtation. On the outrider's step stood "Loyal and Honest," the fat lackey, all four cheeks leaping up and down with the shaking of the coach; and the drollest thing was that between the tails of his lackey's livery one could see the brisk flourishes of a cow tail.

This spectacle tempted me. In an access of daring I seized the wagging tail in a quick grasp and swung myself right foot forward onto the running board. I might just as soon have jumped on the stovelid of hell's kitchen when it is busy cooking the banquet for grandmother's birthday. There was a gale of laughter from Lucinda as if someone was tickling her; a yell on my part as if I were being run onto a spit; a backward somersault; and then I lay full-length on the roadway, in the unfortunate position of a cockchafer which has landed on its back.

I crawled aside into the ditch, groaning. The fire damage was considerable; but I did not need to pull off my boot for the sake of closer inspection, for my right foot was bare to the sky, its aspect that of a single blister. This brought on a lively desire for someone to come along who might give me a lift.

Finally, in the morning mist, a rustic vehicle slowly rumbled up. In front on a bundle of straw sat a little peasant. Early morning though it was, he was singing in the greatest good humor:

> Higher, Gretchen, skip and dash,
> Make your dainty stockings flash!
> White, the two, as any snow,
> Hey, whirly-oh!

And behind him stood a long plain box of spruce wood as the only piece of freight.

The compassionate carrier had hardly noticed my state of distress when he stopped the cart and helped me climb up on it; and I found a quite acceptable seat on the box.

We hadn't been under way long when my friendly coachman turned around to me and said:

"You are in luck! I am just driving to Dr. Schnorz's, to town. He knows his business. With him it's zip-zap and that does it. I'm taking that one to him, official-like."

At these last words, he rapped on the box with his whip handle, and because I didn't quite understand what he meant, I lifted the lid.

"It's Tony!" I cried in horror.

"That may well be his name," remarked the little peasant. "I would say he was bitten by an adder out in the forest. Now he must see the doctor, and there's an end of it!"

"But he's dead!" I cried.

"That's why! And he's the better for it, and that's the end of it!" replied the charioteer.

He resumed his merry song, but without words this time, merely by way of oral flute play, at which he proved to be remarkably proficient.

I, meanwhile, was spending a somewhat restless time. A certain icy discomfort of a nether origin was creeping up my spine and under my hat; I was glad therefore, I am bound to say, when finally—it was getting on for eleven—we stopped in front of the doctor's domicile.

Not without some anxiety due to prejudice, I slowly limped into the doctor's office. Doctor Schnorz was already in action. He did not look quite as cruel, for that matter, as I had expected. On the contrary. His fresh color, his full lips, his prominent roguish eyes, his rolled-up sleeves, the businesslike apron over his round belly, all this gave him something of the look of a butcher universally popular for his sanitary ways.

He was just then interrogating a countryman, whose features depicted a profound anxiety.

"Why, how old is your wife?"

"Well," said the peasant. "Fifty to sixty, thereabouts."

"Kill the old woman off. There's nothing more to be done for her. Good-bye!"

As the peasant, whose features had grown quite serene, passed me, I heard him say:

"There's a doctor for you! When he recognizes that there's no help for something, he saves you the expense."

Now it was a fat lady's turn.

"Oh, doctor," she started complaining, "I don't know, I can't get any rest. Every hour of the night I hear the watchman's horn, and I'm so afraid of mice and wicked men; I'm sure it's my nerves."

"A newfangled word!" said the doctor. "Used to be called a bad conscience. Those symptoms, exactly. Keep a tight rein on your tongue, my dear madam. Be kind to your servants. Lots of water! Easy on liqueurs! Hope you improve, madam!"

The lady for her part did not appear to be at all satisfied with Doctor Schnorz's salutary counsel as she sailed out.

And now it was my turn.

"Ah!" exclaimed Schnorz in joyous surprise. "Do my eyes play me a trick or . . . ? Permit me, just a moment. It's just a test."

As he was throwing off these remarks, he had already cut off my big toe and was putting it under his magnifying glass.

"Thought so!" he said with satisfaction. "A virulent gangrene, the real article. Off with it is the best thing."

"Is there a risk to my life?" I inquired timidly.

"Why not?" retorted the doctor. "But don't lose heart; should anything go wrong, the world, at a pinch, will get along without you. Just look at me. If I die today, there'll be another here tomorrow, and I am already enjoying the thought that the Jews won't make any money." *

With this, he pressed me back into a comfortable easychair, strapped me down, took hold of the saw without much ado and threw himself into his work. At every cut a short groaning ha! was squeezed from him. First it went gnauch! gnauch!

---

* The import of this phrase eludes the translator.

Then it went tseek! tsawk! At last it went bump. There! My foot was rid of me.

The further treatment took a similarly swift and auspicious course; and after only a fortnight the good doctor, who had by then had two beautiful crutches made for me, could allow himself the treat of conducting me before the mirror. The person I saw in it was not to my liking. Head: bald; nose: red; neck: twisted; beard: shaggy; half a tailcoat, half a leg; grand total: a gargoyle. And that was me.

But before I had time to burst out crying, the doctor exclaimed in triumph:

"Eh? Well? What do you say now? Picture of a lad, as I live! Marry a rich wife. Everything in tip-top shape! Congratulations! Bon voyage!"

Touched and grateful, I pressed the fleshy hand of the doctor (who had taken no money for all this) and left the town for the open country, with the intention of begging my way on by stages until I finally reached home.

This last came about sooner than I had thought.

Late autumn had arrived; a chilly wind blew; my outfit, so fetching at one time, was all fluttering rags like a scarecrow. Thus I judged it a very hopeful prospect for my purpose when I heard that someone in a certain house had departed this life; for as we all know, the dead are apt to leave perfectly serviceable clothes behind which no one quite sees his way to claiming.

I was not mistaken. Grandfather had died. The fortunate heirs, who understandably had felt a little discommoded for quite some time by the tardiness of a man so advanced in age, and who were therefore in a mellow and charitable mood now, were pleased to make me a present, without a great deal of importuning, of the third-best suit of the deceased, which he had favored for daily use until his blessed demise. I retired into the cattle barn to don it. It is true that the trousers were too ample and the twill coat too long for me by a large margin, but the cuddly woolly cap, a trifle greasy but capable of sliding far down over the ears, made up for it by suiting my needs perfectly. Thus, well-armed against severe weather, I continued my arduous limping pilgrimage. No farther than the next house, the Beggar Bailiff caught me and at the point of his spear drove me into the local prison, called the "Dog Hole," where after a short interrogation it was decided to pass me on without delay.

The shock of it was severe, yet it turned out to be a lucky turn; confirming the truth of the naive saying:

> Hardship despised:
> Blessing disguised.

Since no community could seem to see me as a productive fellow citizen—and who could blame them—each hastened to deport me with a minimum of formality into the next, until, by the nature of the case, the last of them very smoothly deposited me onto the familiar territory of the town of Geckelbeck, where the future was generously left entirely to my own discretion.

The wind was northerly and the snow whirling merrily when in the evening I made my weary entry, on two crutches and one leg, at the paternal farmstead I had left so easily on two legs long ago.

I first peeped shyly through the window. In the easychair sat Gottlieb, looking considerably more sedate than formerly; between his knees stood a boy of three or four, for whom he was making a whip. Near the tile stove stood a cradle, and next to it sat Katharina, nursing a chubby infant at her buxom breast. The maid was setting the table. Father was missing.

Something had gone wrong with my breathing as I took this in. I almost turned back; but the cruel weather prompted me to enter and ask for a night's shelter.

The unknown stranger's request was granted without much ado and with the greatest good nature.

"Or," Gottlieb asked the boy, "should we chase him out again into wind and weather? What do you think, Peter?"

"No, no!" cried the softhearted boy. "Poor man stay here; eat lots of sausage, make leg grow back!"

That night I spent in the horse barn with the hired hand, and from him I learned the full story.

After many years of fruitless waiting, Father, firmly convinced that I had been dragged into Grummel Mere by the Muddy Butt, had made the place over to Gottlieb and Katharina. He had become more and more silent. One morning they found him dead.

During this account my soul, to put it mildly, had been wrenched inside out. I meant to work; I meant to lie patiently in the bed I had made for myself; and never—with this firm vow I went to sleep—were these dear people, who had taken me in so warmly, to find out who I was.

I got up early. Some clothes of little Peter's, in need of repair and draped over the banister of the stairs biding their fate, gave my urge for action the necessary direction. In the table drawer in the parlor I found needle and thread.

By the time the family gathered for the morning soup, my work was ready. It was subjected to a searching inspection and earned delighted acclaim from all those who had a mature judgment in such matters.

I was urged to stay a few more days. The days turned into weeks, the weeks have become years. Rich experience increased my skill not merely in the restoration of the worn and derelict; I even started creating new things on my own without stint. The fame of my art penetrated into Geckelbeck, and

Frau Knippipp, my former master's wife, long widowed now, went so far as to have an honorable proposal of marriage conveyed to me. It met with a flat refusal.

Questioned by Gottlieb, I had called myself Fritz Fröhlich. Funny little Peter, my favorite, called me Hobble-Fritz; an apt name, which has since gained general currency, even among people who do not have the honor of my close acquaintance.

And so I have kept on living here as a quiet, patient, useful domestic animal. I pay no more attention to butterflies. I have fitted out the little attic room in the gable as a comfortable workshop.

The witches still ride by there. The other night, Walpurgis Night, when I was sitting there, busy with the writing of this story, Lucinda peeped into the window. She laughed like a fool; she was just as pretty as ever.

I gave her a calm look, whistled, took a pinch of snuff, and went kerchooh!

Personally

(WAS MICH BETRIFFT)

It may seem odd; but, since others have written about me, I felt like trying it myself just once. I doubt that I can make the reader, with his deep insight into his own heart, believe that it is undertaken with reluctance. It will be a pleasant surprise to him, though, to find me brief.

I was born on April 5, 1832, at Wiedensahl, as the first of seven children.

My father was a shopkeeper; small, curly-haired, active, frugal, and conscientious; always solicitous, never tender; inclined to jesting, but intolerant of pranks. He was forever smoking pipes, but never cigars, being averse to any innovations. He never took to safety matches either, but stayed with tinder, flint, and steel, or used spills. Every evening he would stroll through the village alone; or in the forest if it was nightingale season. My mother, quiet, hardworking, devout, would read after supper. The two lived in concord and such domesticity that at one time twenty years passed without their driving out together.

What else do I remember of the time before I was three? Heinrich, the farm hand, making beautiful flutes for me, and himself playing the jew's harp; the grass so tall in the garden and the peas taller still; behind the straw-thatched house, next to the well, a water trough; and seeing my little sister lie in it like a picture under glass; and when mother came she could barely be brought back to life. Today (1886) I live in her house.

Hymn-books, stories from the Bible, and a selection of Anderson's fairy tales were my earliest reading.

When I had turned nine, it was decided that I should be entrusted to my mother's brother at Ebergötzen. I looked forward to it, not without melancholy. On the eve of departure, I trailed my hand in the rain barrel, which was overhung by a bush of white roses, and sang Christine! Christine! to myself like a dolt. Before dawn the fat little Pomeranian cob was thrust between the poles of the haywagon. The luggage has been loaded, the chief item being the well-preserved carcass of an old clonkedy-ding of a piano, whose awkwardly sprawling underpinnings had to be left behind—a sombre omen of my future as a musician. The travelers get in; grandmother, mother, four children, and a nursemaid; Heinrich last. Off we rumble through the Schaumburg Forest. A herd of stags scampering across the road; the stars wandering overhead; twanging noises from the piano rump. After two overnight stays with relatives, the Ebergötzen vicarage is reached.

Uncle (past eighty at this writing and spry) was a fine figure of a man, a calm observer of nature, and extremely mild-tempered. Only once (though my deserts would have called for more) did some lashes, with a dry Georgina stalk, come my way, because I had teased the village idiot. On the very day of my arrival I formed a friendship with the miller's son. It proved durable. I visit him every year and still find myself sleeping very well to the rumbles and bumps of the millworks and the noise of the rushing millstream.

1886

I made an older friend in the person of the innkeeper and merchant of the village. Hair growing right up to his eyes, down into his neckband, out again from his coat sleeves, and on over his fingernails; always wearing a yellowish green jacket which seldom strove to hide the hinder histrionics of his blue trousers, and down-at-heel leather slippers; indistinct in his speech, vehement, never finishing a sentence; addicted to snuff; a flower grower of some taste; thrice married; a dear man and a delight to me to the day of his death.

In his house I found a fat volume of songs, which I duly fingered my way through on the piano, and many of the liberal religious tracts of that period, which I devoured avidly.

The schoolmaster of the village youth, not being my own teacher, had no power over me—while he was alive. He hanged himself, though, fell down, cut his throat, and was buried in the churchyard almost under my bedroom window. Henceforth, he forced me every night, even in hottest summer, to sleep completely under the covers. Freethinker in the daytime, haunted by ghosts at night. My studies naturally fell into two categories, those I liked and those I disliked. Among the former I counted fairy tales, drawing, trout-catching, and bird-trapping. In between all this, there constantly hovered the graceful image of a fairhaired child, for whose good opinion (and my own aggrandizement) it seemed imperative to deploy fabulous riches, display supernatural agility, and even enact the obligatory rescue from a fiery death with subsequent demise at the beloved's feet.

About the year 1845, we moved to the parish of Lüthorst. Through my window I hear the murmur of the brook; right across it there is a house, a stage of marital discord. The would-be master of the house is cast in the role of the fallen tyrant. A pretty piece of natural theater; vice succumbs, to be sure, but virtue does not triumph. At this point metrics stole into the lesson plan. The great native poets were read; also Shakespeare. At the same time Kant's *Critique of Pure Reason* fell into my hands; though not fully understood, it nevertheless nourished a tendency to amble in the more secluded arbors and byways of the brain—exceedingly shady places, as we know.

Sixteen years old, equipped with a sonnet and a dubious acquaintance with the four operations of arithmetic, I was granted admission to the Polytechnical School at Hannover, within whose walls I rose to an "*A* with distinction" in pure mathematics. In the year 1848, I duly carried a shooting-iron (which by order was never to be loaded with live ammunition) and in the guardroom victoriously secured the rights, not theretofore appreciated, of smoking and beer drinking; two achievements of March,* of which the first was sturdily maintained, while the second has begun to wither noticeably under the inroads of old age.

After hanging on three or four years at Hannover, I betook myself, encouraged by a painter, to the Hall of Classical Statuary at Düsseldorf. There, applying india rubber, the soft core of a wheat roll, and chalk, I mastered the popular method of "dabbing" by which the charming lithographic "grain" is produced.

From Düsseldorf I passed on to the painting academy at Antwerp.

I lived at the corner of Cheese Bridge at a barber's. His name was Jan, hers Mie. Of a mild evening hour, I would sit just outside the door with them in a green dressing-gown, a clay pipe in my mouth; and the neighbors would join us: the basket-weaver, the clockmaker, the tinsmith; their daughters wore black varnished clogs. Jan and Mie were an affectionate little pair, she fat, he thin; they used to barber me by turns, they looked after me during an illness, and at my leavetaking in the cool season presented me with a warm red jacket and three oranges.

How it saddened me to return to this same corner again years later, full of warmth and gratitude, and find everything new, Jan and Mie dead, and only the tinsmith still tinkering in his little old house, looking over his spectacles at me, dimly and without comprehension.

The German Artists' Club, which consisted of a few painters and some political refugees and emigration agents, rarely saw me, but I was sensible of the honor of having a few jokes accepted by their *Kneipzeitung* (*Tipplers' Journal*).

At Antwerp I saw the works of old masters for the first time in my life: Rubens, Brouwer, Teniers; later Frans Hals. Their

---

*The reference is to the limited and transient liberties achieved by the abortive revolutionary movement of 1848.

divine ease of rendering, where there is no dabbling, scratching, or scraping, that ingenuousness of an easy conscience which has no need for hushing anything up; combined with the sensuous appeal of a shimmering jewel, won my love and admiration forever; and gladly do I pardon them for having quelled me so thoroughly that I never really dared to earn my bread by painting, as many another was doing.

It wasn't for lack of trying, to be sure; for work clamors to be done, and even the pickpocket goes to the job daily. A well-meaning fellow human might even make so bold as to assume that these attempts, the results of which are for the most part lost to me, continued steadily all down the chain of circumstances which ultimately allotted me my modest place.

After Antwerp I made a sojourn at Wiedensahl. What people told each other "ût ôler welt" ("from times of yore") fell oddly on my ear. I listened more closely. The person who knew most was an old, quiet, usually taciturn man. Of an evening he would sit all by himself in the dark. At my knock at the window, he would happily light the oil wick. His ear-hugger chair stands in the stove corner. From the wall at his right he gets down the short pipe, artfully lodged upright in a cotton bag; from the stove on his left, the jar full of local tobacco; and having stuffed, puffed, and made smoke, he is launched on the tales inherited from Mum and Gran. He takes his time about the story; but at moments of drama he gets up and changes places with each interlocuter: at which times his tasseled cap, which generally just gives a little nod now and then, gets involved in complex pendulum motions.

From Wiedensahl I visited my uncle at Lüthorst. An amateur theater in the neighboring township drew me into the pleasant circle of its doings; but my mind was more seriously engaged and fascinated by the miraculous life of the bee tribe and by the polemics concerning parthenogenesis then raging, in which my uncle, a deft writer and observer, took a decisive and successful part. A cherished plan to emigrate to Brazil, the beekeeper's Eldorado, remained unrealized. Even the notion that I made a hobby of beekeeping is a well-meaning error.

In the course of such dabbling in the natural sciences, Darwin was read among others. He remained unforgotten when, years later, I steeped myself with passion and persistence in Schopenhauer. Both these enthusiasms have somewhat abated.

The keys they offer do appear to me to fit a variety of doors in the enchanted castle of this world, but not the exit.

From Lüthorst the wind blew me to Munich, where, given the academic current then prevailing, the little boat from Antwerp, not very expertly skippered as it was, soon found itself on the rocks.

The Artists' Club beckoned all the more enticingly. I deplore the publication of the jokes perpetrated there, especially the personal persiflage. But what's the use? Silly pranks, even when launched in confidence, are apt, willy nilly, to catch up with their author.

It may have been in '59 that *Fliegende Blätter* received my first contribution: two men on the ice, of whom one loses his head. I had to narrate on wood. The old handy line was at my disposal as it was at anyone's; delight in the varied interplay of things envisaged and their growing and taking shape was mine too. Thus originated the continuous picture tales, whose random evolution over the years brought their author more acclaim than he had any right to expect. Whoever takes them to hand in a kindly spirit, as he might music boxes, may find that despite their slovenly appearance there is a good deal in them that has been annealed in the furnace of life, forged with diligence, and assembled not without purposeful craft. I did almost all of them at Wiedensahl without consulting anyone and (with the exception of a few products of a craving for nourishment) to please the author. However, should the muse have stepped on one or the other worthy spectator's toes as she went dancing along in her clogs without a care in the world, let it be said that this is the sort of thing no one apologizes for at rustic festivities. To be sure, she is not a strikingly virtuous wench. But while, on one hand, she blushingly rejects any myrtle branch from the hand of undue benevolence, she is also quite undaunted by the rheumy gaze of any elderly esthete who may find a speck of guano in his eye as he cultivates his own plot.

The author whom this muse inspires has been taken for a bookworm and an eccentric; the former erroneously, the latter with some justice. His negligence in the matter of epistolary traffic with strangers has repeatedly, it is rumored, been visited with the death penalty in absentia. As for society, he is not well enough trained either to appreciate its pleasures to the full or to indulge them in comfort. An evening's entertainment in some neutral smoky nook under four or, at most, six eyes may, however, still find him capable of the kind of staying power which scarcely retreats before advancing dawn.

This much I wished to say about myself.

The habit of complaining about old acquaintances is one I have long decided to leave to shrews and gossips; during the present enterprise, though, I have even judged it seemly to remain silent about some persons I love and revere.

II

Someone who happens to be engrossed in a ballet; who is having a champagne party to celebrate his nameday; who chances to be reading his own poems; who is playing skat or tarock, is doing well enough for himself, to be sure.

Unfortunately, these justly popular means of temporary salvation are not always at everyone's disposal. Often you are well off if someone able to raise a wind will at some point merely send up a faintly philosophical little kite pasted together from waste paper. You set your pack down, throw your stick beside it, take off the hot overcoat of existence, sit down on the moleheap of most strenuous observation and gaze after the long-tailed thing as it noses higher and higher aloft and proudly disports itself for a while on high, until the string grows shorter and it sinks lower and lower, to lie down at last, weary and flat, on the dry stubble whence it took off.

Where I am concerned, at least, anyone is welcome to come up and prove to me that time, and this or that other thing, are merely figments, hereditary brain defects, stubborn and incurable until the last skull has spun its last; let him go ahead, take me out on the ice, let him strap on his gleaming skates and describe his clever figures and curlicues. I will follow him with fascinated interest, I will be grateful to him; only let it not get cold enough to freeze my nose, or I will prefer to tuck myself in behind any sort of tangible stove—be it only a quite modest one of simple tile—fit to get a little warmth from.

Yes, time spins airy threads, especially those one keeps sequestered and often draws far out into the so-called future in order to hang up one's worries and wishes like auntie's laundry for the wind to scatter—as though the crowding of the present moment were not quite enough to deal with.

And then, take that dear, cozy, partly sinister and wholly bizarre haunted closet of memory, full of apparently wilted and decayed stuff; which nevertheless continues acting, oppressing, pinching, delighting, often by its own druthers, not at all ours; that sits there quite at ease, however uninvited; that makes its adieus when we want it to stay. A little chamber subdivided into compartments with white doors and red; even black ones, behind which hide the old follies and pratfalls.

It happens to be winter, shall we say. The flakes tumble down across your window in a quiet throng. A little white door opens. Just look how distinctly everything is outlined there: as in a brightly lit doll's house. The lighted tree, the garlands of raisins, the gilded apples and nuts, the gingerbread men baked all brown; happy parents, ecstatic children. You gaze with kindness at the little boy there, for he was you; but also ruefully, because he has not turned into anything better and more respectable than what you are now.

Close it again. Open this little red door here. The picture of a woman in the bloom of youth looks at you earnestly and tenderly, as if it still existed, and were not merely a phantom of what once was.

Let that go. Keep your eye on that little black door. There is a rumbling noise behind it. Keep it closed! Yes, that's all very well; provided you can. Wham, something, you don't know from where, deals you a blow to the heart, the liver, the stomach, or the wallet. You let go of the doorknob. Night comes, quiet, lonesome, dark. Ghosts walk about the brainpan and spook all through your bones, while you hurl yourself from the hot corner of your pillow to the cool and back and forth, until the noise of the dawning day is delightful music to your ears.

Not you, my rosy teenager! You lie there in your white bedcap and snowy little gown, you fold your slim fingers, close those innocent, dreamy blue eyes, and in utter peace of mind slumber your way through to the milk and rolls of the morning and even to your piano lesson; for you have been very good about practicing.

But I, madam! And you, madam! and your wedded lord, who insists on having lobster for supper, let anyone say what they like. But no panic: there is no need to let those wicked people know absolutely everything. I, for instance, am going to be jolly careful; all I'm doing here is letting out a few wretched figures which have somehow come to squat in my brain, as though they had any rights there.

It is night in the royal city, celebrated for its art and its beer. I have come from the pub, needless to say, but have already reached the suburb on the course I have set for my lonely couch. On my left the gangplank, on my right the ditch. Behind me a city full of empty beer mugs, before me the nebulous teetering silhouette of some slouch, well on in years. Now he will tenderly hug the plank, now be magically drawn to the ditch, until finally the plank, tired of the deceitful game, deals him a contemptuous jolt which plunges him instantly into the yielding arms of the ditch, not without jettisoning his left felt slipper. I pull him out by the legs like a wheelbarrow. He wipes his ears and wails piteously: "Y'know what it is, I don't see aright no more. . . ." Surely a most suitable alibi for middle-aged gentlemen in a great number of complex circumstances.

Same route, another day. In front of me a tender couple. Her apron is dragging after her by the strings. I fish it up with my stick and call out ingratiatingly: "Miss, you are losing something." She does not hear me. It is the moment before a lover's tiff. He knocks her down, audibly stamps three times on her chest and is off. That was quick! And what a strange sound it makes, a foot brought down on a woman's heart. Dull, not sonorous. Neither kettle drum nor bass drum. More like a leather suitcase; full of love and loyalty perhaps. I offer her my arm by which to scramble upright and recover herself; for one is often touched and gallant without being drunk.

Another route; another time. I'm invited to lunch with a famous painter. Proud of him and of my silver-gilt box, I walk down a lonely street and quickly roll myself another cigarette. Someone comes shuffling up behind me; shuffling past me. "Beggar folk, sure, nobody fancies *them*; no one cares for cadgers." He says it quietly and humbly, not looking either sideways or over his shoulder; just shuffling on. Hands stuck in a blackish grey cloak; blackish grey hat down on his neck, trousers blackish grey ending in fringes; where hat and coat collar meet, you can see a bit of pale ear on either side. A poor colorless fellow. Even ten marks would probably do a good deal for him. To be sure—the tailor—the trip to the Tyrol—

when all is said and done he'll just waste it on drink. Oh, never mind. Give it to him anyway! Meanwhile he has turned the corner, irretrievable forever.

Quickly, another door. Well, well! Between two hills, a brook running right through it, the little village of my childhood. Much of it thrown into bright relief by the sunlight of early impressions; a lot of it shaded by more than forty years past; some of it only visible through the picket fence of things lived and things known by hearsay. Everything as serene as though it never rained in those days.

But here, too, there are poor little people. Those were the good old days, when an itinerant journeyman, if taken ill, was helped across the village boundary and gently bedded in the ditch so that he might die without embarrassment; although the indigent's corpse still retains a certain market value—to the carrier, for one, who hauls him to the morgue to sell.

Off to one side in the little village, over there behind those dim windowpanes, let us say, there sits "Hunchback Nancy," spinning away. She has renounced the joys of life. But three days after her death—at that point at least she looks forward to a really cozy party, i.e., an honest funeral with all her limbs intact, in a black varnished coffin, in the home cemetery. She has no mind for "the professor who cuts up dead people"; why, for one thing, she would be so embarrassed to face the student gentlemen because she is so very small and lean and hunchbacked. That's why she keeps busy from dawn to dusk begging and musing and spinning.—Oh my! Too soon the sister with the scissors cuts off the flaxen thread of life. Nancy did not make it. Now it's going to be, after all, "Off with her into the pine box" and "hitch 'em up, George!" Away he creaks with her at the crack of dawn, and anyone who is thinking of a trip may catch a ride. (That would have been just the thing for Auntie Amalia, always so eager to get a lift!)

The person over there who is taking his time and seems disgruntled, sawing wood, looks to me like the "Parisian." "A cold winter night," he used to say in Low German, "a boundary stone out in the fields and a bottle of gut-wash—that would add up to a dandy way to go." Or: "Just let me hang for a quarter of an hour, and I'll bet you I could outhang someone who's been at it all year!" He deprecates the first of these ways out because he can't afford it, and the second because of the troublesome onset. He keeps procrastinating and ends up having to be content with just any old death that comes along.

Here in the yard, on the stone stoop in front of the door, stands a pretty woman. Let's give her crossbands on her shoes, curls at the temples, a tortoiseshell comb in a nest of braids. A strange beggar boy comes in by the garden gate, hair like dry wattle; shirt and skin painted out of the same pot; pants roomy, presumably the present of a charitable grandfather; beggar's pouch lumpy with contents; stick plain, serviceable. "Nothing for you today; we have enough poor people of our own." "So let the Devil quick-fry 'ee summat to choke on!" Upon delivering this blessing, he retreats in order to resume his collections elsewhere. Unsuccessfully, though. From behind the wall, armed with a short spear, a little man quite unexpectedly steps into his path, rids him of his provisions with a subtle smile but perfect ruthlessness, and proceeds to show him the proper exit from the village by periodic pointers to his backside with the blunt end of his weapon.

This vigilant potentate is known as "Old Dan." Since his physical and mental powers have grown inadequate for the position of day laborer, he has been appointed to the office of Beggar Bailiff and carries its emblem, the spear known as "Baddelspit."* By virtue of this appointment, he is regent and protector of all indigenous beggars. For his meals he "goes the rounds." He does his sleeping at night in the horse barn, and in the afternoon, weather permitting, in the orchard behind the house. And here is where one may best observe a certain peculiarity of his, which seems to be characteristic mainly of elderly, impecunious people who have neglected to invest in a new plate. When he inhales, there is a loud snore; when he exhales, a soft whistle. First that old, wrinkled, gray-stubbled mumblemouth is drawn in, forming a spacious, pleasingly rounded crater, then abruptly blown out between hollow cheeks to a pretty protruding point with the finest of holes in the center—a phenomenon which remains interesting to the naturalist even upon frequent repetition.

Unfortunately Old Dan has only a short time left to attend to either his office or his recreation. A certain fine, unusually warm afternoon comes along. Two tow-headed boys, experts in fructicultural matters, happen to pay a visit to a notorious tree of summer pears in a shady orchard, just by way of a routine rundown. Old Dan lies beneath it, the spear by his arm, quiet, pale, stretched full-length; his eyes stare straight up into the plenitude of pears; his mouth is open; two flies crawl in and out. Old Dan is dead. And he has timed it cannily, for the new cemetery is about to be inaugurated. He will still slip into the old one and may look forward to a long rest undisturbed by later boarders. A tasteful arrangement of nettles surrounds his resting place.

Ah, yes, my good, comfortably situated, extant reader! Is one not forced to observe that annoyances abound in this world, and that dying goes on on every hand? You should be cheerful, though. You are still standing there on your native soil as though there could be no two ways about it. And then, when you saunter along, spring's foreboding storms roaring about you, and your heart buoyed with a dauntless spirit, as though you would live forever; when blissful summer blossoms surround you and the loving little birds fill the foliage with their song; when your hand trails along billows of grain in the golden autumn; when in the bright glaze of winter your foot rustles in glittering diamonds, high above you the beneficent sun or the night sky's infinity of winking stars—and when yet, omnipresent in all this magnificence, a subtle, unpleasant fragrance hovers, a tiny quavering note: if then, not being some species of St. Francis, you turn serenely to a well-cooked dinner and twinkle at your charming companion and manage to flirt and have a good time as if nothing else were going on, in that case one may truly call you a thoroughly natural and uninhibited humorist.

Almost all of us are of that kind. You, too, my funny little Johnny, with your mumps, your cheek all swollen, smiling at me through tears out of your puffed, shiny, lopsided face, you too are one; and should you perhaps some time later choose to be a professional jester, who considers it his calling to make gratuitous additions to our already vast store of hilarity, just come and call on us, my good Johnny. We shall be glad to let you have the use of our old anecdotes, for you are worth it.

"Ho-hum! What about that dinner at the famous painter's?" you interrupt me, my valued friend with the double chin. Oh! Short but good; wine, superb; snipe, exquisite. But I can see that I've bored you. I'm insulted, but my liking for you is indestructible. I shall take care of you in some other way: let me refer you to a pregnant dictum from a reliable paper: "Il faut louer Busch pour ce qu'il a fait, et pour ce qu'il n'a pas fait." There you are, friends! Let your gaze sweep from left to right, and stretched out before you lies the promised land of all the good things I haven't done.

If you like heartwarming, sunlit prose, read *Werther*. If you seek imperishable humor, likely to endure as long as a musing brow is found over laughing lips, accompany the knight of La Mancha upon his glorious voyages. If you care to see in a full-size mirror, not in a shard, people of every kind, loving, teasing, fighting each other until everyone has received his due portion, turn to Shakespeare. If you feel a desire for bold riots of enchanting color, go and stand before Peter Paul's altarpiece in the city on the Schelde and let the Virgin Mother and Child shine upon you. Or if you yearn more for the solemn tones of a luminous dusk, visit the Holy Father in his enviable penitentiary and gaze at the Sebastian. And if even this is not enough for you, move to the Arno for all I care, where a covered bridge links two wondrous worlds of art.

This should hold you for a week or so, even if you are as much of a glutton for enjoyment as a traveling tailor from London.

APPENDIXES AND BIBLIOGRAPHY

Appendix I
BIOGRAPHICAL CHRONICLE

1832 April 15, 6:00 A.M., Heinrich Christian Wilhelm Busch is born at Wiedensahl (between Stadthagen and Loccum, the former Cistercian Monastery, in the southernmost wedge of the kingdom of Hannover between the Weser and the Steinhude Mere) to Henriette Dorothee Charlotte née KLEINE and Johann Friedrich Wilhelm BUSCH (legitimized premarital son of J. H. W. EMME), shopkeeper at Wiedensahl.

1841 For the sake of a better education, WB is entrusted as a private pupil and lodger to his uncle, Georg Kleine, Lutheran pastor of the village of Ebergötzen east of Göttingen, prominent apiarist. WB forms a lifelong friendship with the local miller's son, Erich Bachmann; their rambles and mischievous pranks are reflected in *Max und Moritz* twenty years later.

1843–45 Tutorials with uncle Kleine; miscellaneous reading of, inter alia, devotional and homiletic tracts, rationalist and atheistic pamphlets; first drawings and portrait sketches. WB later cites Lebrecht Uhlig's pamphlet *Die Throne im Himmel und auf Erden* and the periodical tracts *Die Blätter für christliche Erbauung* (*Sheets for Christian Edification*) as examples of his reading.

1846 Pastor Kleine moves his household to Lüthorst (north of Dassel and Einbeck in the kingdom of Hannover), a larger parish than Ebergötzen. Before the move, WB pays his first visit home to Wiedensahl (the sixty miles or so then meant two days of travel by coach or cart); his mother fails to recognize him as he passes her in the fields.

1847 WB by age fifteen has come to "doubt the native catechism," as he notes later in a letter to Maria Anderson. He enrolls in the mechanical engineering curriculum at Hannover Polytechnical School, normally a six-year course, staying with his uncle, the titular judicial councillor Eberhardt, and later in digs with a fellow student.

1851–52 WB gives up engineering in March 1851 to take up the study of painting. He is admitted (June/July/October) to the Düsseldorf Academy, directed by the Pre-Raphaelite Wilhelm von Schadow (son of the prominent classicist sculptor Johann Gottfried von Schadow); then in May 1852 transfers to the Royal Academy of Fine Arts at Antwerp. He is overwhelmed and (he later confesses) thwarted for life in his self-confidence as a painter by the mastery of the Netherlands seventeenth-century school (Rubens, Adriaen Brouwer, David Teniers, Jr., Frans Hals). WB's diary records: "Anvers, 26th June, 1852. Saturday. From this day dates a firmer definition of my character as a person and a painter. Let it be my second birthdate." In retrospect he notes some forty years later: "At this town, celebrated for its art, I first saw Rubens, Brouwer, Teniers, Frans Hals. Their divine ease of presenting painterly ideas, combined with the sensuous appeal of a jewel, that ingenuousness of an easy conscience which has no need for any hushing up; that music of colors in which all voices are clearly heard, from the ground bass up—these won my love and admiration forever." An earlier reminiscence (1886) continues: "And gladly do I pardon them for having quelled me so thoroughly that I never really dared to earn my bread by painting, as many another was doing." WB's most influential master at Antwerp was the Fleming Joseph Laurent Dykmans ("the Belgian Dou"), a painter of meticulous small genre pictures. Three impressive portrait studies in oil date from this period. "Rembrandt, Hals, and Steen—they are a piece of our Lord's work," he writes later.

1853 In late March WB falls sick with typhoid fever; he returns to Wiedensahl in early May, out of funds and in a state of physical and spiritual collapse; apparently retreating from the vocation of painting with a sense of crucial failure. With genuine interest, he takes up the fashionable Romantic (Grimm Brothers') pursuit of gathering folk songs, rural tales, and idioms into a collection he calls, in Low German, *Ût ôler Welt* (*From Times of Yore*), eventually published, without scholarly apparatus, in 1910.

1854 In a renewed attempt to make painting his career, WB enters the Munich Academy of Fine Arts; joins the "Young Munich" group of artists, which includes the painters Heinrich von Angeli, Otto Stoeger, Moritz von Beckerath, Theodor Pixis, Andreas Müller, Wilhelm Diez, William Unger, Joseph Munsch, Friedrich Lossow; Otto Bassermann, WB's later publisher; Ernst Hanfstaengel, the lithographer, of the Munich art publishers' family; the composer G. Krempelsetzer, a Franz Lachner pupil; and others. An inner circle of late adjourners to which WB also belonged called themselves "The Order of Night Lights." The thirteen years which follow WB spends largely at Munich, with seasonal retreats to the Bavarian highlands or the home regions of Lower Saxony. The summer is spent with "Young Munich" associates at a painters' camp near Brannenburg on the Inn; home in November.

1857 Publication of the fairy-tale volume miscarries. Extensive sketching of human figures and anatomical detail at Lüthorst. From May WB spends time at Munich, Ammerland, (Lake Starnberg), and Brannenburg. At the painters' camp, WB meets the famous graphic artist, Ludwig Richter, whose sentimental, bucolic scenes and vignettes epitomize the Biedermeier age. His son, Heinrich, later publishes WB's first book, the *Bilderpossen* (*Picture Farces*). On July 6, WB's youngest sister, Anna, dies at Wiedensahl. In October WB's first contributions are accepted by *Fliegende Blätter* (*Flying Leaves*) at Munich, which has already yielded its place as a vehicle of political satire to *Kladderadatsch* (founded at Berlin in 1848) in the wave of feeble cultural pessimism the German democratic movement substituted for revolution after the repression of 1848. Prominent fellow contributors

to *Fliegende Blätter* were the Biedermeier painters Moritz von Schwind (of "The Bookworm" and similar static type-studies of the bourgeoisie) and Adolf Oberländer. This initiates a twelve-year period of steady work on cartoon episodes, captioned or "silent," published in *FB* and *Münchner Bilderbogen* (*Picture Sheets from Munich*), both under Caspar Braun's editorship. The first five years of this relationship produce about 130 items of various sizes, which establish WB's reputation and somewhat stabilize his finances.

In this period WB writes a few comic opera librettos and a farcical puppet play.

1860 In October, an attack of "typhoid fever" (others surmise nicotine poisoning), marked by violent diarrhea ("*Schleimfieber*") prostrates WB for several weeks.

The Young Munich group begins to decline and to pall on WB; it disintegrates around 1863.

1862 The Fasching celebrations at Munich feature a fairy-tale performance produced and directed by WB and attended by the royal court.

1864 In the autumn the four tales of *Bilderpossen* (*Picture Farces*) are published with Heinrich Richter at Dresden, but remain a commercial failure until revived by Bassermann in 1880. *Max und Moritz* is offered to Richter and rejected.

1865 *Max und Moritz* is released by (Caspar) Braun & Schneider at Munich, WB receiving a single lump sum of 1000 *gulden*. It is an instant though controversial success, and is ultimately published in some fifty languages. The chief points of its satire, viz., the vindictive repression of children (and other rebels) by a bourgeoisie thwarted and stunted in its own drive for political liberation, and the amoral nature of "the child," formerly and officially conceived of as innocent, were widely misunderstood but proba-

bly had a subliminal effect. The polemically sharpened cruelty of its episodes in both "crime" and "punishment," in conjunction with a few crudely "patriotic" captioned comics by WB in the Austrian and Franco-Prussian war years, may have stamped him as a Teutonic ogre in Victorian Britain and helped prevent his discovery there to this day.

1867 A contract with E. Hellberger of Stuttgart opens a period of several years of contributions by WB to the middlebrow family journals *Über Land und Meer* and *Die illustrierte Welt. Hans Huckebein* appears under the same imprint.

1868 WB's father dies at Wiedensahl.

WB spends this winter and the next two at Frankfurt in the circle of the Kessler bankers' family, one of several wealthy houses with a fashionable taste for art collecting and patronage of painters. He is shown great personal solicitude and active concern for his professional advancement by Frau Johanna Kessler, taken in as a house guest, and adopted as an uncle by the two young daughters, Nanda and Letty. After the first winter he is supplied with a studio and apartment in the Kesslers' converted coachman's quarters on Wiesenstrasse. He undertakes and completes the graphic work for a revived version of the popular eighteenth-century mock epic tale by K. A. Kortum, *The Jobsiad*. In this connection he studies and copies the work of the leading engraver of domestic satires and theatrical illustrations of the preceding century, the Polish master Daniel Chodowiecki, whose role and gift are reminiscent of Hogarth and who did much of his work in Prussia. WB eventually replaces most of the Kortum text with his own verse and illustrates it brilliantly. *Bilder zur Jobsiade* thus becomes the first artistic triumph of WB's personal genre, the picture tale, not equalled again until *Die fromme Helene*.

WB's close attachment to Johanna Kessler lasts, with varying degrees of devotion and rates of communication, all his life, except for an estrangement of more than a decade over his move to Munich in 1877.

1870 WB's mother dies at Wiedensahl on June 1. He works on *Jobsiade* at Frankfurt early in the year. *Der heilige Antonius von Padua* (*St. Anthony of Padua*), a saucy parody in verse and sketch of a Catholic saint's life, is delivered to Moritz Schauenburg at Lahr, banned by the authorities, and published after acquittal of the editor in a lawsuit. The minor cause célèbre adds further notoriety to the name of the author of *Max und Moritz.**

1871 A firm publishing contract is signed on profitable terms (45 percent of net to author) with Otto Bassermann, one of WB's friends of the Young Munich group. The following picture tales and other items in verse and prose, representing all the new work published by WB in his lifetime, appear under the Bassermann imprint (daggers denote full or partial representation in the present anthology):

1872	*Die fromme Helene* †
	Bilder zur Jobsiade
	Pater Filuzius
1873	*Der Geburtstag, oder Die Partikularisten*
1874	*Dideldum;* † *Kritik des Herzens* †
1875	*Abenteuer eines Junggesellen* †
1876	*Herr und Frau Knopp* †
1877	*Julchen* †
1878	*Die Haarbeutel* †
1879	*Fipps der Affe* †
1880	*Bilderpossen*, 2nd ed.; † *Stippstörchen für Äuglein und Öhrchen*

*Wilhelm Busch's knee-jerk patriotism in national crises as well as his impish irreverence in verse toward orthodox religious legendry offer a striking parallel with Pushkin forty years earlier.

1881	*Der Fuchs. Die Drachen. Zwei lustige Sachen.*
1882	*Plisch und Plum* †
1883	*Balduin Bählamm, der verhinderte Dichter* †
1884	*Maler Klecksel;* † *Wilhelm-Busch-Album: Humoristischer Hausschatz* †
1891	*Eduards Traum*
1893	*Von mir über mich* in anniversary ed. of *Die fromme Helene*
1895	*Der Schmetterling* †
1904	*Zu guter Letzt* †

1872 WB abruptly gives up the Frankfurt studio and flat (March), prompted by a crisis in his relations with Johanna Kessler and/or gossip about them; probably also in renewed disappointment with his painting. He returns to Wiedensahl and moves into his parents' house with his brother Adolf and the latter's wife, Johanna. From here he delivers *Die fromme Helene* to Bassermann in May, and both *Pater Filuzius*, his polemic contribution to Bismarck's *Kulturkampf*, and *Bilder zur Jobsiade* in October. The following month, domestic relations deteriorating, he moves in with his sister Fanny and her husband, Pastor Hermann Nöldeke, at the parsonage. This causes a rift with Adolf and Johanna Busch.

During this and the next few years, WB journeys to art centers like Frankfurt, Munich, Vienna, Berlin, and Dresden; to the Low Countries (Amsterdam, Antwerp, Bruges); and to Italy (Bozen, Venice). In Munich in March and May, he is introduced into the informal Munich artists' circle "Allotria."

1874 Work on *Dideldum!* and *Kritik des Herzens* (*Critique of the Heart*). An epistolary friendship begins with Auguste Gruber of Vienna.

1875 After a cool critical reception of his first volume of poems, *Kritik des Herzens*, WB responds warmly to a letter of homage from the widowed Dutch writer Maria Anderson (1842–1917). A lively correspondence between them—over seventy letters by WB are extant—continues for three years but does not long survive a much-postponed first meeting face to face.

A makeshift studio, occasionally used in later years, is made available to WB by brother Gustav at Wolfenbüttel in Brunswick.

1876 Closer association with the "Allotria" group initiates lifelong friendships with the gifted and sensitive Hermann Levi (1839–1900), an abjectly Germanophile Jewish musician and prominent conductor of Wagner operas; with the sculptor and decorator Lorenz Gedon (1843–83); and with the celebrated society portraitists Friedrich August (von) Kaulbach (1850–1920) and Franz (von) Lenbach (1836–1904).

1877 In January, WB paints in Lenbach's luxurious studio. His work is acclaimed by many, including Prince Ludwig and his consort. On September 8 begins his "second Munich period," which ends on April 12, 1881, and marks his last attempt to "go public" in painting. Gedon arranges and decorates a studio for him.

In December a first draft of *Fipps der Affe* is completed.

WB's friendship with Johanna Kessler suffers a rift, not to be healed until the nineties, over his resuming his painting career in Munich, not Frankfurt.

1878 Pastor Nöldeke dies, and WB assumes responsibility for his three orphaned nephews. He discharges it with great conscientiousness and throughout his life maintains a close and warm rapport with all three and their families. Their reminiscences later constitute an important, if not wholly reliable source of information on the last thirty years of WB's life.

During five summer weeks spent on Borkum Island (North Sea coast), he forms a friendship with Frau Marie Hesse, a Silesian landed proprietor with a second home at Bremen, with whom he later corresponds frequently.

1879   After another four months at Munich, WB sets up a new joint household with his widowed sister in the dowager parsonage at Wiedensahl. Brother Otto, who had held a tutor's position in the Kessler house since 1867 and first introduced WB there, dies in May.

1880   The early eighties show a marked shift in WB's painting to landscapes and open-air scenes. He produces hundreds of small-format oil sketches, which he treats casually and often fails to preserve. The friendship with Hermann Levi, director of the Bavarian Court Orchestra, deepens in these years. Levi's touching warmth of feeling and intuitive understanding of both WB's genius and its crucial inhibitions tend to break down his friend's morbid reserve. Their pursuit of common interests and a more far-ranging intellectual rapport than links WB to other friends takes such forms as music enjoyed and discussed together and exchanges of literature, such as Levi's gift to WB of Dostoevsky's *Crime and Punishment*, which had then just come to the notice of German publishers.

WB's correspondence with Lenbach and Kaulbach continues for many years to produce letters of great literary power and originality of phrasing, suggesting that WB's verbal gift and vigor have begun to rival and divorce themselves from his impulse to paint and draw.

1881   In February, and again in the autumn, WB suffers attacks of nicotine poisoning which require treatment. There are new signs of a severe psychic upheaval and a crisis in his philosophy as he approaches fifty.

1885   WB's aunt Fanny Kleine, his foster mother in the Ebergötzen years, dies at Lüthorst; her husband will live to be over ninety.

The first *Wilhelm-Busch-Album*, ancestor of the many hundreds of thousands of red folio tomes absorbed by German speakers over the century to come, launched by Bassermann with the stuffy subtitle "Home Thesaurus of Humor," begins its career.

In the years following *Maler Klecksel*, which proved to be the last completed work of his picture-tale genre, WB turns to painting and free, i.e., uncaptioned and discontinuous, graphic work, of which only a portion is still extant.

The Swiss cultural historian, John Grand-Cartenet, pays a glowing tribute to the originality and brilliance of WB's work in thirty profusely illustrated pages of his tome, *Les moeurs et la caricature en Allemagne—en Autriche—en Suisse*. "Here we assuredly have the king of caricature and the farcical lampoon. . . . By the power of his genius Busch has contrived to incarnate a manner; he has created a Busch genre." His book first calls WB's attention to the work of the Swiss draftsman Rodolphe Toepffer (1799–1846), who delighted Goethe and was still popular in the eighties in the France of Doré and Daumier.

1886   Trip to Rome in May.

WB supplies the *Frankfurter Zeitung* with an autobiographical sketch, *Was mich betrifft* ("As for Myself," titled "Personally" in this anthology), in response to some errors in a fine biographical analysis by Johannes Proelss, the *Frankfurter*'s literary feature editor. This profile had itself been motivated by an embarrassingly fulsome pamphlet extolling WB by the Düsseldorf painter, Eduard Daelen.

1887–88   WB enjoys the last "Sylvester punch" on New Year's Eve with his brother Gustav, who dies the following May. In August WB visits art centers in Holland again, this time with Lenbach.

1891   The picaresque and surrealist prose fantasy, *Eduards Traum (Edward's Dream)* is delivered to Bassermann and published (5,000 copies) in conjunction with a new edition of *Kritik des Herzens*, first issued seventeen years earlier.

In August, WB accompanies Lenbach on another journey to Holland.

Late in the year WB pays a long visit to Frankfurt, which marks his recent rapprochement with Johanna Kessler. The happier relationship with the Kessler daughters continues, especially with Nanda, now a wife and mother at the stage of life Johanna had been at in the late sixties.

1893   WB reworks and curtails *Was mich betrifft*, trying to make it even less personal and revealing. The result, *Von mir über mich (By Me About Me)* is used to accompany the twentieth-anniversary edition of *Die fromme Helene*.

1895   After working on a piece of prose, thought of as a counterpart to *Eduards Traum*, almost all the preceding year, WB completes it—*Der Schmetterling (The Butterfly)*—at Hermann Busch's at Celle. It is published in late April. The story combines strong ingredients of fairy tale, allegory, and parable (of much autopsychological import) with a lyric vein reminiscent of Eichendorff's famous 1826 romantic fantasy, *Aus dem Leben eines Taugenichts (Memoirs of a Good-for-Nothing)*, as well as a bitter transcendental skepticism showing the lifelong influence of Schopenhauer on WB.

WB grows more inactive in painting, giving it up entirely in 1896, while some graphic work continues. The success of his picture tales steadily increases throughout these years; *Die fromme Helene* is well beyond the 100,000 mark, and the *Album* past 20,000, with the *Knopp* trilogy and the rest keeping pace. A lively correspondence begins with WB's favorite "niece," Grete Meyer-Thomsen, a young musician, daughter of Helene Meyer née Kleine, granddaughter of WB's foster father, Georg Kleine, and sister of Else, who had married his nephew Otto Nöldeke.

1898   WB and Fanny give up the household at Wiedensahl in October and move to Mechtshausen, a village of about 400 inhabitants in the Harz mountains, to live with Otto Nöldeke and his family.

1899   Some ninety of the poems going into the later collection *Zu guter Letzt* are written this year.

WB reads widely; he shows considerable familiarity with foreign classics such as Boswell's *Life of Johnson* and Shakespeare, whom he quotes in English. A passage in a letter to Johanna Kessler contains interesting hints of his view of the contemporary state of painting, with sidelights on himself: "You . . . have seen many beautiful Vandykes at Antwerp. . . . Those bygone gentlemen did bring their business to the point of perfection. Let us not hold it against their epigones, therefore, even if they take us aback at first, that they go separate ways in order to gain some elbowroom and some notice of their own, without always being measured by that grand scale which will always make them seem to fall short. Original fellows will have some pleasing achievements to show for having taken this route. And for that matter, the world is in a fever. Like a delirious patient it tosses and turns now to one side, now to the other, until there too the head feels too hot. That is how it goes in art, politics, philosophy and other things; and this is how it will probably go on as long as there is life in the patient" (excerpted by Friedrich Bohne in his *Wilhelm Busch: Leben, Werk, Schicksal*, [Zurich, 1958], p. 270; translated by W. Arndt).

1902   Celebrations of WB's seventieth birthday take place all over Germany. He evades the messages and visitors by traveling to Ebergötzen and Hattorf (Harz), his nephew Hermann Nöldeke's parish since 1878, and continues his life of almost complete seclusion, seldom reacting to inquiries and requests from would-be biographers and public figures but generously responsive to family and close friends.

1903–04   The volume of late poems, *Zu guter Letzt* (*Winding Up*) is readied and published.

1905   A collection of late graphic work, *Hernach* (*Hereafter*) is turned over to Otto Nöldeke (published in 1908). WB leaves dispositions for his poetic bequest, published in 1909 as *Schein und Sein* (*Appearance and Essence*).

1907   WB's seventy-fifth birthday occasions much homage in the public press and a jubilee edition of the works.

WB pays his last visit to Frankfurt in June.

Erich Bachmann, WB's childhood friend, dies in August.

1908   WB suffers a mild heart attack at Mechtshausen on January 6 and dies in his sleep on January 9.

Appendix II:

GERMAN ORIGINALS OF THE VERSE

Der Eispeter

Als Anno 12 das Holz so rar
Und als der kalte Winter war,
Da blieb ein jeder gern zu Haus;
Nur Peter muss aufs Eis hinaus.
Da draussen, ja, man glaubt es kaum,
Fiel manche Krähe tot vom Baum.
Der Onkel Förster warnt und spricht:
"Mein Peter, heute geht es nicht!"
Auch ist ein Hase bei den Ohren
Ganz dicht am Wege festgefroren.
Doch Peter denkt: Tralitrala!
Und sitzt auf einem Steine da.
Nun möchte Peter sich erheben;
Die Hose bleibt am Steine kleben,
Der Stoff ist alt, die Lust ist gross;
Der Peter reisst sich wieder los.
Na, richtig! Ja, ich dacht' es doch!
Da fällt er schon ins tiefe Loch.
Mit Hinterlassung seiner Mütze
Steigt Peter wieder aus der Pfütze.
Bald schiesst hervor, obschon noch klein,
Ein Zacken Eis am Nasenbein.
Der Zacken wird noch immer besser
Und scharf als wie ein Schlachtermesser.
Der Zacken werden immer mehr,
Der Nasenzacken wird ein Speer.
Und jeder fragt: Wer mag das sein?
Das ist ja ein gefrornes Stachelschwein!
Die Eltern sehen nach der Uhr:
"Ach, ach! Wo bleibt denn Peter nur?"
Da ruft der Onkel in das Haus:
"Der Schlingel ist aufs Eis hinaus!"
Mit einer Axt und stillem Weh
Sucht man den Peter hier im Schnee.
Schon sieht man mit betrübtem Blick
Ein Teil von Peters Kleidungsstück.
Doch grösser war die Trauer da,
Als man den Peter selber sah.
Hier wird der Peter transportiert,
Der Vater weint, die Träne friert.
Behutsam lässt man Peters Glieder
Zu Haus am warmen Ofen nieder.
Juchhe! Die Freudigkeit ist gross;
Das Wasser rinnt, das Eis geht los.
Ach, aber ach! Nun ist's vorbei!
Der ganze Kerl zerrinnt zu Brei.
Hier wird in einen Topf gefüllt
Des Peters traurig Ebenbild.
Jaja! In diesem Topf von Stein,
Da machte man den Peter ein,
Der, nachdem er anfangs hart,
Später weich wie Butter ward.

Max und Moritz

Max und Moritz machten beide,
Als sie lebten, keinem Freude:
Bildlich siehst du jetzt die Possen,
Die in Wirklichkeit verdrossen,
Mit behaglichem Gekicher,
Weil du selbst vor ihnen sicher.
Aber das bedenke stets:
Wie man's treibt, mein Kind, so geht's.

Vorwort

Ach, was muss man oft von bösen
Kindern hören oder lesen!
Wie zum Beispiel hier von diesen,
Welche Max und Moritz hiessen;
Die, anstatt durch weise Lehren
Sich zum Guten zu bekehren,
Oftmals noch darüber lachten
Und sich heimlich lustig machten.
Ja, zur Übeltätigkeit,
Ja, dazu ist man bereit!
Menschen necken, Tiere quälen,
Äpfel, Birnen, Zwetschgen stehlen,
Das ist freilich angenehmer
Und dazu auch viel bequemer,
Als in Kirche oder Schule
Festzusitzen auf dem Stuhle.
Aber wehe, wehe, wehe!
Wenn ich auf das Ende sehe!!
Ach, das war ein schlimmes Ding,
Wie es Max und Moritz ging!
Drum ist hier, was sie getrieben,
Abgemalt und aufgeschrieben.

Erster Streich

Mancher gibt sich viele Müh'
Mit dem lieben Federvieh;
Einesteils der Eier wegen,
Welche diese Vögel legen;

Zweitens: Weil man dann und wann
Einen Braten essen kann;
Drittens aber nimmt man auch
Ihre Federn zum Gebrauch
In die Kissen und die Pfühle,
Denn man liegt nicht gerne kühle.
Seht, da ist die Witwe Bolte,
Die das auch nicht gerne wollte.
Ihrer Hühner waren drei
Und ein stolzer Hahn dabei.
Max und Moritz dachten nun:
Was ist hier jetzt wohl zu tun?
Ganz geschwinde, eins, zwei, drei,
Schneiden sie sich Brot entzwei,
In vier Teile, jedes Stück
Wie ein kleiner Finger dick.
Diese binden sie an Fäden,
Übers Kreuz, ein Stück an jeden,
Und verlegen sie genau
In den Hof der guten Frau.
Kaum hat dies der Hahn gesehen,
Fängt er auch schon an zu krähen:
Kikeriki! Kikikerikih!!—
Tak, tak, tak!—Da kommen sie.
Hahn und Hühner schlucken munter
Jedes ein Stück Brot hinunter;
Aber als sie sich besinnen,
Konnte keines recht von hinnen.
In die Kreuz und in die Quer
Reissen sie sich hin und her,
Flattern auf und in die Höh',
Ach herrje, herrjemine!
Ach, sie bleiben an dem langen,
Dürren Ast des Baumes hangen.
Und ihr Hals wird lang und länger,
Ihr Gesang wird bang und bänger.
Jedes legt noch schnell ein Ei,
Und dann kommt der Tod herbei.
Witwe Bolte in der Kammer
Hört im Bette diesen Jammer;
Ahnungsvoll tritt sie heraus,
Ach, was war das für ein Graus!
"Fliesset aus dem Aug', ihr Tränen!
All mein Hoffen, all mein Sehnen,
Meines Lebens schönster Traum
Hängt an diesem Apfelbaum!"
Tiefbetrübt und sorgenschwer
Kriegt sie jetzt das Messer her,
Nimmt die Toten von den Strängen,
Dass sie so nicht länger hängen,
Und mit stummem Trauerblick
Kehrt sie in ihr Haus zurück.

Dieses war der erste Streich,
Doch der zweite folgt sogleich.

Zweiter Streich

Als die gute Witwe Bolte
Sich von ihrem Schmerz erholte,
Dachte sie so hin und her,
Dass es wohl das beste wär',
Die Verstorbnen, die hienieden
Schon so frühe abgeschieden,
Ganz im stillen und in Ehren
Gut gebraten zu verzehren.
Freilich war die Trauer gross,
Als sie nun so nackt und bloss
Abgerupft am Herde lagen,
Sie, die einst in schönen Tagen
Bald im Hofe, bald im Garten
Lebensfroh im Sande scharrten.—
Ach, Frau Bolte weint aufs neu,
Und der Spitz steht auch dabei
Max und Moritz rochen dieses.
"Schnell aufs Dach gekrochen!" hiess es.
Durch den Schornstein mit Vergnügen
Sehen sie die Hühner liegen,
Die schon ohne Kopf und Gurgeln
Lieblich in der Pfanne schmurgeln.
Eben geht mit einem Teller
Witwe Bolte in den Keller,
Dass sie von dem Sauerkohle
Eine Portion sich hole,
Wofür sie besonders schwärmt,
Wenn er wieder aufgewärmt.
Unterdessen auf dem Dache
Ist man tätig bei der Sache.
Max hat schon mit Vorbedacht
Eine Angel mitgebracht.
Schnupdiwup! Da wird nach oben
Schon ein Huhn heraufgehoben.
Schnupdiwup! Jetzt Numro zwei;
Schnupdiwup! Jetzt Numro drei;
Und jetzt kommt noch Numro vier:
Schnupdiwup! Dich haben wir!
Zwar der Spitz sah es genau,
Und er bellt: Rawau! Rawau!
Aber schon sind sie ganz munter
Fort und von dem Dach herunter.
Na! Das wird Spektakel geben,
Denn Frau Bolte kommt soeben;
Angewurzelt stand sie da,
Als sie nach der Pfanne sah.
Alle Hühner waren fort.—
"Spitz!!"—Das war ihr erstes Wort.

"O du Spitz, du Ungetüm!
Aber wart! Ich komme ihm!"
Mit dem Löffel gross und schwer
Geht es über Spitzen her;
Laut ertönt sein Wehgeschrei,
Denn er fühlt sich schuldenfrei.
Max und Moritz im Verstecke
Schnarchen aber an der Hecke,
Und vom ganzen Hühnerschmaus
Guckt nur noch ein Bein heraus.
Dieses war der zweite Streich,
Doch der dritte folgt sogleich.

Dritter Streich

Jedermann im Dorfe kannte
Einen, der sich Böck benannte.
Alltagsröcke, Sonntagsröcke,
Lange Hosen, spitze Fräcke,
Westen mit bequemen Taschen,
Warme Mäntel und Gamaschen,
Alle diese Kleidungssachen
Wusste Schneider Böck zu machen.
Oder wäre was zu flicken,
Abzuschneiden, anzustücken,
Oder gar ein Knopf der Hose
Abgerissen oder lose,
Wie und wo und was es sei,
Hinten, vorne, einerlei,
Alles macht der Meister Böck,
Denn das ist sein Lebenszweck.
Drum so hat in der Gemeinde
Jedermann ihn gern zum Freunde.
Aber Max und Moritz dachten,
Wie sie ihn verdriesslich machten.
Nämlich vor des Meisters Hause
Floss ein Wasser mit Gebrause.
Übers Wasser führt ein Steg,
Und darüber geht der Weg.
Max und Moritz, gar nicht träge,
Sägen heimlich mit der Säge,
Ritzeratze! voller Tücke,
In die Brücke eine Lücke.
Als nun diese Tat vorbei,
Hört man plötzlich ein Geschrei:
"He, heraus! Du Ziegen-Böck!
Schneider, Schneider, meck, meck, meck!"
Alles konnte Böck ertragen,
Ohne nur ein Wort zu sagen;
Aber wenn er dies erfuhr,
Ging's ihm wider die Natur.
Schnelle springt er mit der Elle
Über seines Hauses Schwelle,

Denn schon wieder ihm zum Schreck
Tönt ein lautes: "Meck, meck, meck!"
Und schon ist er auf der Brücke,
Kracks! Die Brücke bricht in Stücke;
Wieder tönt es: "Meck, meck, meck!"
Plumps! Da ist der Schneider weg!
Grad als dieses vorgekommen,
Kommt ein Gänsepaar geschwommen,
Welches Böck in Todeshast
Krampfhaft bei den Beinen fasst.
Beide Gänse in der Hand,
Flattert er auf trocknes Land.
Übrigens bei alledem
Ist so etwas nicht bequem;
Wie denn Böck von der Geschichte
Auch das Magendrücken kriegte.
Hoch ist hier Frau Böck zu preisen!
Denn ein heisses Bügeleisen,
Auf den kalten Leib gebracht,
Hat es wiedergutgemacht.
Bald im Dorf hinauf, hinunter,
Hiess es: "Böck ist wieder munter!"
Dieses war der dritte Streich,
Doch der vierte folgt sogleich.

Vierter Streich

Also lautet ein Beschluss,
Dass der Mensch was lernen muss.
Nicht allein das Abc
Bringt den Menschen in die Höh';
Nicht allein in Schreiben, Lesen
Übt sich ein vernünftig Wesen;
Nicht allein in Rechnungssachen
Soll der Mensch sich Mühe machen,
Sondern auch der Weisheit Lehren
Muss man mit Vergnügen hören.
Dass dies mit Verstand geschah,
War Herr Lehrer Lämpel da.
Max und Moritz, diese beiden,
Mochten ihn darum nicht leiden;
Denn wer böse Streiche macht,
Gibt nicht auf den Lehrer acht.
Nun war dieser brave Lehrer
Von dem Tobak ein Verehrer,
Was man ohne alle Frage
Nach des Tages Müh und Plage
Einem guten, alten Mann
Auch von Herzen gönnen kann.
Max und Moritz, unverdrossen,
Sinnen aber schon auf Possen,
Ob vermittelst seiner Pfeifen
Dieser Mann nicht anzugreifen.
Einstens, als es Sonntag wieder

Und Herr Lämpel, brav und bieder,
In der Kirche mit Gefühle
Sass vor seinem Orgelspiele,
Schlichen sich die bösen Buben
In sein Haus und seine Stuben,
Wo die Meerschaumpfeife stand;
Max hält sie in seiner Hand;
Aber Moritz aus der Tasche
Zieht die Flintenpulverflasche,
Und geschwinde, stopf, stopf, stopf!
Pulver in den Pfeifenkopf. —
Jetzt nur still und schnell nach Haus,
Denn schon ist die Kirche aus. —
Eben schliesst in sanfter Ruh
Lämpel seine Kirche zu;
Und mit Buch und Notenheften
Nach besorgten Amtsgeschäften
Lenkt er freudig seine Schritte
Zu der heimatlichen Hütte,
Und voll Dankbarkeit sodann
Zündet er sein Pfeifchen an.
"Ach!"—spricht er—"Die grösste Freud
Ist doch die Zufriedenheit!!"
Rums!!—Da geht die Pfeife los
Mit Getöse, schrecklich gross.
Kaffeetopf und Wasserglas,
Tobaksdose, Tintenfass,
Ofen, Tisch und Sorgensitz—
Alles fliegt im Pulverblitz. —
Als der Dampf sich nun erhob,
Sieht man Lämpel, der gottlob
Lebend auf dem Rücken liegt;
Doch er hat was abgekriegt.
Nase, Hand, Gesicht und Ohren
Sind so schwarz als wie die Mohren,
Und des Haares letzter Schopf
Ist verbrannt bis auf den Kopf.
Wer soll nun die Kinder lehren
Und die Wissenschaft vermehren?
Wer soll nun für Lämpel leiten
Seine Amtestätigkeiten?
Woraus soll der Lehrer rauchen,
Wenn die Pfeife nicht zu brauchen?
Mit der Zeit wird alles heil,
Nur die Pfeife hat ihr Teil.
Dieses war der vierte Streich,
Doch der fünfte folgt sogleich.

Fünfter Streich

Wer in Dorfe oder Stadt
Einen Onkel wohnen hat,
Der sei höflich und bescheiden,
Denn das mag der Onkel leiden.

Morgens sagt man: "Guten Morgen!
Haben Sie was zu besorgen?"
Bringt ihm, was er haben muss:
Zeitung, Pfeife, Fidibus.
Oder sollt' es wo im Rücken
Drücken, beissen oder zwicken,
Gleich ist man mit Freudigkeit
Dienstbeflissen und bereit.
Oder sei's nach einer Prise,
Dass der Onkel heftig niese,
Ruft man: "Prosit!" alsogleich.
"Danke!"—"Wohl bekomm' es Euch!"
Oder kommt er spät nach Haus,
Zieht man ihm die Stiefel aus,
Holt Pantoffel, Schlafrock, Mütze,
Dass er nicht im Kalten sitze—
Kurz, man ist darauf bedacht,
Was dem Onkel Freude macht.
Max und Moritz ihrerseits
Fanden darin keinen Reiz.
Denkt euch nur, welch schlechten Witz
Machten sie mit Onkel Fritz!
Jeder weiss, was so ein Mai-
Käfer für ein Vogel sei.
In den Bäumen hin und her
Fliegt und kriecht und krabbelt er.
Max und Moritz, immer munter,
Schütteln sie vom Baum herunter.
In die Tüte von Papiere
Sperren sie die Krabbeltiere.
Fort damit und in die Ecke
Unter Onkel Fritzens Decke!
Bald zu Bett geht Onkel Fritze
In der spitzen Zippelmütze;
Seine Augen macht er zu,
Hüllt sich ein und schläft in Ruh.
Doch die Käfer, kritze, kratze!
Kommen schnell aus der Matratze.
Schon fasst einer, der voran,
Onkel Fritzens Nase an.
"Bau!"—schreit er—"Was ist das hier?!!"
Und erfasst das Ungetier.
Und den Onkel, voller Grausen,
Sieht man aus dem Bette sausen.
"Autsch!!"—Schon wieder hat er einen
Im Genicke, an den Beinen;
Hin und her und rundherum
Kriecht es, fliegt es mit Gebrumm.
Onkel Fritz, in dieser Not,
Haut und trampelt alles tot.
Guckste wohl! Jetzt ist's vorbei
Mit der Käferkrabbelei!
Onkel Fritz hat wieder Ruh

Und macht seine Augen zu.
Dieses war der fünfte Streich,
Doch der sechste folgt sogleich.

Sechster Streich

In der schönen Osterzeit,
Wenn die frommen Bäckersleut'
Viele süsse Zuckersachen
Backen und zurechte machen,
Wünschten Max und Moritz auch
Sich so etwas zum Gebrauch.
Doch der Bäcker, mit Bedacht,
Hat das Backhaus zugemacht.
Also will hier einer stehlen,
Muss er durch den Schlot sich quälen.
Ratsch! Da kommen die zwei Knaben
Durch den Schornstein, schwarz wie Raben.
Puff! Sie fallen in die Kist',
Wo das Mehl darinnen ist.
Da! Nun sind sie alle beide
Rundherum so weiss wie Kreide.
Aber schon mit viel Vergnügen
Sehen sie die Brezeln liegen.
Knacks!!—Da bricht der Stuhl entzwei;
Schwapp!!—Da liegen sie im Brei.
Ganz von Kuchenteig umhüllt
Stehn sie da als Jammerbild.
Gleich erscheint der Meister Bäcker
Und bemerkt die Zuckerlecker.
Eins, zwei, drei!—Eh' man's gedacht,
Sind zwei Brote draus gemacht.
In dem Ofen glüht es noch—
Ruff!!—damit ins Ofenloch!
Ruff!!—man zieht sie aus der Glut;
Denn nun sind sie braun und gut.
Jeder denkt, die sind perdü!
Aber nein!—Noch leben sie!
Knusper, knasper!—wie zwei Mäuse
Fressen sie durch das Gehäuse;
Und der Meister Bäcker schrie:
"Ach herrje! Da laufen sie!"
Dieses war der sechste Streich,
Doch der letzte folgt sogleich.

Letzter Streich

Max und Moritz, wehe euch!
Jetzt kommt euer letzter Streich!
Wozu müssen auch die beiden
Löcher in die Säcke schneiden??
Seht, da trägt der Bauer Mecke
Einen seiner Maltersäcke.
Aber kaum dass er von hinnen,
Fängt das Korn schon an zu rinnen.

Und verwundert steht und spricht er:
"Zapperment! Dat Ding werd lichter!"
Hei! Da sieht er voller Freude
Max und Moritz im Getreide.
Rabs!!—in seinen grossen Sack
Schaufelt er das Lumpenpack.
Max und Moritz wird es schwüle,
Denn nun geht es nach der Mühle.
"Meister Müller, he, heran!
Mahl er das, so schnell er kann!"
"Her damit!" Und in den Trichter
Schüttet er die Bösewichter.
Rickeracke! Rickeracke!
Geht die Mühle mit Geknacke.
Hier kann man sie noch erblicken,
Fein geschroten und in Stücken.
Doch sogleich verzehret sie
Meister Müllers Federvieh.

Schluss

Als man dies im Dorf erfuhr,
War von Trauer keine Spur.
Witwe Bolte, mild und weich,
Sprach: "Sieh da, ich dacht' es gleich!"
"Jajaja!" rief Meister Böck.
"Bosheit ist kein Lebenszweck!"
Drauf so sprach Herr Lehrer Lämpel:
"Dies ist wieder ein Exempel!"
"Freilich," meint' der Zuckerbäcker,
"Warum ist der Mensch so lecker!"
Selbst der gute Onkel Fritze
Sprach: "Das kommt von dumme Witze!"
Doch der brave Bauersmann
Dachte: Wat geiht meck dat an!
Kurz, im ganzen Ort herum
Ging ein freudiges Gebrumm:
"Gott sei Dank! Nun ist's vorbei
Mit der Übeltäterei!"

Hans Huckebein, der Unglücksrabe

Hier sieht man Fritz, den muntern Knaben,
Nebst Huckebein, dem jungen Raben.
Und dieser Fritz, wie alle Knaben,
Will einen Raben gerne haben.
Schon rutscht er auf dem Ast daher,
Der Vogel, der misstraut ihm sehr.
Schlapp! macht der Fritz von seiner Kappe
Mit Listen eine Vogelklappe.
Beinahe hätt' er ihn! Doch ach!

Der Ast zerbricht mit einem Krach.
In schwarzen Beeren sitzt der Fritze,
Der schwarze Vogel in der Mütze.
Der Knabe Fritz ist schwarz betupft;
Der Rabe ist in Angst und hupft.
Der schwarze Vogel ist gefangen,
Er bleibt im Unterfutter hangen.
"Jetzt hab' ich dich, Hans Huckebein!
Wie wird sich Tante Lotte freu'n!"
Die Tante kommt aus ihrer Tür;
"Ei!"—spricht sie—"Welch ein gutes Tier!"
Kaum ist das Wort dem Mund entflohn,
Schnapp! hat er ihren Finger schon.
"Ach!"—ruft sie—"Er ist doch nicht gut!
Weil er mir was zuleide tut!"
Hier lauert in des Topfes Höhle
Hans Huckebein, die schwarze Seele.
Den Knochen, den er Spitz gestohlen,
Will dieser jetzt sich wieder holen.
Sie ziehn mit Knurren und Gekrächz,
Der eine links, der andre rechts.
Schon denkt der Spitz, dass er gewinnt,
Da zwickt der Rabe ihn von hint.
O weh! Er springt auf Spitzens Nacken,
Um ihm die Haare auszuzwacken.
Der Spitz, der ärgert sich bereits
Und rupft den Raben seinerseits.
Derweil springt mit dem Schinkenbein
Der Kater in den Topf hinein.
Da sitzen sie und schau'n und schau'n.—
Dem Kater ist nicht sehr zu trau'n.
Der Kater hackt den Spitz, der schreit,
Der Rabe ist voll Freudigkeit.
Schnell fasst er, weil der Topf nicht ganz,
Mit schlauer List den Katerschwanz.
Es rollt der Topf. Es krümmt voll Quale
Des Katers Schweif sich zur Spirale.
Und Spitz und Kater fliehn im Lauf.—
Der grösste Lump bleibt obenauf!!—
Nichts Schönres gab's für Tante Lotte
Als Schwarze-Heidelbeer-Kompotte.
Doch Huckebein verschleudert nur
Die schöne Gabe der Natur.
Die Tante naht voll Zorn und Schrecken;
Hans Huckebein verlässt das Becken.
Und schnell betritt er, angstbeflügelt,
Die Wäsche, welche frisch gebügelt.
O weh! Er kommt ins Tellerbord;
Die Teller rollen rasselnd fort.
Auch fällt der Korb, worin die Eier—
Ojemine!—und sind so teuer!
Patsch! fällt der Krug. Das gute Bier
Ergiesst sich in die Stiefel hier.

Und auf der Tante linken Fuss
Stürzt sich des Eimers Wasserguss.
Sie hält die Gabel in der Hand,
Und auch der Fritz kommt angerannt.
Perdums! Da liegen sie.—Dem Fritze
Dringt durch das Ohr die Gabelspitze.
Dies wird des Raben Ende sein—
So denkt man wohl—, doch leider nein!
Denn—schnupp!—der Tante Nase fasst er;
Und nochmals triumphiert das Laster!
Jetzt aber naht sich das Malheur,
Denn dies Getränke ist Likör.
Es duftet süss.—Hans Huckebein
Taucht seinen Schnabel froh hinein.
Und lässt mit stillvergnügtem Sinnen
Den ersten Schluck hinunterrinnen.
Nicht übel!—Und er taucht schon wieder
Den Schnabel in die Tiefe nieder.
Er hebt das Glas und schlürft den Rest,
Weil er nicht gern was übriglässt.
Ei, ei! Ihm wird so wunderlich,
So leicht und doch absunderlich.
Er krächzt mit freudigem Getön
Und muss auf einem Beine stehn.
Der Vogel, welcher sonsten fleugt,
Wird hier zu einem Tier, was kreucht.
Und Übermut kommt zum Beschluss,
Der alles ruinieren muss.
Er zerrt voll roher Lust and Tücke
Der Tante künstliches Gestricke.
Der Tisch ist glatt—der Böse taumelt—
Das Ende naht—sieh da! Er baumelt!
"Die Bosheit war sein Hauptpläsier,
Drum"—spricht die Tante—"Hängt er hier!"

Die fromme Helene

Lenchen kommt aufs Land

Wie der Wind in Trauerweiden
Tönt des frommen Sängers Lied,
Wenn er auf die Lasterfreuden
In den grossen Städten sieht.
Ach, die sittenlose Presse!
Tut sie nicht in früher Stund
All die sündlichen Exzesse
Schon den Bürgersleuten kund?!
Offenbach ist im Thalia,
Hier sind Bälle, da Konzerts.
Annchen, Hannchen und Maria

Hüpft vor Freuden schon das Herz.
Kaum trank man die letzte Tasse,
Putzt man schon den irdschen Leib.
Auf dem Walle, auf der Gasse
Wimmelt man zum Zeitvertreib.
Wie sie schauen, wie sie grüssen!
Hier die zierlichen Mosjös,
Dort die Damen mit den süssen
Himmlisch hohen Prachtpopös.
Und der Jud mit krummer Ferse,
Krummer Nas' und krummer Hos'
Schlängelt sich zur hohen Börse
Tiefverderbt und seelenlos.
Schweigen will ich von Lokalen,
Wo der Böse nächtlich prasst,
Wo im Kreis der Liberalen
Man den Heilgen Vater hasst.
Schweigen will ich von Konzerten,
Wo der Kenner hochentzückt
Mit dem seelenvoll-verklärten
Opernglase um sich blickt,
Wo mit weichen Wogebusen
Man so warm zusammensitzt,
Wo der hehre Chor der Musen,
Wo Apollo selber schwitzt.
Schweigen will ich vom Theater,
Wie von da, des Abends spät,
Schöne Mutter, alter Vater
Arm in Arm nach Hause geht.
Zwar man zeuget viele Kinder,
Doch man denket nichts dabei.
Und die Kinder werden Sünder,
Wenn's den Eltern einerlei.
"Komm, Helenchen!" sprach der brave
Vormund.—"Komm, mein liebes Kind!
Komm aufs Land, wo sanfte Schafe
Und die frommen Lämmer sind.
Da ist Onkel, da ist Tante,
Da ist Tugend und Verstand,
Da sind deine Anverwandte!"
So kam Lenchen auf das Land.

Des Onkels Nachthemd

"Helene!"—sprach der Onkel Nolte—
"Was ich schon immer sagen wollte!
Ich warne dich als Mensch und Christ:
Oh, hüte dich vor allem Bösen!
Es macht Pläsier, wenn man es ist,
Es macht Verdruss, wenn man's gewesen!"
"Ja leider!"—sprach die milde Tante—
"So ging es vielen, die ich kannte!
Drum soll ein Kind die weisen Lehren

Der alten Leute hochverehren!
Die haben alles hinter sich
Und sind, gottlob! recht tugendlich."
Nun gute Nacht! Es ist schon späte!
Und, gutes Lenchen, bete, bete!"
Helene geht.—Und mit Vergnügen
Sieht sie des Onkels Nachthemd liegen.
Die Nadel her, so schnell es geht!
Und Hals und Ärmel zugenäht!
Darauf begibt sie sich zur Ruh
Und deckt sich warm und fröhlich zu.
Bald kommt der Onkel auch herein
Und scheint bereits recht müd zu sein.
Erst nimmt er seine Schlummerprise,
Denn er ist sehr gewöhnt an diese.
Und nun vertauscht er mit Bedacht
Das Hemd des Tags mit dem der Nacht.
Doch geht's nicht so, wie er wohl möcht',
Denn die Geschichte will nicht recht.
"Potz tausend, das ist wunderlich!"
Der Onkel Nolte ärgert sich.
Er ärgert sich, doch hilft es nicht.
Ja, siehste wohl! Da liegt das Licht!
Stets grösser wird der Ärger nur,
Es fällt die Dose und die Uhr.
Rack!—stösst er an den Tisch der Nacht,
Was einen grossen Lärm gemacht.
Hier kommt die Tante mit dem Licht.—
Der Onkel hat schon Luft gekriegt.
"O sündenvolle Kreatur!
Dich mein' ich dort!—Ja, schnarche nur!"
Helene denkt: Dies will ich nun
Auch ganz gewiss nicht wieder tun.

Vetter Franz

Helenchen wächst und wird gescheit
Und trägt bereits ein langes Kleid.—
"Na, Lene! Hast du's schon vernommen?
Der Vetter Franz ist angekommen."
So sprach die Tante früh um achte,
Indem sie grade Kaffee machte.
"Und, hörst du, sei fein hübsch manierlich
Und zeige dich nicht ungebührlich,
Und sitz bei Tische nicht so krumm,
Und gaffe nicht so viel herum.
Und ganz besonders muss ich bitten:
Das Grüne, was so ausgeschnitten—
Du ziehst mir nicht das Grüne an,
Weil ich's nun mal nicht leiden kann."
Ei!—denkt Helene—Schläft er noch?
Und schaut auch schon durchs Schlüsselloch.
Der Franz, ermüdet von der Reise,

Liegt tief versteckt im Bettgehäuse.
"Ah, ja ja jam!"—so gähnt er eben—
"Es wird wohl Zeit, sich zu erheben
Und sich allmählich zu bequemen,
Die Morgenwäsche vorzunehmen."
Zum ersten: ist es mal so schicklich,
Zum zweiten: ist es sehr erquicklich,
Zum dritten: ist man sehr bestaubt,
Und viertens: soll man's überhaupt,
Denn fünftens: ziert es das Gesicht.
Und schliesslich: schaden tut's mal nicht!
Wie fröhlich ist der Wandersmann,
Zeiht er das reine Hemd sich an.
Und neugestärkt und friedlich-heiter
Bekleidet er sich emsig weiter.
Und erntet endlich stillerfreut
Die Früchte seiner Reinlichkeit.
Jetzt steckt der Franz die Pfeife an,
Helene eilt, so schnell sie kann.
Plemm!—stösst sie an die alte Brause,
Die oben steht im Treppenhause.
Sie kommt auf Hannchen hergerollt,
Die Franzens Stiefel holen wollt.
Die Lene rutscht, es rutscht die Hanne;
Die Tante trägt die Kaffeekanne.
Da geht es klirr! und klipp! und klapp!
Und auch der Onkel kriegt was ab.

Der Frosch

Der Franz, ein Schüler hochgelehrt,
Macht sich gar bald beliebt und wert.
So hat er einstens in der Nacht
Beifolgendes Gedicht gemacht:
Als ich so von ungefähr
Durch den Wald spazierte,
Kam ein bunter Vogel, der
Pfiff und quinquilierte.
Was der bunte Vogel pfiff,
Fühle und begreif' ich:
Liebe ist der Inbegriff,
Auf das andre pfeif' ich.
Er schenkt's Helenen, die darob
Gar hocherfreut und voller Lob.
Und Franz war wirklich angenehm,
Teils dieserhalb, teils ausserdem.
Wenn in der Küche oder Kammer
Ein Nagel fehlt—Franz holt den Hammer!
Wenn man den Kellerraum betritt,
Wo's öd und dunkel—Franz geht mit!
Wenn man nach dem Gemüse sah
In Feld und Garten—Franz ist da!—
Oft ist z. B. an den Stangen

Die Bohne schwierig zu erlangen.
Franz aber fasst die Leiter an,
Dass Lenchen ja nicht fallen kann.
Und ist sie dann da oben fertig—
Franz ist zur Hilfe gegenwärtig.
Kurzum! Es sei nun, was es sei—
Der Vetter Franz ist gern dabei.
Indessen ganz insonderheit
Ist er voll Scherz und Lustbarkeit.
Schau, schau! Da schlupft und hupft im Grün
Ein Frosch herum.—Gleich hat er ihn!
Und setzt ihn heimlich nackt und bloss
In Nolten seine Tabaksdos'.
Wie nun der sanfte Onkel Nolte
Sich eine Prise schöpfen wollte—
Hucks da! Mit einem Satze sass
Der Frosch an Nolten seiner Nas.
Platsch! springt er in die Tasse gar,
Worin noch schöner Kaffee war.
Schlupp! sitzt er in der Butterbemme,
Ein kleines Weilchen in der Klemme.
Putsch!—Ach, der Todesschreck ist gross!
Er hupft in Tante ihren Schoss.
Der Onkel ruft und zieht die Schelle:
"He, Hannchen, Hannchen, komme schnelle!"
Und Hannchen ohne Furcht und Bangen
Entfernt das Scheusal mit der Zangen.
Nun kehrt die Tante auch zum Glück
Ins selbstbewusste Sein zurück.
Wie hat Helene da gelacht,
Als Vetter Franz den Scherz gemacht!
Eins aber war von ihm nicht schön:
Man sah ihn oft bei Hannchen stehn!
Doch jeder Jüngling hat wohl mal
'n Hang fürs Küchenpersonal,
Und sündhaft ist der Mensch im ganzen!
Wie betet Lenchen da für Franzen!
Nur einer war, der heimlich grollte:
Das ist der ahnungsvolle Nolte.
Natürlich tut er dieses bloss
In Anbetracht der Tabaksdos'.
Er war auch wirklich voller Freud,
Als nun vorbei die Ferienzeit,
Und Franz mit Schrecken wiederum
Zurück muss aufs Gymnasium.

Der Liebesbrief

Und wenn er sich auch ärgern sollte,
Was schert mich dieser Onkel Nolte!
So denkt Helene leider Gotts!
Und schreibt dem Onkel grad zum Trotz:
"Geliebter Franz!

Du weisst es ja, Dein bin ich ganz!
Wie reizend schön war doch die Zeit,
Wie himmlisch war das Herz erfreut,
Als in den Schnabelbohnen drin
Der Jemand eine Jemandin,
Ich darf wohl sagen: herzlich küsste.—
Ach Gott, wenn das die Tante wüsste!
Und ach! Wie ist es hierzuland
Doch jetzt so schrecklich anigant!
Der Onkel ist, gottlob! recht dumm,
Die Tante nöckert so herum,
Und beide sind so furchtbar fromm;
Wenn's irgend möglich, Franz, so komm
Und trockne meiner Sehnsucht Träne!
10000 Küsse von   Helene."
Jetzt Siegellack!—Doch weh! Alsbald
Ruft Onkel Nolte donnernd: "Halt!"
Und an Helenens Nase stracks
Klebt das erhitzte Siegelwachs.

Eine unruhige Nacht

In der Kammer, still und donkel,
Schläft die Tante bei dem Onkel.
Mit der Angelschnur versehen,
Naht sich Lenchen auf den Zehen.
Zupp—Schon lüftet sich die Decke
Zu des Onkels grossem Schrecke.
Zupp!—Jetzt spürt die Tante auch
An dem Fuss den kalten Hauch.
"Nolte!" ruft sie. "Lasse das,
Denn das ist ein dummer Spass!"
Und mit Murren und Gebrumm
Kehrt man beiderseits sich um.
Schnupp!—Da liegt man gänzlich bloss,
Und die Zornigkeit wird gross;
Und der Schlüsselbund erklirrt,
Bis der Onkel flüchtig wird.
Autsch! Wie tut der Fuss so weh!
An der Angel sitzt der Zeh.
Lene hört nicht auf zu zupfen,
Onkel Nolte, der muss hupfen.
Lene hält die Türe zu.
O du böse Lene du!
Stille wird es nach und nach,
Friede herrscht im Schlafgemach.
Am Morgen aber ward es klar,
Was nachts im Rat beschlossen war.
Kalt, ernst und dumpf sprach Onkel Nolte:
"Helene, was ich sagen wollte:—"
"Ach!"—rief sie—"Ach! Ich will es nun
Auch ganz gewiss nicht wieder tun!"

"Es ist zu spät!—Drum stante pe'
Pack deine Sachen!—So!—Ade!"

Interimistische Zerstreuung

Ratsam ist und bleibt es immer
Für ein junges Frauenzimmer,
Einen Mann sich zu erwählen
Und womöglich zu vermählen.
Erstens: will es so der Brauch.
Zweitens: will man's selber auch.
Drittens: Man bedarf der Leitung
Und der männlichen Begleitung;
Weil bekanntlich manche Sachen,
Welche grosse Freude machen,
Mädchen nicht allein verstehn;
Als da ist: Ins Wirtshaus gehn.—
Freilich oft, wenn man auch möchte,
Findet sich nicht gleich der Rechte;
Und derweil man so allein,
Sucht man sonst sich zu zerstreu'n.
Lene hat zu diesem Zwecke
Zwei Kanari in der Hecke,
Welche Niep und Piep genannt.
Zierlich frassen aus der Hand
Diese goldignetten Mätzchen;
Aber Mienzi hiess das Kätzchen.
Einstens kam auch auf Besuch
Kater Munzel, frech und klug.
Alsobald so ist man einig.—
Festentschlossen, still und schleunig
Ziehen sie voll Mörderdrang
Niep und Piep die Hälse lang.
Drauf so schreiten sie ganz heiter
Zu dem Kaffeetische weiter.—
Mienzi mit den sanften Tätzchen
Nimmt die guten Zuckerplätzchen.
Aber Munzels dicker Kopf
Quält sich in den Sahnetopf.
Grad kommt Lene, welche drüben
Eben einen Brief geschrieben,
Mit dem Licht und Siegellack
Und bemerkt das Lumpenpack.
Mienzi kann noch schnell enteilen,
Aber Munzel muss verweilen;
Denn es sitzt an Munzels Kopf
Festgeschmiegt der Sahnetopf.
Blindlings stürzt er sich zur Erd.
Klacks!—Der Topf ist nichts mehr wert.
Aufs Büfett geht es jetzunder;
Flaschen, Gläser—alles 'runter!
Sehr in Ängsten sieht man ihn
Aufwärts sausen am Kamin.

Ach!—Die Venus ist perdü—
Klickradoms!—von Medici!
Weh! Mit einem Satze ist er
Vom Kamine an dem Lüster;
Und da geht es Klingelingelings!
Unten liegt das teure Dings.
Schnell sucht Munzel zu entrinnen,
Doch er kann nicht mehr von hinnen.—
Wehe, Munzel!—Lene kriegt
Tute, Siegellack und Licht.
Allererst tut man die Tute
An des Schweifs behaarte Rute;
Dann das Lack, nachdem's erhitzt,
Auf die Tute, bis sie sitzt.
Drauf hält man das Licht daran,
Dass die Tute brennen kann.
Jetzt lässt man den Munzel los—
Mau!—Wie ist die Hitze gross!

Der Heiratsentschluss

Wenn's einer davon haben kann,
So bleibt er gerne dann und wann
Des Morgens, wenn das Wetter kühle,
Noch etwas liegen auf dem Pfühle
Und denkt sich so in seinem Sinn:
Na, dämmre noch 'n bissel hin!
Und denkt so hin und denkt so her,
Wie dies wohl wär', wenn das nicht wär'.—
Und schliesslich wird es ihm zu dumm.—
Er wendet sich nach vorne um,
Kreucht von der warmen Lagerstätte
Und geht an seine Toilette.
Die Propretät ist sehr zu schätzen,
Doch kann sie manches nicht ersetzen.
Der Mensch wird schliesslich mangelhaft.
Die Locke wird hinweggerafft.—
Mehr ist hier schon die Kunst zu loben,
Denn Schönheit wird durch Kunst gehoben.—
Allein auch dieses, auf die Dauer,
Fällt doch dem Menschen schliesslich sauer.—
"Es sei!"—sprach Lene heute früh—
"Ich nehme Schmöck und Companie!"
G. I. C. Schmöck, schon längst bereit,
Ist dieserhalb gar hoch erfreut.
Und als der Frühling kam ins Land,
Ward Lene Madam Schmöck genannt.

Die Hochzeitsreise

's war Heidelberg, das sich erwählten
Als Freudenort die Neuvermählten.—
Wie lieblich wandelt man zu zwein
Das Schloss hinauf im Sonnenschein.

"Ach, sieh nur mal, geliebter Schorsch,
Hier diese Trümmer alt und morsch!"
"Ja!"—sprach er—"Aber diese Hitze!
Und fühle nur mal, wie ich schwitze!"
Ruinen machen vielen Spass.—
Auch sieht man gern das grosse Fass.
Und—alle Ehrfurcht!—muss ich sagen,
Alsbald, so sitzt man froh im Wagen
Und sieht das Panorama schnelle
Vorüberziehn bis zum Hotelle;
Denn Spargel, Schinken, Kotteletts
Sind doch mitunter auch was Netts.
"Pist! Kellner! Stell'n Sie eine kalt!
Und, Kellner, aber möglichst bald!"
Der Kellner hört des Fremden Wort.
Es saust der Frack. Schon eilt er fort.
Wie lieb und luftig perlt die Blase
Der Witwe Klicko in dem Glase.—
Gelobt seist du viel tausend Mal!
Helene blättert im Journal.
"Pist! Kellner! Noch einmal so eine!"—
—Helene ihre Uhr ist neune.—
Der Kellner hört des Fremden Wort.
Es saust der Frack. Schon eilt er fort.
Wie lieb und luftig perlt die Blase
Der Witwe Klicko in dem Glase.
"Pist! Kellner! Noch so was von den!"—
—Helenen ihre Uhr ist zehn.—
Schon eilt der Kellner emsig fort.—
Helene spricht ein ernstes Wort.—
Der Kellner leuchtet auf der Stiegen.
Der fremde Herr ist voll Vergnügen.
Pitsch!—Siehe da!
Er löscht das Licht.
Plumps! liegt er da
und rührt sich nicht.

Löbliche Tätigkeit

Viele Madams, die ohne Sorgen,
In Sicherheit und wohlgeborgen,
Die denken: Pa! Es hat noch Zeit!—
Und bleiben ohne Frömmigkeit.—
Wie lobenswert ist da Helene!
Helene denkt nicht so wie jene.—
Nein, nein! Sie wandelt oft und gerne
Zur Kirche hin, obschon sie ferne.
Und Jean, mit demutsvollem Blick,
Drei Schritte hinterwärts zurück,
Das Buch der Lieder in der Hand,
Folgt seiner Herrin unverwandt.
Doch ist Helene nicht allein
Nur auf sich selbst bedacht.—O nein!—

Ein guter Mensch gibt gerne acht,
Ob auch der andre was Böses macht;
Und strebt durch häufige Belehrung
Nach seiner Bessrung und Bekehrung.
"Schang!" sprach sie einstens—"Deine Taschen
Sind oft so dick! Schang! Tust du naschen?
Ja, siehst du wohl! Ich dacht' es gleich!
O Schang! Denk an das Himmelreich!"
Dies Wort drang ihm in die Natur,
So dass er schleunigst Bessrung schwur.
Doch nicht durch Worte nur allein
Soll man dem andern nützlich sein.—
Helene strickt die guten Jacken,
Die so erquicklich für den Nacken;
Denn draussen wehen rauhe Winde.—
Sie fertigt auch die warme Binde;
Denn diese ist für kalte Mägen
Zur Winterszeit ein wahrer Segen.
Sie pflegt mit herzlichem Pläsier
Sogar den fränk'schen Offizier,
Der noch mit mehren dieses Jahr
Im deutschen Reiche sesshaft war.—
Besonders aber tat ihr leid
Der armen Leute Bedürftigkeit.—
Und da der Arzt mit Ernst geraten,
Den Leib in warmem Wein zu baden,
So tut sie's auch. Oh, wie erfreut
Ist nun die Schar der armen Leut;
Die, sich recht innerlich zu laben,
Doch auch mal etwas Warmes haben.

Geistlicher Rat

Viel Freude macht, wie männiglich bekannt,
Für Mann und Weib der heilige Ehestand!
Und lieblich ist es für den Frommen,
Der die Genehmigung dazu bekommen,
Wenn er sodann nach der üblichen Frist
Glücklicher Vater und Mutter ist.—
—Doch manchmal ärgert man sich bloss,
Denn die Ehe bleibt kinderlos.—
—Dieses erfuhr nach einiger Zeit
Helene mit grosser Traurigkeit.—
Nun wohnte allda ein frommer Mann,
Bei Sankt Peter dicht nebenan,
Von Frau'n und Jungfrau'n weit und breit
Hochgepriesen ob seiner Gelehrsamkeit.—
(Jetzt war er freilich schon etwas kränklich.)
"O meine Tochter!" sprach er bedenklich—
"Dieses ist ein schwierig Kapitel;
Da helfen allein die geistlichen Mittel!
Drum, meine Beste, ist dies mein Rat:
Schreite hinauf den steilen Pfad

Und folge der seligen Pilger-Spur
Gen Chosemont de bon secours,
Denn dorten, berühmt seit alter Zeit,
Stehet die Wiege der Fruchtbarkeit.
Und wer allda sich hinverfügt,
Und wer allda die Wiege gewiegt,
Der spürete bald nach selbiger Fahrt,
Dass die Geschichte anders ward.
Solches hat noch vor etlichen Jahren
Leider Gotts! eine fromme Jungfer erfahren,
Welche, indem sie bis dato in diesen
Dingen nicht sattsam unterwiesen,
Aus Unbedacht und kindlichem Vergnügen
Die Wiege hat angefangen zu wiegen.—
Und ob sie schon nur ein wenig gewiegt,
Hat sie dennoch ein ganz kleines Kind
      gekriegt.—
Auch kam da ein frecher Pilgersmann,
Der rühret aus Vorwitz die Wiegen an.
Darauf nach etwa etlichen Wochen,
Nachdem er dieses verübt und verbrochen,
Und——Doch, meine Liebe, genug für heute!
Ich höre, dass es zur Metten läute.
Addio! Und Trost sei dir beschieden!
Zeuge hin in Frieden!"

Die Wallfahrt

Hoch von gnadenreicher Stelle
Winkt die Schenke und Kapelle.
Aus dem Tale zu der Höhe,
In dem seligen Gedränge
Andachtsvoller Christenmenge
Fühlt man froh des andern Nähe;
Denn hervor aus Herz und Munde,
Aus der Seele tiefstem Grunde
Haucht sich warm und innig an
Pilgerin und Pilgersmann.—
Hier vor allen, schuhbestaubt,
Warm ums Herze, warm ums Haupt,
Oft erprobt in ernster Kraft,
Schreitet die Erzgebruderschaft.—
Itzo kommt die Jungferngilde,
Auf den Lippen Harmonie,
In dem Busen Engelsmilde,
In der Hand das Paraplü.—
Oh, wie lieblich tönt der Chor!
Bruder Jochen betet vor.—
Aber dort im Sonnenscheine
Geht Helene traurig-heiter,
Sozusagen, ganz alleine,
Denn ihr einziger Begleiter,
Stillverklärt im Sonnenglanz,

Ist der gute Vetter Franz,
Den seit kurzem die Bekannten
Nur den "heil'gen" Franz benannten.—
Traulich wallen sie zu zweit
Als zwei fromme Pilgersleut.
Gott sei Dank, jetzt ist man oben!
Und mit Preisen und mit Loben
Und mit Eifer und Bedacht
Wird das Nötige vollbracht.
Freudig eilt man nun zur Schenke,
Freudig greift man zum Getränke,
Welches schon seit langer Zeit
In des Klosters Einsamkeit,
Ernstbesonnen, stillvertraut,
Bruder Jakob öfters braut.
Hierbei schaun sich innig an
Pilgerin und Pilgersmann.
Endlich nach des Tages Schwüle
Naht die sanfte Abendkühle.
In dem goldnen Mondenscheine
Geht Helene froh und heiter,
Sozusagen, ganz alleine,
Denn ihr einziger Begleiter,
Stillverklärt im Mondesglanz,
Ist der heil'ge Vetter Franz.
Traulich ziehn sie heim zu zweit
Als zwei gute Pilgersleut.—
Doch die Erzgebruderschaft
Nebst den Jungfern tugendhaft,
Die sich etwas sehr verspätet,
Kommen jetzt erst angebetet.
O wie lieblich tönt der Chor!
Bruder Jochen betet vor.
Schau, da kommt von ungefähr
Eine Droschke noch daher.—
Er, der diese Droschke fuhr,
Frech und ruchlos von Natur,
Heimlich denkend: Papperlapp!
Tuet seinen Hut nicht ab.—
Weh! Schon schau'n ihn grollend an
Pilgerin und Pilgersmann.—
Zwar der Kutscher sucht mit Klappen
Anzuspornen seinen Rappen,
Aber Jochen schiebt die lange
Jungfernbundesfahnenstange
Durch die Hinterräder quer—
Schrupp!—und's Fuhrwerk geht nicht mehr.—
Bei den Beinen, bei dem Rocke
Zieht man ihn von seinem Bocke.
Jungfer Nanni mit der Krücke
Stösst ihm häufig ins Genicke.
Aber Jungfer Adelheid

Treibt die Sache gar zu weit,
Denn sie sticht in Kampfeshitze
Mit des Schirmes scharfer Spitze;
Und vor Schaden schützt ihn bloss
Seine warme Lederhos'.—
Drauf so schau'n sich fröhlich an
Pilgerin und Pilgersmann.—
Fern verklingt der Jungfernchor,
Bruder Jochen betet vor.—
Doch der böse Kutscher, dem
Alles dieses nicht genehm,
Meldet eilig die Geschichte
Bei dem hohen Stadtgerichte.
Dieses ladet baldigst vor
Jochen und den Jungfernchor.
Und das Urteil wird gesprochen:
Bruder Jochen kriegt drei Wochen;
Aber Jungf- und Bruderschaften
Sollen für die Kosten haften.—
Ach! Da schau'n sich traurig an
Pilgerin und Pilgersmann.

Die Zwillinge

Wo kriegten wir die Kinder her,
Wenn Meister Klapperstorch nicht wär'?
Er war's, der Schmöcks in letzter Nacht
Ein kleines Zwillingspaar gebracht.
Der Vetter Franz, mit mildem Blick,
Hub an und sprach: "O welches Glück!
Welch kleine, freundliche Kollegen!
Das ist fürwahr zwiefacher Segen!
Drum töne zwiefach Preis und Ehr!
Herr Schmöck, ich gratuliere sehr!"
Bald drauf um zwölf kommt Schmöck herunter,
So recht vergnügt und frisch und munter.
Und emsig setzt er sich zu Tische,
Denn heute gibt's Salat und Fische.
Autsch!—Eine Gräte kommt verquer,
Und Schmöck wird blau und hustet sehr;
Und hustet, bis ihm der Salat
Aus beiden Ohren fliegen tat.
Bums! Da! Er schliesst den Lebenslauf.
Der Jean fängt schnell die Flasche auf.
"Oh!"—sprach der Jean—"Es ist ein Graus!
Wie schnell ist doch das Leben aus!"

Ein treuloser Freund

"O Franz!"—spricht Lene—und sie weint.
"O Franz! Du bist mein einz'ger Freund!"
"Ja!"—schwört der Franz mit mildem Hauch
"Ich war's, ich bin's und bleib' es auch!"
Nun gute Nacht! Schon tönt es zehn!

Will's Gott! Auf baldig Wiedersehn!
Die Stiegen steigt er sanft hinunter.—
Schau, schau! Die Kathi ist noch munter.
Das freut den Franz.—Er hat nun mal
'n Hang fürs Küchenpersonal.
Der Jean, der heimlich näher schlich,
Bemerkt die Sache zorniglich.
Von grosser Eifersucht erfüllt,
Hebt er die Flasche rasch und wild.
Und—kracks!—Es dringt der scharfe Schlag
Bis tief in das Gedankenfach.
's ist aus!—Der Lebensfaden bricht.—
Helene naht.—Es fällt das Licht.—

Die Reue

Ach, wie ist der Mensch so sündig!—
Lene, Lene! Gehe in dich!—
Und sie eilet tieferschüttert
Zu dem Schranke schmerzdurchzittert.
Fort! Ihr falschgesinnten Zöpfe,
Schminke und Pomadetöpfe!
Fort! Du Apparat der Lüste!
Hochgewölbtes Herzgerüste!
Fort vor allem mit dem Übel
Dieser Lust- und Sündenstiebel!
Trödelkram der Eitelkeit,
Fort, und sei der Glut geweiht!
Oh, wie lieblich sind die Schuhe
Demutsvoller Seelenruhe!—
Sieh, da geht Helene hin,
Eine schlanke Büsserin!

Versuchung und Ende

Es ist ein Brauch von alters her:
Wer Sorgen hat, hat auch Likör!
"Nein!"—ruft Helene—"Aber nun
Will ich's auch ganz—und ganz—und ganz—
und ganz gewiss nicht wieder tun!"
Sie kniet von ferne fromm und frisch.
Die Flasche stehet auf dem Tisch.
Es lässt sich knien auch ohne Pult.
Die Flasche wartet mit Geduld.
Man liest nicht gerne weit vom Licht.
Die Flasche glänzt und rührt sich nicht.
Oft liest man mehr als wie genug.
Die Flasche ist kein Liederbuch.
Gefährlich ist des Freundes Nähe.
O Lene, Lene! Wehe, Wehe!
Oh, sieh!—Im sel'gen Nachtgewande
Erscheint die jüngstverstorbne Tante.
Mit geisterhaftem Schmerzgetöne—
"Helene!"—ruft sie—"O Helene!"

Umsonst!—Es fällt die Lampe um,
Gefüllt mit dem Petroleum.
Und hilflos und mit Angstgewimmer
Verkohlt dies fromme Frauenzimmer.
Hier sieht man ihre Trümmer rauchen.
Der Rest ist nicht mehr zu gebrauchen.

Triumph des Bösen

Hu! Draussen welch ein schrecklich Grausen!
Blitz, Donner, Nacht und Sturmesbrausen!—
Schon wartet an des Hauses Schlote
Der Unterwelt geschwänzter Bote.
Zwar Lenens guter Genius
Bekämpft den Geist der Finsternus.
Doch dieser kehrt sich um und packt
Ihn mit der Gabel zwiegezackt.
O weh, o weh! Der Gute fällt!
Es siegt der Geist der Unterwelt.
Er fasst die arme Seele schnelle
Und fährt mit ihr zum Schlund der Hölle.
Hinein mit ihr!—Huhu! Haha!
Der heil'ge Franz ist auch schon da.

Epilog

Als Onkel Nolte dies vernommen,
War ihm sein Herze sehr beklommen.
Doch als er nun genug geklagt:
"Oh!" sprach er—"Ich hab's gleich gesagt!
Das Gute—dieser Satz steht fest—
Ist stets das Böse, was man lässt!
Ei ja!—Da bin ich wirklich froh!
Denn, Gott sei Dank! Ich bin nicht so!"

Die Knopp-Trilogie

Abenteuer eines Junggesellen
Herr und Frau Knopp
Julchen

Abenteuer eines Junggesellen

Die Sache wird bedenklich

Sokrates, der alte Greis,
Sagte oft in tiefen Sorgen:
"Ach, wieviel ist doch verborgen,
Was man immer noch nicht weiss."
Und so ist es.—Doch indessen
Darf man eines nicht vergessen;
Eines weiss man doch hinieden,

Nämlich, wenn man unzufrieden.—
Dies ist auch Tobias Knopp,
Und er ärgert sich darob.
Seine zwei Kanarienvögel,
Die sind immer froh und kregel,
Während ihn so manches quält,
Weil es ihm bis dato fehlt.
Ja, die Zeit entfliehet schnell;
Knopp, du bist noch Junggesell!—
Zwar für Stiefel, Bett, Kaffee
Sorgt die gute Dorothee;
Und auch, wenn er dann und wann
Etwas nicht alleine kann,
Ist sie gleich darauf bedacht,
Dass sie es zurechte macht.
Doch ihm fehlt Zufriedenheit.—
Nur mit grosser Traurigkeit
Bleibt er vor dem Spiegel stehn,
Um sein Bildnis zu besehn.
Vornerum ist alles blank;
Aber hinten, Gott sei Dank,
Denkt er sich mit frohem Hoffen,
Wird noch manches angetroffen.
Oh, wie ist der Schreck so gross!
Hinten ist erst recht nichts los;
Und auch hier tritt ohne Frage
Nur der pure Kopf zutage.—
Auch bemerkt er ausserdem,
Was ihm gar nicht recht bequem,
Dass er um des Leibes Mitten
Längst die Wölbung überschritten,
Welche für den Speiseschlauch,
Bei natürlichem Gebrauch,
Wie zum Trinken, so zum Essen,
Festgesetzt und abgemessen.—
Doch es bietet die Natur
Hierfür eine sanfte Kur.
Draussen, wo die Blumen spriessen,
Karelsbader Salz geniessen
Und melodisch sich bewegen
Ist ein rechter Himmelssegen;
Und es steigert noch die Lust,
Wenn man immer sagt: Du musst.
Knopp, der sich dazu entschlossen,
Wandelt treu und unverdrossen.
Manchmal bleibt er sinnend stehn;
Manchmal kann ihn keiner sehn.
Aber bald so geht er wieder
Treu beflissen auf und nieder.—
Dieses treibt er vierzehn Tage;
Darnach steigt er auf die Waage;
Und da wird es freudig kund:

Heissa, minus zwanzig Pfund!
Wieder schwinden vierzehn Tage,
Wieder sitzt er auf der Waage,
Autsch, nun ist ja offenbar
Alles wieder, wie es war.
Ach, so denkt er, diese Welt
Hat doch viel, was nicht gefällt.
Rosen, Tanten, Basen, Nelken
Sind genötigt zu verwelken;
Ach, und endlich auch durch mich
Macht man einen dicken Strich.
Auch von mir wird man es lesen:
Knopp war da und ist gewesen.
Ach, und keine Träne fliesst
Aus dem Auge, was es liest:
Keiner wird, wenn ich begraben,
Unbequemlichkeiten haben;
Keine Seele wird geniert,
Weil man keinen Kummer spürt.
Dahingegen spricht man dann:
Was geht dieser Knopp uns an?
Dies mag aber Knopp nicht leiden.
Beim Gedanken, so zu scheiden
In ein unverziertes Grab,
Drückt er eine Träne ab.
Sie liegt da, wo er gesessen,
Seinem Schmerze angemessen.
Dieses ist ja fürchterlich.
Also, Knopp, vermähle dich.
Mach dich auf und sieh dich um.
Reise mal 'n bissel 'rum.
Sieh mal dies, und sieh mal das,
Und pass auf, du findest was.
Einfach ist für seine Zwecke
Das benötigte Gepäcke;
Und die brave Dorothee
Ruft: "Herr Knopp, nanu adje!"

Eine alte Flamme

Allererst und alsofort
Eilet Knopp an jenen Ort,
Wo sie wohnt, die Wohlbekannte,
Welche sich Adele nannte;
Jene reizende Adele,
Die er einst mit ganzer Seele
Tiefgeliebt und hochgeehrt,
Die ihn aber nicht erhört,
So dass er, seit dies geschah,
Nur ihr süsses Bildnis sah.
Transpirierend und beklommen
Ist er vor die Tür gekommen,
Oh, sein Herze klopft so sehr,

Doch am Ende klopft auch er.
"Himmel," ruft sie, "welches Glück!"
(Knopp sein Schweiss, der tritt zurück.)
"Komm, geliebter Herzensschatz,
Nimm auf der Berschäre Platz!
Nur an dich bei Tag und Nacht,
Süsser Freund, hab' ich gedacht.
Unaussprechlich inniglich,
Freund und Engel, lieb' ich dich!"
Knopp, aus Mangel an Gefühl,
Fühlt sich wieder äusserst schwül;
Doch in dieser Angstsekunde
Nahen sich drei fremde Hunde.
"Hilfe, Hilfe!" ruft Adele.
"Hilf, Geliebter meiner Seele!"
Knopp hat keinen Sinn dafür.
Er entfernt sich durch die Tür.—
Schnell verlässt er diesen Ort
Und begibt sich weiter fort.

Ein schwarzer Kollege

Knopp verfügt sich weiter fort
Bis an einen andern Ort.
Da wohnt einer, den er kannte,
Der sich Förster Knarrtje nannte.—
Unterwegs bemerkt er bald
Eine schwärzliche Gestalt,
Und nun biegt dieselbe schräg
Ab auf einen Seitenweg.
Sieh, da kommt ja Knarrtje her!
"Alter Knopp, das freut mich sehr!"
Traulich wandeln diese zwei
Nach der nahen Försterei.
"So, da sind wir, tritt hinein;
Meine Frau, die wird sich freun!"
"He, zum Teufel, was ist das?
Allez, Waldmann, allez fass!
Oh, du du verruchtes Weib,
Jetzt kommt Knarrtje dir zu Leib!"
Knopps Vermittlung will nicht glücken.
Wums! Da liegt er auf dem Rücken.
Schnell verlässt er diesen Ort
Und begibt sich weiter fort.

Rektor Debisch

Knopp begibt sich weiter fort
Bis an einen andern Ort.
Da wohnt einer, den er kannte,
Der sich Rektor Debisch nannte.
Er erteilte seinem Sohn
Eben eine Lektion,
Die er aber unterbricht,

Als er Knopp zu sehen kriegt.
Zu dem Sohne spricht er dann:
"Kuno, sag' ich, sieh mich an!
Höre zu und merke auf!
Richte itzo deinen Lauf
Dahin, wo ich dir befehle,
Nämlich in die Kellerhöhle.
Dorten lieget auf dem Stroh
Eine Flasche voll Bordeaux.
Diese Flasche, sag' ich dir,
Zieh herfür und bringe mir."
Kuno eilet froh und prompt,
Dass er in den Keller kommt,
Wo er still und wohlgemut
Etwas von dem Traubenblut
In sich selbst hinüberleitet,
Was ihm viel Genuss bereitet.
Die dadurch entstandne Leere
Füllt er an der Regenröhre.
Rotwein ist für alte Knaben
Eine von den besten Gaben:
Gern erhebet man das Glas.
Aber Knopp, der findet was.
"Ei," spricht Debisch, "dieses ist
Sozusagen Taubenmist.
Ei, wie käme dieses dann?
Kuno, sag' ich, sieh mich an!"
Drauf nach diesem strengen Blick
Kommt er auf den Wein zurück.
Aber Knopp verschmäht das Glas,
Denn schon wieder sieht er was.
"Dies," spricht Debisch, "scheint mir ein
Neugeborner Spatz zu sein.
Ei, wie käme dieses dann?
Kuno, sag' ich, sieh mich an!
Deiner Taten schwarzes Bild
Ist vor meinem Blick enthüllt;
Und nur dieses sage ich:
Pfui, mein Sohn, entferne dich!"
Das ist Debisch sein Prinzip:
Oberflächlich ist der Hieb.
Nur des Geistes Kraft allein
Schneidet in die Seele ein.
Knopp vermeidet diesen Ort
Und begibt sich weiter fort.

Ländliches Fest

Knopp begibt sich weiter fort
Bis an einen andern Ort.
Da wohnt einer, den er kannte,
Der sich Meister Druff benannte.

Druff hat aber diese Regel:
Prügel machen frisch und kregel
Und erweisen sich probat
Ganz besonders vor der Tat.
Auch zum heut'gen Schützenfeste
Scheint ihm dies für Franz das beste.
Drum hört Knopp von weitem schon
Den bekannten Klageton.
Darnach wandelt man hinaus
Schön geschmückt zum Schützenhaus.—
Gleich verschafft sich hier der Franz
Eines Schweines Kringelschwanz,
Denn er hat es längst beachtet,
Dass der Wirt ein Schwein geschlachtet;
Und an Knoppens Fracke hing
Gleich darauf ein krummes Ding.—
Horch, da tönet Horngebläse,
Und man schreitet zur Française.
Keiner hat so hübsch und leicht
Sich wie unser Knopp verbeugt;
Keiner weiss sich so zu wiegen
Und den Tönen anzuschmiegen;
Doch die höchste Eleganz
Zeiget er im Solotanz.
Hoch erfreut ist jedermann,
Dass Herr Knopp so tanzen kann.
Leider ist es schon vorbei.
Und er schreitet stolz und frei
Wiederum zu seinem Tische,
Dass er etwas sich erfrische.
Rums!—Der Franz entfernt die Bank,
So dass Knopp nach hinten sank!—
Zwar er hat sich aufgerafft,
Aber doch nur mangelhaft.
Und er fühlt mit Angst und Beben:
Knopp, hier hat es Luft gegeben!—
Schnell verlässt er diesen Ort
Und begibt sich weiter fort.

Die stille Wiese

Knopp begibt sich weiter fort
Bis an einen stillen Ort.
Hier auf dieser Blumenwiese,
Denn geeignet scheinet diese,
Kann er sich gemütlich setzen,
Um die Scharte auszuwetzen
Und nach all den Angstgefühlen
Sich ein wenig abzukühlen.
Hier ist alles Fried und Ruh.
Nur ein Häslein schauet zu.
Sieh, da kommt der Bauer Jochen.

Knopp hat sich nur leicht verkrochen,
Doch mit Jochen seiner Frau
Nimmt er es schon mehr genau.
Kurz war dieser Aufenthalt.
Und mit Eifer alsobald
Richtet Knopp sein Augenmerk
Auf das angefangne Werk.—
Kaum hat er den Zweck erreicht,
Wird er heftig aufgescheucht,
Und es zeigt sich, ach herrje,
Jetzt sind Damen in der Näh'.
Plumps!—Man kommt.—Indes von Knopp
Sieht man nur den Kopf, gottlob!—
Wie erschrak die Gouvernante,
Als sie die Gefahr erkannte.
Ängstlich ruft sie: "Oh, mon dieu!
C'est un homme, fermez les yeux!"
Knopp, auf möglichst schnelle Weise,
Schlüpfet in sein Beingehäuse.
Dann verlässt er diesen Ort
Und begibt sich weiter fort.

Babbelmann

Knopp begibt sich weiter fort
Bis an einen andern Ort.
Da wohnt einer, den er kannte,
Der sich Babbelmann benannte,
Der ihm immer so gefallen
Als der Lustigste von allen.
Schau, da tritt er aus der Tür.
"Na," ruft Knopp, "jetzt bleib' ich hier!"
Worauf Babbelmann entgegnet:
"Werter Freund, sei mir gesegnet!"
"Erstens in betreff Logis,
Dieses gibt es nicht allhie,
Denn ein Pater hochgelehrt
Ist soeben eingekehrt.
Zweitens dann: Für Essen, Trinken
Seh' ich keine Hoffnung blinken.
Heute mal wird nur gebetet,
Morgen wird das Fleisch getötet,
Übermorgen beichtet man,
Und dann geht das Pilgern an.
Ferner drittens, teurer Freund—
Pst!—, denn meine Frau erscheint!"
Knopp, dem dieses ungelegen,
Wünscht Vergnügen, Heil und Segen
Und empfiehlt sich alsobald
Äusserst höflich, aber kalt.—
Schnelle flieht er diesen Ort
Und begibt sich weiter fort.

Wohlgemeint wird abgelehnt

Knopp verfügt sich weiter fort
Bis an einen andern Ort.
Da wohnt einer, den er kannte,
Der sich Küster Plünne nannte.
Knopp, der tritt durchs Gartengatter.
Siehe, da ist Hemdgeflatter,
Woraus sich entnehmen lässt:
Plünnens haben Waschefest.
Dieses findet Knopp bekräftigt
Dadurch, wie der Freund beschäftigt.
Herzlich wird er aufgenommen.
Plünne rufet: "Ei, willkommen!
Gleich besorg' ich dir zu essen,
Halte mal das Kind indessen."
Knopp ist dieses etwas peinlich.
Plünne machet alles reinlich.
Knopp, der fühlt sich recht geniert.
Plünne hat derweil serviert.
Jetzt eröffnet er das Bette
Der Familienlagerstätte.
In dem Bette, warm und schön,
Sieht man eine Schale stehn.
Nämlich dieses weiss ein jeder:
Wärmehaltig ist die Feder.
Hat man nun das Mittagessen
Nicht zu knappe zugemessen,
Und, gesetzt den Fall, es wären
Von den Bohnen oder Möhren
Oder, meinetwegen, Rüben
Ziemlich viel zurückgeblieben,
Dann so ist das allerbeste,
Dass man diese guten Reste
Aufbewahrt in einem Hafen,
Wo die guten Eltern schlafen,
Weil man, wenn der Abend naht,
Dann sogleich was Warmes hat.
Diese praktische Methode
Ist auch Plünnens ihre Mode.
"So," ruft Plünne, "Freund, nanu,
Setz dich her und lange zu."
Knopp hat aber, wie man sieht,
Keinen rechten Appetit.
Schnell verlässt er diesen Ort
Und begibt sich weiter fort.

Freund Mücke

Knopp begibt sich weiter fort
Bis an einen andern Ort.
Da wohnt einer, den er kannte,
Welcher Mücke sich benannte.

Wie es scheint, so lebt Herr Mücke
Mit Frau Mücke sehr im Glücke.
Eben hier, bemerken wir,
Küsst er sie und spricht zu ihr:
"Also, Schatz, ade derweil!
Ich und Knopp, wir haben Eil.
Im historischen Verein
Wünscht er eingeführt zu sein."
Bald so öffnet sich vor ihnen
Bei der Kirche der Kathrinen
Im Hotel zum blauen Aal
Ein gemütliches Lokal.
Mücke scheinet da nicht fremd,
Er bestellt, was wohlbekömmt.
Junge Hähnchen, sanft gebraten,
Dazu kann man dringend raten,
Und man darf getrost inzwischen
Etwas Rheinwein drunter mischen.
Nötig ist auf alle Fälle,
Dass man dann Mussö bestelle.
Nun erfreut man sich selbdritt,
Denn Kathinka trinket mit!—
"So, jetzt wären wir soweit,
Knopp, du machst wohl Richtigkeit."
Lustig ist man fortspaziert
Zum Hotel, wo Knopp logiert.
Heftig bollert man am Tor,
Der Portier kommt nicht hervor.
"Komm," ruft Mücke, "Knopp, komm hier,
Du logierst die Nacht bei mir!"
Schwierig, aus verschiednen Gründen,
Ist das Schlüsselloch zu finden.
So, so, so! Jetzt nur gemach,
Tritt hinein, ich komme nach.
Knopp schiebt los. Indessen Mücke
Bleibt mit Listigkeit zurücke.
Schrupp!—Wie Knopp hineingekommen,
Wird er an die Wand geklommen.
"Wart!" ruft Mückens Ehgemahl.
"Warte, Lump, schon wieder mal!"
Weil sie ihn für Mücken hält,
Hat sie ihm so nachgestellt.
Hei! Wie fühlt sich Knopp erfrisch,
Als der Besen saust und zischt.
Bums! Er fällt in einen Kübel,
Angefüllt mit dem, was übel.
Oh, was macht der Besenstiel
Für ein schmerzliches Gefühl!
Und als regellose Masse
Findet Knopp sich auf der Gasse.
Schnell verlässt er diesen Ort
Und begibt sich weiter fort.

Ein frohes Ereignis

Knopp verfügt sich weiter fort
Bis an einen andern Ort.
Da wohnt einer, den er kannte,
Der sich Sauerbrot benannte.
Sauerbrot, der fröhlich lacht,
Hat sich einen Punsch gemacht.
"Heissa!" rufet Sauerbrot.
"Heissa! Meine Frau ist tot!!
Hier in diesem Seitenzimmer
Ruhet sie bei Kerzenschimmer.
Heute stört sie uns nicht mehr,
Also, Alter, setz dich her,
Nimm das Glas und stosse an,
Werde niemals Ehemann,
Denn als solcher, kann man sagen,
Muss man viel Verdruss ertragen.
Kauf Romane und Broschüren,
Zahle Flechten und Turnüren,
Seidenkleider, Samtjacketts,
Zirkus- und Konzertbilletts—
Ewig hast du Nöckerei.
Gott sei Dank, es ist vorbei!"
Es schwellen die Herzen,
Es blinkt der Stern.
Gehabte Schmerzen,
Die hab' ich gern.
Knarr!—Da öffnet sich die Tür.
Wehe! Wer tritt da herfür?
Madam Sauerbrot, die schein-
Tot gewesen, tritt herein.
Starr vor Schreck wird Sauerbrot,
Und nun ist er selber tot.—
Knopp vermeidet diesen Ort
Und begibt sich eilig fort.

O weh!

Knopp verfügt sich weiter fort
Bis an einen andern Ort.
Da wohnt einer, den er kannte,
Welcher Piepo sich benannte.—
Aus dem Garten tönt Gelächter.
Piepo ist's und seine Töchter.
"Dies, mein lieber Knopp, ist Hilda.
Dort die ältre heisst Klotilda
Hilda hat schon einen Freier,
Morgen ist Verlobungsfeier,
Doch Klotilda, ei ei ei,
Die ist noch bis dato frei."—
Oh, wie ist der Abend milde!
Knopp der wandelt mit Klotilde,

Die ihm eine Rose pflückt.—
Und er fühlt es tief beglückt:
Knopp, in diesem Augenblick,
Da erfüllt sich dein Geschick.—
Drauf hat Piepo ihn geleitet,
Wo sein Lager zubereitet.
"Hier," so spricht er, "dieser Saal
Ist für morgen Festlokal.
Hier zur Rechten ist die Klause,
Stillberühmt im ganzen Hause;
Und hier links, da schlummerst du.
Wünsche recht vergnügte Ruh!"
Knopp ist durch und durch Gedanke
An Klotilde, jene Schlanke,
Und er drückt in süssem Schmerz
Ihre Rose an sein Herz.
"O Klotilde, du allein
Sollst und musst die Meine sein."—
Darauf ist ihm so gewesen:
Knopp, du musst noch etwas lesen.—
Gern erfüllt er sein Verlangen;
Still ist er hinausgegangen
Und bei seiner Kerze Strahl
Hingewandelt durch den Saal.—
Oftmals kann man müde sein,
Setzt sich hin und schlummert ein.—
Erst des Morgens so um achte,
Als die Sonne freundlich lachte,
Dachte Knopp an sein Erwachen.—
Er erwacht durch frohes Lachen.—
Dieses tut die Mädchenschar,
Welche schon beschäftigt war,
Um an dieses Festes Morgen
Für des Saales Schmuck zu sorgen.—
Ewig kannst du hier nicht sein,
Denket Knopp voll Seelenpein.
Und so strömt er wohlverdeckt
Da hervor, wo er gesteckt.
Gross ist seines Laufes Schnelle;
Aber ach, die Kammerschwelle
Ist ihm äusserst hinderlich.
Hopsa!—Er entblättert sich.—
Heimlich flieht er diesen Ort
Und begibt sich weiter fort.

Abschreckendes Beispiel

Knopp begibt sich eilig fort
Bis zum höchsten Bergesort.
Hier in öder Felsen Ritzen
Sieht er einen Klausner sitzen.
Dieser Klausner alt und greis
Tritt aus seinem Steingehäus.

Und aus Knoppen seiner Tasche
Hebt er ernst die Wanderflasche.
"Ich," so spricht er, "heisse Krökel,
Und die Welt ist mir zum Ekel.
Alles ist mir einerlei.
Mit Verlaub! Ich bin so frei.
O ihr Bürsten, o ihr Kämme,
Taschentücher, Badeschwämme,
Seife und Pomadenbüchse,
Strümpfe, Stiefel, Stiefelwichse,
Hemd und Hose, alles gleich,
Krökel, der verachtet euch.
Mir ist alles einerlei.
Mit Verlaub, ich bin so frei.
O ihr Mädchen, o ihr Weiber,
Arme, Beine, Köpfe, Leiber,
Augen mit den Feuerblicken,
Finger, welche zärtlich zwicken,
Und was sonst für dummes Zeug—
Krökel, der verachtet euch.
Mir ist alles einerlei.
Mit Verlaub, ich bin so frei.
Nur die eine, himmlisch Reine,
Mit dem goldnen Heilgenscheine
Ehre, liebe, bet' ich an;
Dich, die keiner kriegen kann,
Dich, du süsse, ei jaja,
Heil'ge Emerentia.
Sonst ist alles einerlei.
Mit Verlaub, ich bin so frei."
Hiermit senkt der Eremit
Sich nach hinten.—Knopp entflieht.—
Knopp, der denkt sich: Dieser Krökel
Ist ja doch ein rechter Ekel;
Und die Liebe per Distanz,
Kurz gesagt, missfällt mir ganz.
Schnell verlassend diesen Ort,
Eilet er nach Hause fort.

Heimkehr und Schluss

Knopp, der eilt nach Hause fort,
Und, sieh da, schon ist er dort.
Grade lüftet seine nette,
Gute Dorothee das Bette.
"Mädchen," spricht er, "sag mir, ob . . ."
Und sie lächelt: "Ja, Herr Knopp!"
Bald so wird es laut verkündet:
Knopp hat ehlich sich verbündet,

> Tobias Knopp
> Dorothea Lickefett

Erst nur flüchtig und zivil,
Dann mit Andacht und Gefühl.—
Na, nun hat er seine Ruh.
Ratsch!—Man zieht den Vorhang zu.

Herr und Frau Knopp

Ermahnungen und Winke

O wie lieblich, o wie schicklich,
Sozusagen herzerquicklich,
Ist es doch für eine Gegend,
Wenn zwei Leute, die vermögend,
Ausserdem mit sich zufrieden,
Aber von Geschlecht verschieden,
Wenn nun diese, sag' ich, ihre
Dazu nötigen Papiere,
So wie auch die Haushaltssachen
Endlich mal in Ordnung machen
Und in Ehren und beizeiten
Hin zum Standesamte schreiten,
Wie es denen, welche lieben,
Vom Gesetze vorgeschrieben,
Dann ruft jeder freudiglich:
"Gott sei Dank, sie haben sich!"
Dass es hierzu aber endlich
Kommen muss, ist selbstverständlich.—
Oder liebt man Pfänderspiele?
So was lässt den Weisen kühle.
Oder schätzt man Tanz und Reigen?
Von Symbolen lasst uns schweigen.
Oder will man unter Rosen
Innig miteinander kosen?—
Dies hat freilich seinen Reiz;
Aber elterlicherseits
Stösst man leicht auf so gewisse
Unbequeme Hindernisse,
Und man hat, um sie zu heben,
Als verlobt sich kundzugeben.—
Das ist allerdings was Schönes;
Dennoch mangelt dies und jenes.
Traulich im Familienkreise
Sitzt man da und flüstert leise,
Drückt die Daumen, küsst und plaudert,
Zehne schlägt's, indes man zaudert,
Mutter strickt und Vater gähnt,
Und, eh' man was Böses wähnt,
Heisst es: "Gute Nacht, bis morgen!"
Tief im Paletot verborgen,
Durch die schwarzen, nassen Gassen,
Die fast jeder Mensch verlassen,
Strebt man unmutvoll nach Hause

In die alte, kalte Klause,
Wühlt ins Bett sich tief und tiefer,
Schnatteratt! So macht der Kiefer,
Und so etwa gegen eine
Kriegt man endlich warme Beine.
Kurz, Verstand sowie Empfindung
Dringt auf ehliche Verbindung.—
Dann wird's aber auch gemütlich.
Täglich, stündlich und minütlich
Darf man nun vereint zu zween
Arm in Arm spazierengehen;
Ja, was irgend schön und lieblich,
Segensreich und landesüblich
Und ein gutes Herz ergetzt,
Prüft, erfährt und hat man jetzt.

Ehliche Ergötzlichkeiten

Ein schönes Beispiel, dass obiges wahr,
Bieten Herr und Frau Knopp uns dar.
Hier ruht er mit seiner getreuen Dorette
Vereint auf geräumiger Lagerstätte.
Früh schon erhebt man die Augenlider,
Lächelt sich an und erkennt sich wieder,
Um alsobald mit einem süssen
Langwierigen Kusse sich zu begrüssen.
Knopp aber, wie er gewöhnlich pflegt,
Ist gleich sehr neckisch aufgelegt.
Ganz unvermutet macht er: Kieks!
Hierauf erhebt sich ein lautes Gequieks.
Dorette dagegen weiss auch voll List,
Wo Knopp seine lustige Stelle ist.
Nämlich er hat sie unten am Hals.
Kiewieks! Jetzt meckert er ebenfalls.
Nun freilich möchte sich Knopp erheben
Und schnell vom Lager hinweg begeben,
Wird aber an seines Kleides Falten
Spiralenförmig zurückgehalten.
Husch, er nicht faul, eh' man sich's denkt,
Hat sich nach hinten herumgeschwenkt
Und unter die Decke eingebohrt,
Wo man recht fröhlich herumrumort.—
Nach diesen gar schönen Lustbarkeiten
Wird's Zeit, zur Toilette zu schreiten.
Gern wendet Frau Doris anitzo den Blick
Auf Knopp sein Beinbekleidungsstück,
Welches ihr immer besonders gefiel
Durch Ausdruck und wechselndes Mienenspiel.
Bald schaut's so drein mit Grimm und Verdruss,
Bald voller Gram und Bekümmernus.
Bald zeigt dies edle Angesicht
Nur Stolz und kennt keinen Menschen nicht.
Aber bald schwindet der Übermut;

Es zeigt sich von Herzen sanft und gut,
Und endlich nach einer kurzen Zeit
Strahlt es in voller Vergnüglichkeit.—
Dorettens Freude hierüber ist gross.
Knopp aber ist auch nicht freudenlos;
Denn ihm lächelt friedlich und heiter,
Nach unten spitzig, nach oben breiter,
Weisslich blinkend und blendend schön,
Ein hocherfreuliches Phänomen.
Besonders zeigt sich dasselbe beim Sitzen,
In der Mädchensprache heisst man's: Blitzen.
"Madam, es blitzt!" ruft Knopp und lacht.
Schlupp! wird die Sache zugemacht.

Der alte Junge hat's gut

Die Frühstückszeit hat Knopp vor allen,
Weil sehr behaglich, sehr gefallen.
Nachdem die Liese aufgetischt,
Hat Doris ihm den Trank gemischt.
Und ausserdem geniesst er heute
Noch eine ganz besondre Freude.
Frau Doris schenkt ihm eine Mütze,
Die rings mit Perlen und mit Litze
In Form von einem Kranz der Reben
Gar schön umwunden und umgeben.
Sehr freut ihn dieser Kopfbehälter,
Denn nach Micheli wird es kälter
Und weht schon oft ein herber Hauch,
Und ausserdem verziert es auch.
Stolz sitzt er da auf seinem Sitze;
Das Haupt verschönt die Morgenmütze;
Die Pfeife ist ihm Hochgenuss,
Und Doris hält den Fidibus.
Schnell flieht der Morgen.—Unterdessen
Bereitet man das Mittagessen.—
Was dies betrifft, so muss man sagen,
Kann Knopp sich wirklich nicht beklagen.
Zum Beispiel könnt' er lange suchen
Nach solchem guten Pfannekuchen.
Hierin ist Doris ohne Fehl.
Stets nimmt sie einen Löffel Mehl,
Die nöt'ge Milch, dazu drei Eier,
Ja vier sogar, wenn sie nicht teuer,
Quirlt dies sodann und backt es braun,
Mit Sorgfalt und mit Selbstvertraun;
Und jedesmal spricht Knopp vergnüglich:
"Der Pfannekuchen ist vorzüglich!"
Oh, wie behaglich kann er nun
An Doris' treuem Busen ruhn.
Gern hat er hierbei auf der Glatze
Ein loses leises Kribbelkratze.

So schläft er mit den Worten ein:
"Wie schön ist's, Herr Gemahl zu sein!"

Ein Missgriff

Der Samstag ist meistens so ein Tag,
Den der Vater nicht leiden mag.
Es wirbelt der Staub, der Besen schwirrt,
Man irrt umher und wird verwirrt.—
Hier oben auf der Fensterbank
Steht Liese und macht die Scheiben blank.
Knopp, welcher seine Pfeife vermisst
Und gar nicht weiss, wo sie heute ist,
Schweift sorgenschwer im Haus umher,
Ob sie nicht wo zu finden wär'.
Er denkt: Wo mag die Pfeife sein?
Und zwickt der Liese ins Bein hinein.
Obgleich dies nur ganz unten geschehen,
Frau Doris hat es nicht gern gesehen.
Sie ruft: "Das bitt' ich mir aber aus!
Abscheuliches Mädchen, verlasse das Haus!"
So wären denn Knoppens also mal
Ohne weibliches Dienstpersonal,
Und morgens in früher Dämmerung
Hat Knopp eine schöne Beschäftigung.—
Alsbald so steht es im Wochenblatt,
Dass man Bedienung nötig hat.
Infolgedessen mit sanfter Miene
Erscheint eine Jungfrau Namens Kathrine,
Welche hochheilig und teuer versprochen,
Stets fleissig zu putzen, beten, backen und
   kochen.
Hierin ist sie auch einerseits rühmlich,
Andererseits aber recht eigentümlich!
Erglänzt zum Beispiel am Siruptopfe
Der unvermeidliche zähe Tropfe—
Schluppdiwutsch!—, so schafft sie ihn dort
Mit schnellem Schwunge der Zunge fort.
Oder wenn sich beim Backen vielleicht
Irgendwo irgendwie irgendwas zeigt—
Schluppdiwutsch!—, sie entfernt es gleich
Durch einen doppelten Bogenstreich.—
Obschon dies sehr geschickt geschehen,
Frau Knoppen hat es nicht gern gesehen.
Sie ruft: "Das bitt' ich mir aber aus!
Abscheuliches Mädchen, verlasse das Haus!"—
So wären denn Knoppens zum andern Mal
Ohne weibliches Dienstpersonal.
Knopp aber in früher Dämmerung
Hat eine schöne Beschäftigung.
Alsbald so setzt man ins Wochenblatt,
Dass man ein Mädchen nötig hat!
Hierauf erscheint nach kurzer Zeit

Eine Jungfer mit Namen Adelheid,
Welche hochheilig und teuer versprochen,
Stets fleissig zu putzen, beten, backen und
  kochen.
Auch kann sie dieses; und augenscheinlich
Ist sie in jeder Beziehung sehr reinlich.
Pünktlich pflegt sie und ohne Säumen
Die ehliche Kammer aufzuräumen.
Recht angenehm ist dann der Kamm,
Pomade und Seife von Madam.
Doch für die Zähne verwendet sie gern
Den Apparat des gnädigen Herrn.—
Obgleich dies zu guten Zwecken geschehen,
Frau Knoppen hat es nicht gern gesehen.
Sie ruft: "Das bitt' ich mir aber aus!
Abscheuliches Mädchen, verlasse das Haus!"
Knopp aber in früher Dämmerung
Hat eine neue Beschäftigung.—

Knopp geht mal aus

Bekanntlich möchte in dieser Welt
Jeder gern haben, was ihm gefällt.
Gelingt es dann mal dem wirklich Frommen,
An die gute Gabe dranzukommen,
Um die er dringend früh und spat
Aus tiefster Seele so inniglich bat,
Gleich steht er da, seufzt, hustet und spricht:
"Ach, Herr, nun ist es ja doch so nicht!"—
Auch Knopp ist heute etwas ergrimmt
Und über sein ehliches Glück verstimmt.
Grad gibt es den Abend auch Frikadellen,
Die unbeliebt in den meisten Fällen.
Er lehnt sie ab mit stillem Dank,
Zieht seinen Frack aus dem Kleiderschrank,
Und, ohne sich weiter an was zu kehren,
Wandelt er trotzig zum Goldenen Bären!—
"Potztausend, also auch mal hier!"
So rufen freudig beim Öffnen der Tür
Der kunstreiche Doktor Pelikan
Und Bello, der Förster und Jägersmann.
Knopp aber redet nicht eben viel;
Hat auch nicht Lust zum Solospiel;
Sondern tief in sich selbst gekehrt,
Hat er sein Schöppchen Bier geleert.
Punkt zehn Uhr schliesst er die Rechnung ab
Und begibt sich nach Haus in gelindem Trab.

Unfreundlicher Empfang

Grollend hat Madam soeben
Sich bereits zur Ruh begeben.
Freundlich naht sich Knopp und bang—
"Bäh!" Nicht gut ist der Empfang.

Demutsvoll und treu und innig
Spricht er: "Doris, schau, da bin ich!"
Aber heftig stösst dieselbe—
Bubb!—ihn auf sein Leibgewölbe.
Dieses hat ihn sehr verdrossen.
Tief gekränkt, doch fest entschlossen,
Schreitet er mit stolzem Blick
Wieder ins Hotel zurück.
Heissa, jetzt ist Knopp dabei,
Kartenspiel und was es sei.
Elfe, zwölfe schlägt die Glocke;
Man geniesst verschiedne Grocke.
Dreimal kräht des Hauses Hahn,
Bis der letzte Trunk getan.

Heimkehr

Knopp ist etwas schwach im Schenkel,
Drum so führt man ihn am Henkel.
Glücklich hat es sich getroffen,
Dass das Küchenfenster offen.
Man erhebt ihn allgemach,
Und dann schiebt man etwas nach.
Düster ist der Küchenraum;
Platsch! Man fällt und sieht es kaum.
Ratsam ist es, nachzuspähen,
Wo die Schwefelhölzer stehen.
Kracks! Da stösst das Nasenbein
Auf den offnen Küchenschrein.
Peinlich ist ihm das Gefühl;
Aber er verfolgt sein Ziel.
Oha!—Wieder geht er irr.
Dieses ist das Milchgeschirr.
Dies dagegen ist die volle
Sanftgeschmeid'ge Butterstolle.
Doch hier hinten in der Ecke
Kommt er jetzt zu seinem Zwecke.
"Autsch!" Er schreit mit lautem Schalle
Und sitzt in der Mausefalle.
Jetzo kommt ihm der Gedanke,
Nachzuspüren auf dem Schranke.
Ach! Von Kopfe bis zu Fuss
Rinnt das gute Zwetschgenmus.
Doch zugleich mit dieser Schwärze
Kriegt er Feuerzeug und Kerze.
Freilich muss er häufig streichen,
Ohne etwas zu erreichen.
Aber endlich und zuletzt
Hat er's richtig durchgesetzt.
Jetzt zur Ruh sich zu begeben,
Ist sein sehnlichstes Bestreben.
Hier ist nun die Kammertür.
Ach, man schob den Riegel für.

Demnach muss er sich bequemen,
Auf der Schwelle Platz zu nehmen.
So ruht Knopp nach alledem
Fest, doch etwas unbequem.

Donner und Blitz

Hier sitzt Knopp am selbigen Morgen
Greulich brütend im Stuhl der Sorgen;
Tyrann vom Scheitel bis zur Zeh;
Und heftig tut ihm der Daumen weh.
Ei schau! Die Liese ist wiedergekommen!
Ist Knopp egal. Man hört ihn brommen.
Reumütig nahet Frau Doris sich.
Knopp zeigt sich als schrecklicher Wüterich.
Perdatsch!—Mit einem grossen Geklirr
Entfernt er das schöne Porzlangeschirr.
Dann klopft er über den ganzen Graus,
Ohne Rücksicht zu nehmen, die Pfeife aus.
Mit Tränen tritt Frau Doris hervor
Und sagt ihm ein leises Wörtchen ins Ohr.
Dies Wort fährt ihm wie Donner und Blitz
Durch Kopf, Herz, Leib in den Sorgensitz;
Und tief erschüttert und alsogleich
Zeigt er sich milde, gerührt und weich.

Ängstlicher Übergang und friedlicher Schluss

Wohlbekannt im ganzen Orte,
Mit der Klingel an der Pforte,
Ist die Brave, Ehrenwerte,
Ofterprobte, Vielbegehrte,
Welche sich Frau Wehmut schrieb;
Und ein jeder hat sie lieb.—
Mag es regnen oder schneen,
Mag der Wind auch noch so wehen,
Oder wär' sie selbst nicht munter,
Denn das kommt ja mal mitunter—
Kaum ertönt an ihrer Klingel
Das bekannte: Pingelpingel!
Gleich so ist Frau Wehmut wach
Und geht ihrer Nahrung nach.
Heute ist sie still erschienen,
Um bei Knoppens zu bedienen.
Auf dem Antlitz Seelenruhe,
An den Füssen milde Schuhe,
Wärmt sie sorglich ihre Hände,
Denn der Sommer ist zu Ende.
Also tritt sie sanft und rein
Leise in die Kammer ein.
Auch den Doktor Pelikan
Sieht man ernstbedächtig nahn,
Und es sagt sein Angesicht:

Wie es kommt,
das weiss man nicht.—
Oh, was hat in diesen Stunden
Knopp für Sorgen durchempfunden.
Rauchen ist ihm ganz zuwider.
Seine Pfeife legt er nieder.
Ganz vergebens tief im Pult
Sucht er Tröstung und Geduld.
Oben auf dem hohen Söller,
Unten in dem tiefen Keller,
Wo er sich auch hinverfüge,
Angst verkläret seine Züge.
Ja, er greifet zum Gebet,
Was er sonst nur selten tät.—
Endlich öffnet sich die Türe,
Und es heisst: "Ich gratuliere!"
Friedlich lächelnd, voller Demut,
Wie gewöhnlich, ist Frau Wehmut.—
Stolz ist Doktor Pelikan,
Weil er seine Pflicht getan.—
Aber unser Vater Knopp
Ruft in einem fort: "Gottlob!"
Na, jetzt hat er seine Ruh.—
Ratsch! Man zieht den Vorhang zu.

Julchen

Vorbemerk

Vater werden ist nicht schwer,
Vater sein dagegen sehr.
Ersteres wird gern geübt,
Weil es allgemein beliebt.
Selbst der Lasterhafte zeigt,
Dass er gar nicht abgeneigt;
Nur will er mit seinen Sünden
Keinen guten Zweck verbinden,
Sondern, wenn die Kosten kommen,
Fühlet er sich angstbeklommen.
Dieserhalb besonders scheut
Er die fromme Geistlichkeit,
Denn ihm sagt ein stilles Grauen:
Das sind Leute, welche trauen.—
So ein böser Mensch verbleibt
Lieber gänzlich unbeweibt.—
Ohne einen hochgeschätzten
Tugendsamen Vorgesetzten
Irrt er in der Welt umher,
Hat kein reines Hemde mehr,
Wird am Ende krumm und faltig,
Grimmig, greulich, ungestaltig,
Bis ihn denn bei Nacht und Tag

Gar kein Mädchen leiden mag.
Onkel heisst er günst'gen Falles,
Aber dieses ist auch alles.—
Oh, wie anders ist der Gute!
Er erlegt mit frischem Mute
Die gesetzlichen Gebühren,
Lässt sich redlich kopulieren,
Tut im stillen hocherfreut
Das, was seine Schuldigkeit,
Steht dann eines Morgens da
Als ein Vater und Papa
Und ist froh aus Herzensgrund,
Dass er dies so gut gekunnt.

Julchen, das Wickelkind

Also, wie bereits besprochen:
Madame Knoppen ist in Wochen,
Und Frau Wehmut, welche kam
Und das Kind entgegennahm,
Rief und hub es in die Höh:
"Nur ein Mädel, ach herrje!"
(Oh, Frau Wehmut, die ist schlau;
So was weiss sie ganz genau!)
Freilich Knopp, der will sich sträuben,
Das Gesagte gleich zu gläuben;
Doch bald überzeugt er sich,
Lächelt etwas säuerlich
Und mit stillgefassten Zügen
Spricht er: "Na, denn mit Vergnügen!"
Dieses Kind hat eine Tante,
Die sich Tante Julchen nannte;
Demnach kommt man überein,
Julchen soll sein Name sein.
Julchen, als ein Wickelkind,
Ist so, wie so Kinder sind.
Manchmal schläft es lang und feste,
Tief versteckt in seinem Neste.
Manchmal mit vergnügtem Sinn
Duselt es so für sich hin.
Manchmal aber wird es böse,
Macht ein lautes Wehgetöse
Und gibt keine Ruhe nicht,
Bis es was zu lutschen kriegt.—
Sein Prinzip ist überhaupt:
Was beliebt, ist auch erlaubt;
Denn der Mensch als Kreatur
Hat von Rücksicht keine Spur.—
O ihr, die ihr Eltern seid,
Denkt doch an die Reinlichkeit!
Wahrlich, hier gebührt Frau Knopp
Preis und Ehre, Dank und Lob.
Schon in früher Morgenstund

Öffnet sie den Wickelbund,
Gleichsam wie ein Postpaket,
Worauf Knopp beiseite geht.
Mit Interesse aber sieht
Er, was fernerhin geschieht.
Macht man Julchens Nase reinlich,
So erscheint ihm "dieses" peinlich.
Wie mit Puder man verfährt,
Dünkt ihm höchst bemerkenswert.
Freudevoll sind alle drei,
Wenn die Säuberung vorbei.
Nun mag Knopp sich gern bequemen,
Julchen auch mal hinzunehmen.
Flötend schöne Melodien,
Schaukelt er es auf den Knien.
Auf die Backe mit Genuss
Drückt er seinen Vaterkuss.

Eine unruhige Nacht

Eins, zwei, drei! Im Sauseschritt
Läuft die Zeit; wir laufen mit.
Julchen ist hübsch kugelrund
Und schon ohne Wickelbund.—
Es ist Nacht.—Frau Doris ruht,
Während Knopp das Seine tut.
Aber Julchen in der Wiegen
Will partout nicht stille liegen.
Er bedenkt, dass die Kamille
Manchmal manche Schmerzen stille.
Wirkungslos ist dieser Tee.
Julchen macht: "Rabä, rabä!"
Lieber Gott, wo mag's denn fehlen?
Oder sollte sonst was quälen?
Oh, wie gern ist Knopp erbötig,
Nachzuhelfen, wo es nötig.
Aber weh, es will nicht glücken,
Und nun klopft er sanft den Rücken.—
Oder will's vielleicht ins Bette,
Wo auf warmer Liegestätte
Beide Eltern in der Näh?
Nein, es macht: "Rabä, rabä!"
Schau! Auf einmal wird es heiter.—
Knopp begibt sich eilig weiter
Und bemerkt nur dieses noch:
"Ei, potztausend! Also doch!"

Ein festlicher Morgen

Eins, zwei, drei! Im Sauseschritt
Läuft die Zeit; wir laufen mit.—
Julchen ist schon sehr verständig
Und bewegt sich eigenhändig.—
Heut ist Feiertag; und siehe!

Schon streicht Knopp in aller Frühe
Luftig losen Seifenschaum
Auf des Bartes Stachelflaum.
Heut will er zur Messe gehn,
Denn da singt man dann so schön.
Frau Dorette trägt getreu
Frack und Biberhut herbei.
Julchen gibt indessen acht,
Was der gute Vater macht.
Bald ist seine Backe glatt,
Weil er darin Übung hat.
In die Kammer geht er nun.
Julchen macht sich was zu tun.
Gern ergreift sie die Feder
An des Vaters Schreibkatheder.
Reizend ist die Kunstfigur
Einer Ticktacktaschenuhr.
Ach herrje! Es geht klabum!
Julchen schwebt; der Stuhl fällt um.
Allerdings kriegt Julchen bloss
Einen leichten Hinterstoss,
Doch die Uhr wird sehr versehrt
Und die Tinte ausgeleert.—
Schmiegsam, biegsam, mild und mollig
Ist der Strumpf, denn er ist wollig.
Drum wird man ihn gern benutzen,
Um damit was abzuputzen.—
Wohlbesorgt ist dieses nun.
Julchen kann was andres tun.
Keine Messer schneiden besser
Wie des Vaters Putzemesser.
Wozu nützen, warum sitzen
An dem Frack die langen Spitzen?
Hier ein Schnitt und da ein Schnitt,
Ritscheratsche, weg damit.—
Wohlbesorgt ist dieses nun.
Julchen kann was andres tun.—
In des Vaters Pfeifenkopf
Setzt sich oft ein fester Pfropf,
Ja, was schlimmer, die bewusste
Alte, harte, schwarze Kruste;
Und der Raucher sieht es gerne,
Dass man sie daraus entferne.
Wohlbesorgt ist dieses nun.
Julchen kann was andres tun.—
Stattlich ist der Biberhut;
Manchmal passt er nur nicht gut.
Niemals soll man ihn benützen,
Um bequem darauf zu sitzen.
Seht, da kommt der Vater nun,
Um den Frack sich anzutun.

Schmerzlich sieht er, was geschehn,
Und kann nicht zur Messe gehn.

Böse Knaben

Eins, zwei, drei! Im Sauseschritt
Läuft die Zeit; wir laufen mit.—
Unsre dicke, nette Jule
Geht bereits schon in die Schule,
Und mit teilnahmsvollem Sinn
Schaut sie gern nach Knaben hin.
Einer, der ihr nicht gefiel,
Das ist Dietchen Klingebiel.
Ferdinandchen Mickefett
Scheint ihr nicht besonders nett.
Peter Sutitt, frech und dick,
Hat natürlich auch kein Glück.
Försters Fritze, blond und kraus,
Ja, der sieht schon besser aus.
Keiner kann wie er so schön
Grade auf dem Kopfe stehn;
Und das Julchen lacht und spricht:
"So wie Fritze könnt ihr's nicht!"
Kränkend ist ein solches Wort.
Julchen eilt geschwinde fort.
Knubbs! Da stossen die drei Knaben
Julchen in den feuchten Graben.
Und sie fühlen sich entzückt,
Dass der Streich so gut geglückt.
Wartet nur, da kommt der Fritze!
Schwapp, sie liegen in der Pfütze.
Fritz ist brav und sanft und spricht:
"Gutes Julchen, weine nicht!"
Julchens Kleid ist zu beklagen.
Knopp, der muss die Kosten tragen.

Vatersorgen

Eins, zwei, drei! Im Sauseschritt
Läuft die Zeit; wir laufen mit.—
Julchen ist nun wirklich gross,
Pfiffig, fett und tadellos,
Und der Vater ruft: "Was seh' ich?
Die Mamsell ist heiratsfähig!"
Dementsprechend wäre ja
Mancher gute Jüngling da.
Da ist Sutitt; aber der
Praktiziert als Vetrinär.
Da ist Mickefett; doch dieser
Ist Apthekereiproviser.
Da ist Klingebiel; was ist er?
Sonntags Kanter, alltags Küster.
Und dann Fritz, der Forstadjunkt,

Das ist auch kein Anhaltspunkt.
Einfach bloss als Mensch genommen
Wäre dieser höchst willkommen,
Nur muss Knopp sich dann entschliessen,
Ganz bedeutend zuzuschiessen.——
Kurz gesagt mit wenig Worten,
Ob auch Knopp nach allen Orten
Seine Vaterblicke richte,
Nirgends passt ihm die Geschichte.—
Anderseits, wie das so geht,
Mangelt jede Pietät.
Man ist fürchterlich verliebt,
Ohne dass man Achtung gibt
Oder irgendwie bedenkt,
Ob man alte Leute kränkt.
Selten fragt sich so ein Tor:
"Was geht in den Eltern vor?"—
Ja, so ist die Jugend heute!—
Schrecklich sind die jungen Leute
Hinter Knoppens Julchen her,
Und recht sehr gefällt es der.—
Was hat Knopp doch für Verdruss,
Wenn er das bemerken muss!—
Hier zum Beispiel abends spät,
Wie er still nach Hause geht;
Sieht er nicht mit Stirnefalten,
Wie drei männliche Gestalten
Emsig spähend da soeben
Starr vor Julchens Fenster kleben?
Zornig mit dem Wanderstab
Stochert er sie da herab.
Er verursacht grossen Schreck,
Doch den Ärger hat er weg.

Herzverlockende Künste

Wohl mit Recht bewundert man
Einen Herrn, der reiten kann.—
Herzgewinnend zeigt sich hier
Sutitt auf dem Sattelier.—
Doch die Wespen in der Mauer
Liegen heimlich auf der Lauer;
Sie sind voller Missvertrauen,
Als sie einen Reiter schauen.
Hopps! Der Rappe springt und schnaubt,
Hebt den Schwanz und senkt das Haupt;
Und am Halse hängt der Reiter.—
Er ist ängstlich, Knopp ist heiter.—
Dahingegen Klingebiel
Hofft vermittelst Saitenspiel
Julchens Seele zu entzücken
Und mit Tönen zu umstricken.

Dazu hat er sich gedichtet,
Aufgesetzt und hergerichtet
Ein gar schönes Schlummerlied,
Horch! Er singt es voll Gemüt.

Ständchen

Der Abend ist so mild und schön.
Was hört man da für ein Getön?
"Sei ruhig, Liebchen, das bin ich,
Dein Dieterich,
Dein Dietrich singt so inniglich!
Nun kramst du wohl bei Lampenschein
Herum in deinem Kämmerlein;
Nun legst du ab der Locken Fülle,
Das Oberkleid, die Unterhülle;
Nun kleidest du die Glieder wieder
In reines Weiss und legst dich nieder.
Oh, wenn dein Busen sanft sich hebt,
So denk, dass dich mein Geist umschwebt.
Und kommt vielleicht ein kleiner Floh
Und krabbelt so—
Sei ruhig, Liebchen, das bin ich,
Dein Dieterich,
Dein Dietrich, der umflattert dich!"
Platsch!—Verstummt ist schnell und bang
Nachtgesang und Lautenklang.
Eilig strömt der Sänger weiter;
Er ist traurig, Knopp ist heiter.—

Die Tante auf Besuch

Unvermutet, wie zumeist,
Kommt die Tante zugereist.
Herzlich hat man sie geküsst,
Weil sie sehr vermöglich ist.
Unser Julchen, als es sah,
Dass die gute Tante da,
Weiss vor Freude nicht zu bleiben
Und hat allerlei zu schreiben.—
Sutitt hielt vor grossem Kummer
Grade einen kleinen Schlummer.
Froh wird er emporgeschnellt,
Als er dies Billett erhält:
"Weisst Du, wo die Rose blüht?
Komm zu mir, wenn's keiner sieht!"
Stolz und schleunig diese Zeilen
Mickefetten mitzuteilen,
Eilt er zur Aptheke hin.
Ach, wie wurde dem zu Sinn;
Plump! So fällt ihm wie ein Stein
Neidgefühl ins Herz hinein.
Aber sagen tut er nichts.—

Scheinbar heitern Angesichts
Mischt er mancherlei Essenzen,
Um's dem Freunde zu kredenzen
Unter Glück- und Segenswunsch;
Und dem Freunde schmeckt der Punsch.—
Hoffnungsvoll, beredt und heiter
Schlürft er arglos immer weiter.
Aber plötzlich wird er eigen,
Fängt sehr peinlich an zu schweigen
Und erhebt sich von dem Sitz.
"Ei," ruft Mickefett, "potzblitz!
Bleib doch noch ein wenig hier!"
Schnupp! Er ist schon aus der Tür.—
Mickefett voll List und Tücke
Wartet nicht, bis er zurücke,
Sondern schleicht als falscher Freund,
Wo ihm Glück zu winken scheint.—
Seht, da steigt er schon hinein.
Freudig zittert sein Gebein.
Und er küsst die zarte Hand,
Die er da im Dunkeln fand.
Und er hält mit Liebeshast
Eine Nachtgestalt umfasst.—
Mickefett! Das gibt Malheur,
Denn die Tante liebt nicht mehr!—
Ängstlich schnelle, laut und helle
Schwingt sie in der Hand die Schelle.
Schwerbewaffnet kommt man jetzt.
Mickefett ist höchst entsetzt.
Schamverwirrt und voller Schrecken
Will er sich sogleich verstecken.
Aber autsch! Der Säbel ritzt,
Weil er vorne zugespitzt.
Schmerzgefühl bei grosser Enge
Wirkt ermüdend auf die Länge.
Bratsch! Mit Rauschen und Geklirr
Leert sich jedes Waschgeschirr.
Man ist sehr verwirrt und feucht.
Mickefett entschwirrt und fleucht.
Schmerzlich an den Stoff der Hose.
Heftet sich die Dornenrose.

Das Gartenhaus

Liebe—sagt man schön und richtig—
Ist ein Ding, was äusserst wichtig.
Nicht nur zieht man in Betracht,
Was man selber damit macht,
Nein, man ist in solchen Sachen
Auch gespannt, was andre machen.—
Allgemein von Mund zu Munde
Geht die ahnungsvolle Kunde,

Sozusagen ein Gemunkel,
Dass im Garten, wenn es dunkel,
Julchen Knopp mit Försters Fritze
Heimlich wandle oder sitze.—
Diese Sage hat vor allen
Drei Personen sehr missfallen,
Die sich leider ganz entzweit
Durch die Eifersüchtigkeit.
Jeder hat sich vorgenommen:
Ei, da muss ich hinter kommen.
Hier schleicht Sutitt schlau heraus
Zu Herrn Knoppens Gartenhaus,
Wo das Gartenbaugerät
Wohlverwahrt und trocken steht.
Husch! Er schlüpft in das Salett,
Denn es naht sich Mickefett.
Husch! Der zögert auch nicht viel,
Denn es naht sich Klingebiel.
Husch! Auch der drückt sich hinein,
Denn hier naht im Mondenschein,
Wie wohl zu vermuten war,
Das bewusste Liebespaar.
Oh, wie peinlich muss es sein,
Wenn man so als Feind zu drein
Engbedrückt zusammen sitzt
Und vor Zorn im Dunkeln schwitzt!—
Siehste wohl! Da geht es plötzlich
Rumpelpumpel, ganz entsetzlich.
Alles Gartenutensil
Mischt sich in das Kampfgewühl;
Und, rabum! Zum Überfluss
Löst sich laut der Flintenschuss.
Husch! Da schlupfen voller Schreck
Fritz und Julchen ins Versteck;
Denn schon zeigt sich in der Ferne
Vater Knopp mit der Laterne.
Knipp, der Hund, kratzt an der Tür.
Knopp, der denkt: Was hat er hier?
Starr und staunend bleibt er stehn
Mit dem Ruf: "Was muss ich sehn?"
Dann mit Fassung in den Zügen
Spricht er: "Na, ihr könnt euch kriegen!"
Jetzt kommt Mutter, jetzt kommt Tante,
Beide schon im Nachtgewande.
Oh, das war mal eine schöne
Rührende Familienszene!—

Ende

Feierlich, wie sich's gebührt,
Ward die Trauung ausgeführt.—
Hierbei leitet Klingebiel

Festgesang und Orgelspiel
Unter leisem Tränenregen,
Traurig, doch von Amtes wegen;
Während still im Kabinett
Sutitt und Herr Mickefett
Hinter einer Flasche Wein
Ihren Freundschaftsbund erneu'n.
Knopp, der hat hienieden nun
Eigentlich nichts mehr zu tun.—
Er hat seinen Zweck erfüllt.—
Runzlig wird sein Lebensbild.—
Mütze, Pfeife, Rock und Hose
Schrumpfen ein und werden lose,
So dass man bedenklich spricht:
"Hört mal, Knopp gefällt mir nicht!"
In der Wolke sitzt die schwarze
Parze mit der Nasenwarze,
Und sie zwickt und schneidet, schnapp!
Knopp sein Lebensbändel ab.
Na, jetzt hat er seine Ruh!
Ratsch! Man zieht den Vorhang zu.

Die Haarbeutel

Einleitung

Der Weise, welcher sitzt und denkt
Und tief sich in sich selbst versenkt,
Um in der Seele Dämmerschein
Sich an der Wahrheit zu erfreun,
Der leert bedenklich seine Flasche,
Hebt seine Dose aus der Tasche,
Nimmt eine Prise, macht hapschie!
Und spricht: "Mein Sohn, die Sach ist die!
Eh' man auf diese Welt gekommen
Und noch so still vorliebgenommen,
Da hat man noch bei nichts was bei;
Man schwebt herum, ist schuldenfrei,
Hat keine Uhr und keine Eile
Und äusserst selten Langeweile.
Allein man nimmt sich nicht in acht,
Und schlupp! ist man zur Welt gebracht.
Zuerst hast du es gut, mein Sohn,
Doch pass mal auf, man kommt dir schon!
Bereits dein braves Elternpaar
Erscheint dir häufig sonderbar.
Es saust der Stab, dann geht es schwapp!
Sieh da, mein Sohn, du kriegst was ab!
Und schon erscheint dir unabwendlich

Der Schmerzensruf: Das ist ja schändlich!
Du wächst heran, du suchst das Weite,
Jedoch die Welt ist voller Leute;
Vorherrschend Juden, Weiber, Christen,
Die dich ganz schrecklich überlisten
Und die, anstatt dir was zu schenken,
Wie du wohl möchtest, nicht dran denken.
Und wieder scheint dir unabweislich
Der Schmerzensruf: Das ist ja scheusslich!
Doch siehe da, im trauten Kreis
Sitzt Jüngling, Mann und Jubelgreis,
Und jeder hebt an seinen Mund
Ein Hohlgemäss, was meistens rund,
Um draus in ziemlich kurzer Zeit
Die drin enthaltne Flüssigkeit
Mit Lust und freudigem Bemühn
Zu saugen und herauszuziehn.
Weil jeder dies mit Eifer tut,
So sieht man wohl, es tut ihm gut.
Man setzt sich auch zu diesen Herrn,
Man tut es häufig, tut es gern,
Und möglichst lange tut man's auch;
Die Nase schwillt, es wächst der Bauch,
Und bald, mein Sohn, wirst du mit Graun
Im Spiegelglas dein Bildnis schaun,
Und wieder scheint dir unerlässlich
Der Schmerzensruf: Das ist ja grässlich!!
Mein lieber Sohn, du tust mir leid,
Dir mangelt die Enthaltsamkeit.
Enthaltsamkeit ist das Vergnügen
An Sachen, welche wir nicht kriegen.
Drum lebe mässig, denke klug.
Wer nichts gebraucht, der hat genug!"
So spricht der Weise, grau von Haar,
Ernst, würdig, sachgemäss und klar,
Wie sich's gebührt in solchen Dingen;
Lässt sich ein Dutzend Austern bringen,
Isst sie, entleert die zweite Flasche,
Hebt seine Dose aus der Tasche,
Nimmt eine Prise, macht hapschie!
Schmückt sich mit Hut und Paraplü,
Bewegt sich mit Bedacht nach Haus
Und ruht von seinem Denken aus.

Silen

Siehe, da sitzet Silen bei der wohlgebildeten
    Nymphe.
Gern entleert er den Krug, was er schon öfters
    getan.—
Endlich aber jedoch erklimmt er den nützlichen
    Esel,

Wenn auch dieses nicht ganz ohne Beschwerde
    geschah.
Fast vergisst er den Thyrsus, woran er sein
    Lebtag gewöhnt ist;
Käme derselbe ihm weg, wär' es ihm schrecklich
    fatal.—
Also reitet er fort und erhebt auf Kunst keinen
    Anspruch;
Bald mal sitzet er so, bald auch wieder mal so.
Horch, wer flötet denn da? Natürlich, Amor, der
    Lausbub;
Aber der Esel erhebt äusserst bedenklich das
    Ohr.
Schlimmer als Flötengetön ist das lautlos
    wirkende Pustrohr;
Pustet man hinten, so fliegt vorne was Spitzes
    heraus.
Ungern empfindet den Schmerz das redlich
    dienende Lasttier;
Aber der Reiter hat auch manche Geschichten
    nicht gern.
Leicht erwischt man den Vogel
    durch List und schlaue Beschleichung;
Wenn er es aber bemerkt, fliegt er meistens
    davon.
Mancher erreichet den Zweck
    durch täuschend geübte Verstellung;
Scheinbar schlummert der Leib, aber die Seele ist
    wach.
Schnupp! Er hat ihn erwischt. Laut kreischt der
    lästige Vogel,
Während der handliche Stab tönend die Backe
    berührt.
Übel wird es vermerkt, entrupft man dem Vogel
    die Feder,
Erstens scheint sie ihm schön, zweitens
    gebraucht er sie auch.
Heimwärts reitet Silen und spielt auf der
    lieblichen Flöte,
Freilich verschiedenerlei, aber doch meistens
    düdellüt!

Der Undankbare

Einen Menschen namens Meier
Schubst man aus des Hauses Tor,
Und man spricht, betrunken sei er;
Selber kam's ihm nicht so vor.
Grade auf des Weges Mitte,
Frisch mit spitzem Kies belegt,
Hat er sich im Schlurferschritte
Knickebeinig fortbewegt.

Plötzlich will es Meiern scheinen,
Als wenn sich die Strasse hebt,
So dass er mit seinen Beinen
Demgemäss nach oben strebt.
Aber Täuschung ist es leider.
Meier fällt auf seinen Bauch,
Wirkt zerstörend auf die Kleider
Und auf die Zigarre auch.
Schnell sucht er sich aufzurappeln.
Weh, jetzt wird die Strasse krumm,
Und es drehn sich alle Pappeln,
Und auch Meiern dreht es um.
Knacks, er fällt auf seine Taschen,
Worin er mit Vorbedacht
Noch zwei wohlgefüllte Flaschen
Klug verwahrt und mitgebracht.
Hilfsbedürftig voller Schmerzen
Sitzt er da in Glas und Kies,
Doch ein Herr mit gutem Herzen
Kam vorbei und merkte dies.
Voller Mitleid und Erbarmen
Sieht er, wie es Meiern geht,
Hebt ihn auf in seinen Armen,
Bis er wieder grade steht.
Puff! Da trifft ein höchst geschwinder
Schlag von Meiern seiner Hand
Auf des Fremden Prachtzylinder,
Dass der Mann im Dunkeln stand.
Ohne Hören, ohne Sehen
Steht der Gute sinnend da;
Und er fragt, wie das geschehen
Und warum ihm das geschah.

Eine milde Geschichte

Selig schwanket Bauer Bunke
Heim von seinem Abendtrunke.
Zwar es tritt auf seinen Wegen
Ihm ein Hindernis entgegen,
Und nicht ohne viel Beschwerden
Kann es überwunden werden.
Aber, siehst du, es gelingt
Schneller, als ihm nötig dünkt.
Pfeife lässt er Pfeife sein,
Drückt sich in sein Haus hinein
Und begibt sich ohne Säumen
Hin zu seinen Zimmerräumen,
Wo Frau Bunke für die Nacht
Einen Teig zurechtgemacht.
Unverzüglich, weil er matt,
Sucht er seine Lagerstatt.
Diese kommt ihm sehr gelegen,

Um darin der Ruh zu pflegen.
Oh, wie wonnig schmiegt das Mus
Sich um Kopf, Leib, Hand und Fuss.
Doch, wie sich der Mund bedeckt,
Wird er ängstlich aufgeschreckt.
Schnell, mit unterdrückter Klage,
Sucht er eine andre Lage.
Auf dem Bauche ruht er milde
Wie die Kröte mit dem Schilde.
Lange bleibt er nicht so liegen.
Ihn verlangt es, Luft zu kriegen.
Ach, Frau Bunke steht erschrocken;
Ihre Lebensgeister stocken.
Traurig führet sie den Besen.
Kummer füllt ihr tiefstes Wesen;
Weinen kann ihr Angesicht,
Aber backen kann sie nicht.

Fritze

Fritze war ein Ladenjüngling,
Dazu braver Eltern Sohn,
Und er stand bei Kaufmann Kunze
Schon ein Jahr in Konditschon.
"Fritze," sagte einstens Kunze,
"Ich muss eben mal wohin;
Mache keine dummen Streiche,
Wenn ich nicht zugegen bin."
Hiemit geht er aus der Türe.
Fritze hält das für ein Glück.
Er ergreift die Kümmelflasche,
Und dann beugt er sich zurück.
Sieh, da naht die alte Grete,
Eine Jungfer ernst und still;
Sie verlangt nach grüner Seife,
Weil sie morgen waschen will.
Auch erhob sie eine Klage,
Dass sie's so im Leibe hat,
Weshalb sie vor allen Dingen
Erst um einen Kümmel bat.
Fritze zeigt sich dienstbeflissen.
Ihm ist recht konfus und wohl.
Statt der grossen Kümmelflasche
Nimmt er die mit Vitriol.
Jungfer Grete, voller Freuden,
Greift begierig nach dem Glas;
Fritz, der grünen Seife wegen,
Beugt sich übers Seifenfass.
Weh, was muss man nun erblicken?
Wo ist Fritzens Gleichgewicht?
Was sind dies für Angstgebärden
Hier auf Gretens Angesicht?

Fritze strampelt mit den Beinen,
Doch die Seife wird sein Grab;
Greten nagt die scharfe Säure
Ihre Mädchenseele ab.
Kümmel zieret keinen Jüngling.
Dazu ist er noch zu klein;
Und ein braves altes Mädchen
Muss nicht mehr so happig sein.

Nur leise

Sehr häufig traf Studiosus Döppe
Paulinen auf des Hauses Treppe,
Wenn sie als Witwe tugendsam
Des Morgens aus der Stube kam.
Da sie Besitzerin vom Haus,
So sprach sich Döppe schliesslich a
Und bat mit Liebe und Empfindun;
Um eine dauernde Verbindung.
"Herr Döppe," sprach Pauline küh
"Ich ehr' und achte Ihr Gefühl,
Doch dies Gepolter auf der Treppe
Fast jede Nacht ist bös, Herr Döppe!"
Worauf denn Döppe fest beschwor,
Die Sache käme nicht mehr vor.
Dies Schwören sollte wenig nützen.
Nachts hat er wieder einen sitzen.
Er kommt nach Haus in später Stund
Mit Pfeife, Rausch und Pudelhund.
Behutsam zieht er auf dem Gang
Die Stiefel aus, die schwer und lang,
Um auf den Socken, auf den weichen,
Geräuschlos sich emporzuschleichen.
Fast ist er schon dem Gipfel nah
Und denkt, der letzte Tritt ist da.
Dies denkt er aber ohne Grund.
Die Pfeife bohrt sich in den Schlund.
Die alte Treppe knackt und knirrt,
Die Pfeife löst sich auf und klirrt;
Erschrecklich tönt der Stiefel Krach,
Dumpf rumpelt Döppe hinten nach.
Der Pudel heult und ist verletzt,
Weil Döppe seinen Schwanz besetzt.
Pauline kommt mit Kerzenlicht;
Beschämt verbirgt er sein Gesicht.
Man hört nichts weiter von Paulinen,
Als: "Döppe, ich verachte Ihnen!"

Vierhändig

Der Mensch, der hier im Schlummer liegt,
Hat seinen Punsch nicht ausgekriegt.

Dies ist dem Affen äusserst lieb;
Er untersucht, was übrigblieb.
Der Trank erscheint ihm augenblicklich
Beachtenswert und sehr erquicklich.
Drum nimmt er auch die Sache gründlich.
Der Schwanz ist aber recht empfindlich.
Der Hauch ist kühlend insoweit,
Doch besser wirkt die Flüssigkeit.
Begierig wird der Rest getrunken
Und froh auf einem Bein gehunken.
Das Trinkgeschirr, sobald es leer,
Macht keine rechte Freude mehr.
Jetzt können wir, da dies geschehn,
Zu etwas anderm übergehn.
Zum Beispiel mit gelehrten Sachen
Kann man sich vielfach nützlich machen.
Hiernach, wenn man es nötig glaubt,
Ist die Zigarre wohl erlaubt.
Man zündet sie behaglich an,
Setzt sich bequem und raucht sodann.
Oft findet man nicht den Genuss,
Den man mit Recht erwarten muss.
So geht es mit Tabak und Rum:
Erst bist du froh, dann fällst du um.
Hier ruhn die Schläfer schön vereint,
Bis dass die Morgensonne scheint.
Im Kopf ertönt ein schmerzlich Summen,
Wir Menschen sagen: Schädelbrummen.

Eine kalte Geschichte

Der Wind, der weht, die Nacht ist kühl.
Nach Hause wandelt Meister Zwiel.
Verständig, wie das seine Art,
Hat er den Schlüssel aufbewahrt.
Das Schlüsselloch wird leicht vermisst,
Wenn man es sucht, wo es nicht ist.
Allmählich schneit es auch ein bissel;
Der kalten Hand entfällt der Schlüssel.
Beschwerlich ist die Bückerei;
Es lüftet sich der Hut dabei.
Der Hut ist nass und äusserst kalt;
Wenn das so fortgeht, friert es bald.
Noch einmal bückt der Meister sich,
Doch nicht geschickt erweist er sich.
Das Wasser in dem Fasse hier
Hat etwa Null Grad Reaumur.
Es bilden sich in diesem Falle
Die sogenannten Eiskristalle.
Der Wächter singt: Bewahrt das Licht!
Der kalte Meister hört es nicht.

Er sitzt gefühllos, starr und stumm,
Der Schnee fällt drauf und drum herum.
Der Morgen kommt so trüb und grau;
Frau Pieter kommt, die Millichfrau;
Auch kommt sogleich mit ihrem Topf
Frau Zwiel heraus und neigt den Kopf.
"Schau schau!" ruft sie in Schmerz versunken.
"Mein guter Zwiel hat ausgetrunken!
Von nun an, liebe Madam Pieter,
Bitt' ich nur um ein Viertel Liter!"

Die ängstliche Nacht

Heut bleibt der Herr mal wieder lang.
Still wartet sein Amöblemang.
Da kommt er endlich angestoppelt.
Die Möbel haben sich verdoppelt.
Was wär' denn dieses hier? Ei ei!
Aus einem Beine werden zwei.
Der Kleiderhalter, sonst so nütze,
Zeigt sich als unbestimmte Stütze.
Oha! Jetzt wird ihm aber schwach,
Die Willenskräfte lassen nach.
Er sucht auf seiner Lagerstatt
Die Ruhe, die er nötig hat.
Auweh! der Fuss ist sehr bedrückt;
Ein harter Käfer beisst und zwickt.
Der Käfer zwickt, der Käfer kneift;
Mit Mühe wird er abgestreift.
Jedoch die Ruhe währt nicht lange;
Schon wieder zwickt die harte Zange.
Er dreht sich um, so schnell er kann;
Da stösst ihn wer von hinten an.
Habuh! Da ist er! Steif und kalt;
Ein Kerl von scheusslicher Gestalt.
Ha, drauf und dran! Du oder ich!
Jetzt heisst es, Alter, wehre dich!
Heiss tobt der Kampf, hoch saust das Bein;
Es mischt sich noch ein dritter drein.
Doch siehe da, der Feind erliegt.
Der Kampf ist aus, er hat gesiegt.
Gottlob, so kommt er endlich nun
Doch mal dazu, sich auszuruhn.
Doch nein, ihm ist so dumpf und bang;
Die Nase wird erstaunlich lang.
Und dick und dicker schwillt der Kopf;
Er ist von Blech, er wird zum Topf;
Wobei ein Teufel voller List
Als Musikus beschäftigt ist.
Wie er erwacht, das sieht man hier:
Ein jedes Haar ein Pfropfenziehr.

Fipps der Affe

Anfang

Pegasus, du alter Renner,
Trag mich mal nach Afrika,
Alldieweil so schwarze Männer
Und so bunte Vögel da.
Kleider sind da wenig Sitte;
Höchstens trägt man einen Hut,
Auch wohl einen Schurz der Mitte;
Man ist schwarz und damit gut.—
Dann ist freilich jeder bange,
Selbst der Affengreis entfleucht,
Wenn die lange Brillenschlange
Zischend von der Palme kreucht.
Kröten fallen auf den Rücken,
Ängstlich wird das Bein bewegt;
Und der Strauss muss heftig drücken,
Bis das grosse Ei gelegt.
Krokodile weinen Tränen,
Geier sehen kreischend zu;
Sehr gemein sind die Hyänen;
Schäbig ist der Marabu.
Nur die Affen, voller Schnacken,
Haben Vor- und Hinterhand;
Emsig mümmeln ihre Backen;
Gerne hockt man beieinand'.
Papa schaut in eine Stelle,
Onkel kratzt sich sehr geschwind,
Tante kann es grad so schnelle,
Mama untersucht das Kind.
Fipps—so wollen wir es nennen.—
Aber wie er sich betrug,
Wenn wir ihn genauer kennen,
Ach, das ist betrübt genug.
Selten zeigt er sich beständig,
Einmal hilft er aus der Not;
Anfangs ist er recht lebendig,
Und am Schlusse ist er tot.

Erstes Kapitel

Der Fipps, das darf man wohl gestehn,
Ist nicht als Schönheit anzusehn.
Was ihm dagegen Wert verleiht,
Ist Rührig- und Betriebsamkeit.
Wenn wo was los, er darf nicht fehlen;
Was ihm beliebt, das muss er stehlen;
Wenn wer was macht, er macht es nach;
Und Bosheit ist sein Lieblingsfach.

Es wohnte da ein schwarzer Mann,
Der Affen fing und briet sie dann.
Besonders hat er junge gern,
Viel lieber als die ältern Herrn.
"Ein alter Herr ist immer zäh!"
So spricht er oft und macht: "Bäbä!"
Um seine Zwecke zu erfüllen,
Wählt er drei leere Kürbishüllen.
Für auf den Kopf die grosse eine,
Für an die Hände noch zwei kleine.
So kriecht er in ein Bündel Stroh,
Macht sich zurecht und wartet so.—
Dies hat nun allerdings den Schein,
Als ob hier schöne Früchte sein.
Fipps, der noch nie so grosse sah,
Kaum sieht er sie, so ist er da.
Er wählt für seinen Morgenschmaus
Sich gleich die allergrösste aus.
Doch wie er oben sich bemüht,
Erfasst ihn unten wer und zieht,
Bis dass an jeder Hinterhand
Ringsum ein Kürbis sich befand.
So denkt ihn froh und nach Belieben
Der böse Mann nach Haus zu schieben.
An dieses Mannes Nase hing
Zu Schmuck und Zier ein Nasenring.
Fipps fasst den Reif mit seinem Schweif.
Der Schwarze wird vor Schrecken steif.
Die Nase dreht sich mehre Male
Und bildet eine Qualspirale.
Jetzt biegt der Fipps den langen Ast,
Bis er den Ring der Nase fasst.
Dem Neger wird das Herze bang,
Die Seele kurz, die Nase lang.
Am Ende gibt es einen Ruck,
Und oben schwebt der Nasenschmuck.
Der Schwarze aber ass seit dieser
Begebenheit fast nur Gemüser.

Zweites Kapitel

Natürlich lässt Fipps die ekligen Sachen,
Ohne neidisch zu sein, von anderen machen.
Dagegen aber, wenn einer was tut,
Was den Anschein hat, als tät' es ihm gut,
Gleich kommt er begierig und hastig herbei,
Um zu prüfen, ob's wirklich so angenehm sei.
Mal sass er an des Ufers Rand
Auf einer Palme, die dorten stand.
Ein grosses Schiff liegt auf dem Meer;
Vom Schiffe schaukelt ein Kahn daher.
Im kleinen Kahn, da sitzt ein Mann,

Der hat weder Schuhe noch Stiefel an;
Doch vor ihm steht ganz offenbar
Ein grosses und kleines Stiefelpaar.
Das kleine, das er mit sich führt,
Ist innen mit pappigem Pech beschmiert;
Und wie der Mann an das Ufer tritt,
Bringt er die zwei Paar Stiefel mit.
Er trägt sie sorglich unter dem Arm
Und jammert dabei, dass es Gott erbarm.
Kaum aber ziehet der Trauermann
Sich einen von seinen Stiefeln an,
So mildern sich schon ganz augenscheinlich
Die Schmerzen, die noch vor kurzem so peinlich,
Und gar bei Stiefel Numero zwei
Zeigt er sich gänzlich sorgenfrei.
Dann sucht er im fröhlichen Dauerlauf
Den kleinen Nachen wieder auf
Und lässt aus listig bedachtem Versehn
Das kleine Paar Stiefel am Lande stehn.
Ratsch, ist der Fipps vom Baum herunter,
Ziehet erwartungsvoll und munter
Die Stiefel an seine Hinterglieder,
Und schau! Der lustige Mann kommt wieder.
O weh! Die Stiefel an Fippsens Bein
Stören die Flucht. Man holt ihn ein.
Vergebens strampelt er ungestüm,
Der Schiffer geht in den Kahn mit ihm.
Zum Schiffe schaukelt und strebt der Kahn,
Das Schiff fährt über den Ozean,
Und selbiger Mann (er schrieb sich Schmidt)
Nimmt Fipps direkt nach Bremen mit.

Drittes Kapitel

Zu Bremen lebt gewandt und still
Als ein Friseur der Meister Krüll,
Und jedermann in dieser Stadt,
Wer Haare und wer keine hat,
Geht gern zu Meister Krüll ins Haus
Und kommt als netter Mensch heraus.
Auch Schmidt lässt sich die Haare schneiden.
Krüll sieht den Affen voller Freuden,
Er denkt: Das wäre ja vor mir
Und meine Kunden ein Pläsier.
Und weil ihn Schmidt veräussern will,
So kauft und hat ihn Meister Krüll.
Es kam mal so und traf sich nun,
Dass Krüll, da anders nichts zu tun,
In Eile, wie er meistens tat,
Das Seitenkabinett betrat,
Wo er die Glanzpomade kocht,
Perücken baut und Zöpfe flocht,

Kurz, wo die kunstgeübte Hand
Vollendet, was der Geist erfand.
Zur selben Zeit erscheint im Laden,
Mit dünnem Kopf und dicken Waden,
Der schlichtbehaarte Bauer Dümmel,
Sitzt auf den Sessel, riecht nach Kümmel
Und hofft getrost, dass man ihn schere,
Was denn auch wirklich nötig wäre.
Wipps—sitzt der Fipps auf seinem Nacken,
Um ihm die Haare abzuzwacken.
Die Schere zwickt, die Haare fliegen;
Dem Dümmel macht es kein Vergnügen.
Oha! Das war ein scharfer Schnitt,
Wodurch des Ohres Muschel litt.
"Hör upp!" schreit Dümmel schmerzensbange.
Doch schon hat Fipps die Kräuselzange.
Das Eisen glüht, es zischt das Ohr,
Ein Dampfgewölk steigt draus hervor.
Die Schönheit dieser Welt verschwindet,
Und nur der Schmerz zieht, bohrt und mündet
In diesen einen Knotenpunkt,
Den Dümmel hier ins Wasser tunkt.—
Der Meister kommt.—
Hoch schwingt die Rechte,
Wie zum Gefechte, eine Flechte.
Der Spiegel klirrt, die Hand erlahmt;
Der Meister Krüll ist eingerahmt.
Mir scheint, ich bin hier unbeliebt!
Denkt Fipps, der sich hinwegbegibt.

Viertes Kapitel

Dämmrung war es, als Adele
Mit dem Freunde ihrer Seele,
Der so gerne Pudding ass,
Traulich bei der Tafel sass.
"Pudding," sprach er, "ist mein Bestes!"
Drum zum Schluss des kleinen Festes
Steht der wohlgeformte grosse
Pudding mit der roten Sosse
Braun und lieblich duftend da,
Was der Freund mit Wonne sah.
Aber, ach du meine Güte,
Plötzlich stockt das Herzgeblüte.—
Angelockt von Wohlgerüchen
Hat sich Fipps herbeigeschlichen,
Um mit seinen gier'gen Händen
Diesen Pudding zu entwenden,
Hergestellt mit grossem Fleiss.
Ätsch! Die Sache ist zu heiss!—
Ärgerlich ist solche Hitze.
Schlapp! Der Freund hat eine Mütze

Tief bis über beide Backen.
Platsch! Und in Adelens Nacken,
Tief bis unten in das Mieder,
Rinnt die rote Sosse nieder.
So wird oft die schönste Stunde
In der Liebe Seelenbunde
Durch Herbeikunft eines Dritten
Mitten durch- und abgeschnitten;
Und im Innern wehmutsvoll
Tönt ein dumpfes Kolleroll!

Fünftes Kapitel

Für Fipps wird es dringende Essenszeit.—
Mit fröhlicher Gelenkigkeit
Durch eine Seitengasse entflieht er
Und schleicht in den Laden von einem Konditer.
Da gibt es schmackhafte Kunstgebilde,
Nicht bloss härtliche, sondern auch milde;
Da winken Krapfen und Mohrenköpfe,
Künstlich geflochtene Brezen und Zöpfe;
Auch sieht man da für gemischtes Vergnügen
Mandeln, Rosinen et cetera liegen.—
"Horch!" ruft voll Sorge Konditor Köck.
"Was rappelt da zwischen meinem Gebäck?"
Die Sorge wandelt sich in Entsetzen,
Denn da steht Fipps mit Krapfen und Brezen.
Die Brezen trägt er in einer Reih
Auf dem Schwanz, als ob es ein Stecken sei,
Und aufgespiesst, gleich wie auf Zapfen,
An allen vier Daumen sitzen die Krapfen.
Zwar Köck bemüht sich, dass er ihn greife
Hinten bei seinem handlichen Schweife,
Doch weil er soeben den Teig gemischt,
So glitscht er ab, und der Dieb entwischt.
Nichts bleibt ihm übrig als lautes Gebröll,
Und grad kommt Mieke, die alte Mamsell.
Unter hellem Gequieke fällt diese Gute
Platt auf die Steine mit Topf und Tute.
Durch ihre Beine eilt Fipps im Sprunge.
Ihn wirft ein schwärzlicher Schusterjunge
Mit dem Stulpenstiefel, der frisch geschmiert,
So dass er die schönen Krapfen verliert.
Auch wartet ein Bettelmann auf der Brücken
Mit einem Buckel und zween Krücken.
Derselbe verspürt ein grosses Verlangen,
Die Brezeln vermittelst der Krücke zu fangen;
Dies kommt ihm aber nicht recht zunütze,
Denn Fipps entzieht ihm die letzte Stütze.—
Da liegt er nun wie ein Käfer am Rücken.—
Fipps aber begibt sich über die Brücken
Und eilet gar sehr beängstigt und matt
Mit der letzten Brezel aus dieser Stadt.—

Schon ist es dunkel und nicht geheuer,
Er schwingt sich über ein Gartengemäuer.
Hier hofft er auf angenehm nächtliche Ruh.
Klapp—schnappt die eiserne Falle zu.—
Sofort tritt aus dem Wohngebäude
Ein Herr und äussert seine Freude.
"Aha!" So ruft er. "Du bist wohl der,
Der Hühner stiehlt? Na, denn komm her!"
Hiermit schiebt er ihn vergnüglich
In einen Sack. Und unverzüglich
Ohne jede weitere Besichtigung
Beginnt er die schmerzhafte Züchtigung.
Drauf schliesst er ihn für alle Fälle
In einen der leeren Hühnerställe,
Damit er am andern Morgen sodann
Diesen Bösewicht näher besichtigen kann.

Sechstes Kapitel

Wer vielleicht zur guten Tat
Keine rechte Neigung hat,
Dem wird Fasten und Kastein
Immerhin erfrischend sein.—
Als der Herr von gestern abend,
Fest und wohl geschlafen habend
(Er heisst nämlich Doktor Fink),
Morgens nach dem Stalle ging,
Um zu sehn, wen er erhascht—
Ei, wie ist er überrascht,
Als bescheiden, sanft und zahm,
Demutsvoll und lendenlahm,
Fipps aus seinem Sacke steigt,
Näher tritt und sich verneigt.
Lächelnd reicht Frau Doktorin
Ihm den guten Apfel hin,
Und das dicke, runde, fette,
Nette Kindermädchen Jette
Mit der niedlichen Elise,
Ei herrje! Wie lachten diese.—
Zwei nur finden's nicht am Platze;
Schnipps, der Hund, und Gripps, die Katze,
Die nicht ohne Missvertrauen
Diesen neuen Gast beschauen.
Fipps ist aber recht gelehrig
Und beträgt sich wie gehörig.
Morgens früh, so flink er kann,
Steckt er Fink die Pfeife an.
Fleissig trägt er dürre Reiser,
Ja, Kaffee zu mahlen weiss er,
Und sobald man musiziert,
Horcht er still, wie sich's gebührt.
Doch sein innigstes Vergnügen
Ist, Elisen sanft zu wiegen,

Oder, falls sie mal verdrossen,
Zu erfreun durch schöne Possen.
Kurz, es war sein schönster Spass,
Wenn er bei Elisen sass.
Dafür kriegt er denn auch nun
Aus verblümtem Zitzkattun
Eine bunte und famose
Hinten zugeknöpfte Hose;
Dazu, reizend von Geschmack,
Einen erbsengrünen Frack;
Und so ist denn gegenwärtig
Dieser hübsche Junge fertig.

Siebentes Kapitel

Elise schläft in ihrer Wiegen.
Fipps passt geduldig auf die Fliegen.—
Indessen denkt die runde Jette,
Was sie wohl vorzunehmen hätte;
Sieht eine Wespe, die verirrt
Am Fenster auf und nieder schwirrt,
Und treibt das arme Stacheltier
In eine Tute von Papier.
Sanft lächelnd reicht sie ihm die Tute,
Damit er Gutes drin vermute.
Er öffnet sie geschickt und gern,
Denn jeder Argwohn liegt ihm fern.
Schnurr pick! Der Stachel sitzt am Finger.
Der Schmerz ist gar kein so geringer.
Doch Fipps hat sich alsbald gefasst,
Zermalmt das Ding, was ihm verhasst,
Setzt sich dann wieder an die Wiegen
Und passt geduldig auf die Fliegen.—
Vor allem eine ist darunter,
Die ganz besonders frech und munter.
Jetzt sitzt sie hier, jetzt summt sie da,
Bald weiter weg, bald wieder nah.
Jetzt krabbelt sie auf Jettens Jacke,
Jetzt wärmt sie sich auf Jettens Backe.
Das gute Kind ist eingenickt.
Kein Wunder, wenn sie nun erschrickt,
Denn, schlapp! Die Fliege traf ein Hieb,
Woran sie starb und sitzenblieb.—
Fipps aber hockt so friedlich da,
Als ob dies alles nicht geschah,
Und schliesset seine Augen zu
Mit abgefeimter Seelenruh.

Achtes Kapitel

Kaum hat mal einer ein bissel was,
Gleich gibt es welche, die ärgert das.—
Fipps hat sich einen Knochen stibitzt,

Wo auch noch ziemlich was drannen sitzt.
Neidgierig hocken im Hintergrund
Gripps, der Kater, und Schnipps, der Hund.
Wauwau! Sie sausen von ihrem Platze.
Happs! macht der Hund, kritzekratze! die Katze,
Dass Fipps in ängstlichem Seelendrang
Eilig auf einen Schrank entsprang,
Allwo man aufbewahren tät
Mancherlei nützliches Handgerät.
Und Gripps, der Kater, und Schnipps, der Hund,
Schleichen beschämt in den Hintergrund.
Fipps aber knüpft mit der Hand gewandt
Den Knochen an ein Band, das er fand,
Und schlängelt dasselbe voller List
Durch einen Korb, welcher löchrig ist.
Sogleich folgt Gripps dem Bratengebein
Bis tief in das Korbgeflecht hinein.
Schwupp—hat ihn der Fipps drin festgedrückt,
Und mit der Zange, die beisst und zwickt,
Entfernt er sorgsam die scharfen Klauen.
Ach, wie so kläglich muss Gripps miauen,
Denn grade in seinen Fingerspitzen
Hat er die peinlichsten Nerven sitzen.
Jetzt wird auch noch der Schweif gebogen
Und durch des Korbes Henkel gezogen.
Mit einer Klammer versieht er ihn,
Damit er nicht leichtlich herauszuziehn.
Schnipps, der Hund, schnappt aber derweilen
Den Knochen und möchte von dannen eilen.
Dieses gelingt ihm jedoch nicht ganz,
Denn Fipps erwischt ihn bei seinem Schwanz
Und schwingt ihn solchermassen im Kreis,
Bis er nichts Gescheits mehr zu denken weiss.
Hiernach, gewissermassen als Schlitten,
Zieht er ihn durch des Hofes Mitten
Und lässt ihn dorten mal soeben
Über dem Abgrund des Brunnens schweben,
Wo ein schwäch- und ängstlich Gemüt
Nur ungern hängt und hinuntersieht.
Drauf so führt er ihn hinten nach
An des Daches Rinne bis auf das Dach
Und lehnt ihn über den Schlot allhier.
Daraus geht ein merklicher Dampf herfür.—
Dem Auge höchst peinlich ist der Rauch,
Auch muss man niesen und husten auch,
Und schliesslich denkt man nichts weiter als
    bloss:
Jetzt wird's mir zu dumm, und ich lasse los.
So wird dieser Rauch immer stärker und stärker,
Schnipps fällt rücküber und auf den Erker,
Doch Gripps, der grad aus der Luke fährt,
Fühlt plötzlich, ihm wird der Korb beschwert.

Hulterpulter, sie rumpeln in grosser Hast
Vom Dach und baumeln an einem Ast.
Hier trennt man sich nicht ohne Pein.
Und jeder ist wieder für sich allein.
Seitdem war Fipps von diesen zween
Als Meister verehrt und angesehn.

Neuntes Kapitel

Mit Recht erscheint uns das Klavier,
Wenn's schön poliert, als Zimmerzier.
Ob's ausserdem Genuss verschafft,
Bleibt hin und wieder zweifelhaft.
Auch Fipps fühlt sich dazu getrieben,
Die Kunst in Tönen auszuüben.
Er zeigt sich wirklich sehr gewandt,
Selbst mit der linken Hinterhand.
Und braucht er auch die Rechte noch,
Den Apfel, den geniesst er doch.
Zu Kattermäng gehören zwei,
Er braucht sich bloss allein dabei.
Piano klingt auf diese Weise
Besonders innig, weich und leise.
Jetzt stimmen ein mit Herz und Mund
Der Kater Gripps und Schnipps, der Hund.
Bei dem Duett sind stets zu sehn
Zwei Mäuler, welche offenstehn.
Oft wird es einem sehr verdacht,
Wenn er Geräusch nach Noten macht.
Der Künstler fühlt sich stets gekränkt,
Wenn's anders kommt, als wie er denkt.

Zehntes Kapitel

Wöhnlich im Wechselgespräch
beim angenehm schmeckenden Portwein
Sassen Professor Klöhn und Fink,
der würdige Doktor.
Aber jener beschloss, wie folgt,
die belehrende Rede:
"O verehrtester Freund!
Nichts gehet doch über die hohe
Weisheit der Mutter Natur.—
Sie erschuf ja so mancherlei Kräuter,
Harte und weiche zugleich,
doch letztere mehr zu Gemüse.
Auch erschuf sie die Tiere,
erfreulich, harmlos und nutzbar;
Hüllte sie aussen in Häute,
woraus man Stiefel verfertigt,
Füllte sie innen mit Fleisch
von sehr beträchtlichem Nährwert;
Aber erst ganz zuletzt,

damit er es dankend benutze,
Schuf sie des Menschen Gestalt
und verlieh ihm die Öffnung des Mundes.
Aufrecht stehet er da,
und alles erträgt er mit Würde."
Also sprach der Professor,
erhub sich und setzte den Hut auf.
Wehe, die Nase hernieder
ins Mundloch rieselt die Tinte.
Wehe, durch Gummi verklebt,
fest haftet das nützliche Sacktuch.
Drohend mit Zorngebärde
erhebt er den schlanken Spazierstock.
Autsch! Ein schmerzlich Geflecht
umschlingt den schwellenden Daumen.
Hastig begibt er sich fort;
indessen die Würde ist mässig.

Elftes Kapitel

Wie gewöhnlich liest die Jette
Wieder nachts in ihrem Bette.
Auf dem Kopf hat sie die Haube,
In der Hand die Gartenlaube.
Hieran will sie sich erfreu'n,
Duselt, nickt und schlummert ein.
An das Unschlittkerzenlicht,
Daran denkt sie freilich nicht.—
Erst brennt nur die Zeitungsecke.
Dann der Vorhang, dann die Decke.
Schliesslich brennt das ganze Haus;
Unten läuft man schon heraus.—
Vater Fink, er läuft nicht schlecht,
Trägt den treuen Stiefelknecht.
Mutter Fink, besorgt vor allen,
Rettet ihre Mausefallen.
Jette schwebt vom Fensterrand;
Sie ist etwas angebrannt.
Doch sie sinkt ins Regenfass,
Wo es drinnen kühl und nass.—
Also sicher wären diese.—
Aber ach, wo ist Elise?
Seht nach oben! Fipps, der Brave,
Hält das Kind, was fest im Schlafe.
Aus dem Fenster, hoch im Raume,
Schwingt er sich zum nächsten Baume.
Höchst besorgt wie eine Amme
Rutscht er abwärts an dem Stamme.
Sanft legt er Elisen nieder.
Sie hat ihre Eltern wieder;
Und die Flasche steht dabei,
Falls Elise durstig sei.—

Zwölftes Kapitel

Fink hat versichert, Gott Lob und Dank,
Bei der Aachener Feuerversicherungs-Bank,
Und nach zwei Jahren so ungefähr
Wohnt er weit schöner als wie vorher.—
Fipps natürlich, der hat es seitdem
In jeder Hinsicht sehr angenehm.—
Dies aber wird ihm im höchsten Grad
Unerträglich und wirklich fad.
Denn, leider Gottes, so ist der Schlechte,
Dass er immer was anderes möchte,
Auch hat er ein höchst verruchtes Gelüst,
Grad so zu sein, wie er eben ist.
Mal traf es sich, dass die Familie Fink
Zusammen aus- und spazierenging,
Um nebst Besorgung von anderen Sachen
Professor Klöhn einen Besuch zu machen.—
Fipps sehnt sich förmlich nach bösen Streichen.
Sein Plan steht fest. Er will entweichen.
Schon ist er im Feld. Die Hasen fliehn.
Einen Wanderer sieht man des Weges ziehn.
Sehr heftig erschrickt der Wandersmann.
Die Töpfersfrau geht still voran.
Zuweilen fällt das Topfgeschirr,
Und dann zerbricht es mit grossem Geklirr.
In jenem Haus da, so fügt's der Himmel,
Wohnt grad der bewusste Bauer Dümmel;
Und Dümmels Küchlein piepsen bang,
Denn Fipps zieht ihnen die Hälse lang.
Da steht auch Dümmels kleiner Sohn
Mit dem Butterbrot.—
Fipps hat es schon.
Des kleinen Dümmels durchdringender Schrei
Lockt seine erschrockene Mutter herbei.
Mit den Schreckensworten: "Da kummt de
    Dübel!"
Fällt sie in einen dastehenden Kübel.
Doch Dümmel schreit und kennt ihn gleich
    wieder:
"Dat is de verdammtige Haaresnieder!"
Schnell fasst er die Flinte, ein Schiesseding,
Was da seit Anno fünfzehn hing.
Auch sammeln sich eilig von jeglicher Seite
Die Nachbarsleute, gerüstet zum Streite.
Sie alle machen grossmächtige Schritte,
Und plötzlich ruft einer: "Kiek, kiek, da sitt'e!"
Jetzt harrt ein jeglicher ängstlich und stumm.
Dümmel legt an.—Er zielt.—Er—drückt.—
Dann geht es: Wumm!
Gross ist der Knall und der Rückwärtsstoss,
Denn jahrelang ging diese Flinte nicht los.

Ende

Wehe! Wehe! Dümmel zielte wacker.
Fipps muss sterben, weil er so ein Racker.—
Wie durch Zufall kommen alle jene,
Die er einst gekränkt, zu dieser Szene.
Droben auf Adelens Dienersitze
Thront der Schwarze mit dem Nasenschlitze.
Miecke, Krüll und Köck mit seinem Bauch,
Wandrer, Töpfersfrau, der Bettler auch;
Alle kommen, doch von diesen allen
Lässt nicht einer eine Träne fallen,
Auch ist eine solche nicht zu sehn
In dem Auge von Professor Klöhn,
Der mit Fink und Frau und mit Elisen
Und mit Jetten wandelt durch die Wiesen.
Nur Elise fasste Fippsens Hand,
Während ihr das Aug voll Tränen stand.
"Armer Fipps!" So spricht sie herzig treu.
Damit stirbt er. Alles ist vorbei.
Man begrub ihn hinten in der Ecke,
Wo in Finkens Garten an der Hecke
All die weissen Doldenblumen stehn.
Dort ist, sagt man, noch sein Grab zu sehn.
Doch, dass Kater Gripps und Schnipps, der
    Hund,
Ganz untröstlich, sagt man ohne Grund.

Balduin Bählamm, der verhinderte Dichter

Erstes Kapitel

Wie wohl ist dem, der dann und wann
Sich etwas Schönes dichten kann!
Der Mensch, durchtrieben und gescheit,
Bemerkte schon seit alter Zeit,
Dass ihm hienieden allerlei
Verdriesslich und zuwider sei.
Die Freude flieht auf allen Wegen;
Der Ärger kommt uns gern entgegen.
Gar mancher schleicht betrübt umher;
Sein Knopfloch ist so öd und leer.
Für manchen hat ein Mädchen Reiz,
Nur bleibt die Liebe seinerseits.
Doch gibt's noch mehr Verdriesslichkeiten.
Zum Beispiel lässt sich nicht bestreiten:
Die Sorge, wie man Nahrung findet,

Ist häufig nicht so unbegründet.
Kommt einer dann und fragt: "Wie geht's?"
Steht man gewöhnlich oder stets
Gewissermassen peinlich da,
Indem man spricht: "Nun, so lala!"
Und nur der Heuchler lacht vergnüglich
Und gibt zur Antwort: "Ei, vorzüglich!"
Im Durchschnitt ist man kummervoll
Und weiss nicht, was man machen soll.—
Nicht so der Dichter. Kaum missfällt
Ihm diese altgebackne Welt,
So knetet er aus weicher Kleie
Für sich privatim eine neue
Und zieht als freier Musensohn
In die Poetendimension,
Die fünfte, da die vierte jetzt
Von Geistern ohnehin besetzt.
Hier ist es luftig, duftig, schön,
Hier hat er nichts mehr auszustehn,
Hier aus dem mütterlichen Busen
Der ewig wohlgenährten Musen
Rinnt ihm der Stoff beständig neu
In seine saubre Molkerei.
Gleichwie die brave Bauernmutter.
Tagtäglich macht sie frische Butter.
Des Abends spät, des Morgens frühe
Zupft sie am Hinterleib der Kühe
Mit kunstgeübten Handgelenken
Und trägt, was kommt, zu kühlen Schränken,
Wo bald ihr Finger, leicht gekrümmt,
Den fetten Rahm, der oben schwimmt,
Beiseite schöpft und so in Masse
Vereint im hohen Butterfasse.
Jetzt mit durchlöchertem Pistille
Bedrängt sie die geschmeidige Fülle.
Es kullert, bullert, quitscht und quatscht,
Wird auf und nieder durchgematscht,
Bis das geplagte Element
Vor Angst in Dick und Dünn sich trennt.
Dies ist der Augenblick der Wonne.
Sie hebt das Dicke aus der Tonne,
Legt's in die Mulde, flach von Holz,
Durchknetet es und drückt und rollt's,
Und sieh, in frohen Händen hält se
Die wohlgeratne Butterwälze.
So auch der Dichter.—Stillbeglückt
Hat er sich was zurechtgedrückt
Und fühlt sich nun in jeder Richtung
Befriedigt durch die eigne Dichtung.
Doch guter Menschen Hauptbestreben
Ist, andern auch was abzugeben.
Der Dichter, dem sein Fabrikat

Soviel Genuss bereitet hat,
Er sehnt sich sehr, er kann nicht ruhn,
Auch andern damit wohlzutun;
Und muss er sich auch recht bemühn,
Er sucht sich wen und findet ihn;
Und sträubt sich der vor solchen Freuden,
Er kann sein Glück mal nicht vermeiden.
Am Mittelknopfe seiner Weste
Hält ihn der Dichter dringend feste,
Führt ihn beiseit zum guten Zwecke
In eine lauschig stille Ecke,
Und schon erfolgt der Griff, der rasche,
Links in die warme Busentasche,
Und rauschend öffnen sich die Spalten
Des Manuskripts, die viel enthalten.
Die Lippe sprüht, das Auge leuchtet,
Des Lauschers Bart wird angefeuchtet,
Denn nah und warm, wie sanftes Flöten,
Ertönt die Stimme des Poeten.—
"Vortrefflich!" ruft des Dichters Freund;
Dasselbe, was der Dichter meint;
Und, was er sicher weiss zu glauben,
Darf sich doch jeder wohl erlauben.
Wie schön, wenn dann, was er erdacht,
Empfunden und zurechtgemacht,
Wenn seines Geistes Kunstprodukt,
Im Morgenblättchen abgedruckt,
Vom treuen Kolporteur geleitet,
Sich durch die ganze Stadt verbreitet:
Das Wasser kocht.—In jedem Hause,
Hervor aus stiller Schlummerklause,
Eilt neu gestärkt und neu gereinigt,
Froh grüssend, weil aufs neu vereinigt,
Hausvater, Mutter, Jüngling, Mädchen
Zum Frühkaffee mit frischen Brötchen.
Sie alle bitten nach der Reihe
Das Morgenblatt sich aus, das neue,
Und jeder stutzt, und jeder spricht:
"Was für ein reizendes Gedicht!"
Durch die Lorgnetten, durch die Brillen,
Durch weit geöffnete Pupillen,
Erst in den Kopf, dann in das Herz,
Dann kreuz und quer und niederwärts
Fliesst's und durchweicht das ganze Wesen
Von allen denen, die es lesen.
Nun lebt in Leib und Seel der Leute,
Umschlossen vom Bezirk der Häute
Und andern warmen Kleidungsstücken,
Der Dichter fort, um zu beglücken,
Bis dass er schliesslich abgenützt,
Verklungen oder ausgeschwitzt.
Ein schönes Los! Indessen doch

Das allerschönste blüht ihm noch.
Denn Laura, seine süsse Qual,
Sein Himmelstraum, sein Ideal,
Die glühend ihm entgegenfliegt,
Besiegt in seinen Armen liegt,
Sie flüstert schmachtend inniglich:
"Göttlicher Mensch, ich schätze dich!
Und dass du so mein Herz gewannst,
Macht bloss, weil du so dichten kannst!"
Oh, wie beglückt ist doch ein Mann,
Wenn er Gedichte machen kann!

Zweites Kapitel

Ein guter Mensch, der Bählamm hiess
Und Schreiber war, durchschaute dies.
Nicht, dass es ihm an Nahrung fehlt.
Er hat ein Amt, er ist vermählt.
Und nicht bloss dieses ist und hat er;
Er ist bereits auch viermal Vater.
Und dennoch zwingt ihn tiefes Sehnen,
Sein Glück noch weiter auszudehnen.
Er möchte dichten, möchte singen,
Er möchte was zuwege bringen
Zur Freude sich und jedermannes;
Er fühlt, er muss, und also kann es.
Der Musse froh, im Paletot,
Verlässt er abends sein Büro.
Er eilt zum Park, um hier im Freien
Den holden Musen sich zu weihen.
Natürlich einer, der wie er
Gefühlvoll und gedankenschwer,
Mag sich an weihevollen Plätzen
Beim Dichten gern auch niedersetzen.
Doch schon besetzt ist jeder Platz
Von Leuten mit und ohne Schatz.
Da lenkt er doch die Schritte lieber
Zum Keller, der nicht fern, hinüber.
Er wählt sich unter vielen Bänken
Die Bank, die angenehm zum Denken.
Zwar erst verwirrte seinen Sinn
Das Nahgefühl der Kellnerin;
Doch führt ihn bald ein tiefer Zug
Zu höherem Gedankenflug.
Schon brennt der Kopf,
Schon glüht der Sitz,
Schon sprüht ein heller Geistesblitz;
Schon will der Griffel ihn notieren;
Allein es ist nicht auszuführen.
Der Hut als Dämpfer der Ekstase
Sinkt plötzlich tief auf Ohr und Nase.
Ein Freund, der viel Humor besass,
Macht sich von hinten diesen Spass.

Empört geht Bählamm fort nach Haus,
Der Freund trinkt seinen Masskrug aus.
Zu Hause hängt er Hut und Rock
An den gewohnten Kleiderstock
Und schmückt in seinem Kabinett
Mit Joppe sich und Samtbarett,
Die, wie die Dichtung Vers und Reim,
Den Dichter zieren, der daheim.
Scharfsinnend geht er hin und wider,
Bald schaut er auf, bald schaut er nieder.
Jetzt steht er still und ruft: "Aha!"
Denn schon ist ein Gedanke da.
Schnell tritt Frau Bählamm in die Tür,
Sie hält in Händen ein Papier.
Sie ruft: "Geliebter Balduin!
Du musst wohl mal den Beutel ziehn.
Siehst du die Rechnung breit und lang?
Der Schuster wartet auf dem Gang."
Besonders tief und voll Empörung
Fühlt man die pekuniäre Störung.
's ist abgetan.—Das Haupt gesenkt,
Steht er schon wieder da und denkt.
Begeistert blickt er in die Höh:
"Willkommen, herrliche Idee!"
Auf springt die Tür. An Bein und Arm
Geräuschvoll hängt der Kinderschwarm.—
"Ho!" ruft der Franzel. "Kinder hört!
Jetzt spielen wir mal Droschkenpferd!
Papa ist Gaul und Kutscher ich."
"Ja!" ruft die Gustel. "Fahre mich!"
"Ich," ruft der Fritz, "will hinten auf!
Hopp hopp, du altes Pferdchen, lauf!"
"Hü!" ruft der kleine Balduin.
"Will er nicht ziehn, so hau' ich ihn!"
Wer kann bei so bewandten Dingen
Ein Dichterwerk zustande bringen?—
Nun meint man freilich, sei die Nacht,
Um nachzudenken, wie gemacht.
Doch oh! Wie sehr kann man sich täuschen!
Es fehlt auch ihr nicht an Geräuschen.
Der Papa hat sich ausgestreckt,
Gewissenhaft sich zugedeckt;
Warm wird der Fuss, der Kopf denkt nach;
Da geht es Bäh!—vielleicht nur schwach.
Doch dieses Bäh erweckt ein zweites,
Dann bäh aus jeder Kehle schreit es.
Aus Mamas Mund ein scharfes Zischen,
Bedrohlich schwellend, tönt dazwischen,
Und Papas Bass, der grad noch fehlte,
Verstärkt zuletzt das Tongemälde.
Wie peinlich dies, ach, das ermisst
Nur der, der selber Vater ist.

Drittes Kapitel

Ein grosser Geist wie Bählamm seiner
Ist nicht so ratlos wie ein kleiner.
Er sieht, ihm mangelt bloss im Grunde
Der stille Ort, die stille Stunde,
Um das, was nötig ist zum Dichten,
Gemächlich einsam zu verrichten;
Und alsogleich spricht der Verstand:
Verlass die Stadt und geh aufs Land!
Wo Biederkeit noch nicht veraltet,
Wo Ruhe herrscht und Friede waltet!—
Leicht reisefertig ist zumeist
Ein Mensch, wenn er als Dichter reist.
Die kleine Tasche, buntgestickt,
Ist schnell gefüllt und zugedrückt.
Ein Hut von Stroh als Sommerzier,
Ein Dichterkragen von Papier,
Das himmelblaue Flattertuch,
Der Feldstuhl, das Notizenbuch,
Ein Bleistift Nr. 4 und endlich
Das Paraplü sind selbstverständlich.
Zum Bahnhof führt ihn die Familie.
Hier spricht er: "Lebe wohl, Cäcilie!
Ich bring' euch auch was Schönes mit!"
Dann schwingt er sich mit leichtem Schritt,
Damit er nicht die Zeit verpasse,
In die bekannte Dichterklasse.
Der Pfiff ertönt, die Glocke schlug.
Fort schlängelt sich der Bummelzug.
Vorüber schnell und schneller tanzen,
Durch Draht verknüpft zu einem Ganzen,
Die schwesterlich verwandten langen
Zahlreichen Telegrafenstangen.
Der Wald, die Wiesen, das Gefilde,
Als unstet wirbelnde Gebilde,
Sind lästig den verwirrten Sinnen.
Gern richtet sich der Blick nach innen.
Ein leichtes Rütteln, sanftes Schwanken
Erweckt und sammelt die Gedanken.
Manch Bild, was sich versteckt vielleicht,
Wird angeregt und aufgescheucht.
Bald fühlt auch Bählamm süssbeklommen
Die herrlichsten Gedanken kommen.—
Ein langer Pfiff.—Da hält er schon
Auf der ersehnten Bahnstation.—
Ein wohlgenährter Passagier
In Nägelschuhen wartet hier.
Er zwängt sich hastig ins Kupee.
Pardon!—Er tritt auf Bählamms Zeh.—
Des Lebens Freuden sind vergänglich;
Das Hühnerauge bleibt empfänglich.

Wie dies sich äussert, ist bekannt.
Krumm wird das Bein und krumm die Hand;
Die Augenlöcher schliessen sich,
Das linke ganz absonderlich;
Dagegen öffnet sich der Mund,
Als wollt er flöten, spitz und rund.
Zwar hilft so eine Angstgebärde
Nicht viel zur Lindrung der Beschwerde;
Doch ist sie nötig jederzeit
Zu des Beschauers Heiterkeit.

Viertes Kapitel

Wie lieb erscheint, wie freundlich winkt
Dem Dichter, der noch etwas hinkt,
Des Dörfleins anspruchloses Bild,
In schlichten Sommerstaub gehüllt.
Hier reitet Jörg, der kleine Knabe,
Auf seinem langen Hakenstabe,
Die Hahnenfeder auf der Mütze,
Kindlich naiv durch eine Pfütze.
Dort, mit dem kurzen Schmurgelpfeifchen,
Auf seinem trauten Düngerhäufchen
Steht Krischan Bopp und füllt die Luft
Mit seines Krautes Schmeichelduft.
Er blickt nach Rieke Mistelfink,
Ein Mädel sauber, stramm und flink.
Sie reinigt grad den Ziegenstall;
Und Friede waltet überall.
Sofort im ländlichen Logis
Geht Bählamm an die Poesie.
Er schwelgt im Sonnenuntergang,
Er lauscht dem Herdenglockenklang,
Und ahnungsfroh empfindet er's:
Glück auf! Jetzt kommt der erste Vers!
Klirrbatsch! Da liegt der Blumentopf.
Es zeigt sich ein gehörnter Kopf,
Das Maulwerk auf, die Augen zu,
Und blärrt posaunenhaft: "Ramuh!"
Erschüttert gehen Vers und Reime
Mitsamt dem Kunstwerk aus dem Leime.
Das tut die Macht der rauhen Töne.
Die Sängerin verlässt die Szene.

Fünftes Kapitel

Die Nacht verstrich. Der Morgen schummert.
Hat unser Bählamm süss geschlummert?
Kennst du das Tierlein leicht beschwingt,
Was, um die Nase schwebend, singt?
Kennst du die andern, die nicht fliegen,
Die leicht zu Fuss und schwer zu kriegen?
Betrachte Bählamm sein Gesicht.
Du weisst Bescheid, drum frage nicht.

Hier auf dem Dreifuss unter'm Flieder
Sitzt er bereits und dichtet wieder.
Der Knabe Jörg, in froher Laune,
Bemerkt ihn durch ein Loch im Zaune.
Er zieht die Nadel aus der Mütze,
Durchbohrt damit die Hakenspitze
Und hat verschmitzt auch schon begonnen
Den kleinen Scherz, den er ersonnen.
Der Dichter greift sich ins Genicke.
Mal wieder, denkt er, eine Mücke.
Er nimmt die Hand in Augenschein.
Es musste doch wohl keine sein.
Kaum hat er dies als wahr befunden,
So kommt ein Stich direkt von unten.
Um diese Gegend zu beschützen,
Kann man das Sacktuch auch benützen.
Insoweit wäre alles gut.
O weh! Wohin entschwebt der Hut?
"Ein leichtes Kräusellüftchen!" rief er,
Holt seinen Hut und setzt ihn tiefer.
Ganz arglos will er sich soeben
Zurück auf seinen Sitz begeben.
Doch die gewohnte Stütze mangelt.
Der Dreifuss wird hinweggeangelt.
Anstatt in den bequemen Sessel,
Setzt er sich in die scharfe Nessel.
Und hell durchblitzt ihn der Gedanke:
Es sitzt wer hinter dieser Planke!
Sehr gut in solchen Fällen ist
Bedachtsamkeit, gepaart mit List.
Verlockend und zugleich gespannt
Setzt er sich wieder vor die Wand.
Aha! Und jetzt wird zugefasst,
Und trefflich hat er's abgepasst;
Denn grad im Zentrum bohrte sich
Durch seine Hand der Nadelstich.
Natürlich macht ihn das nervos.
Der Jörg entfernt sich sorgenlos.

Sechstes Kapitel

In freier Luft, in frischem Grün,
Da wo die bunten Blümlein blühn,
In Wiesen, Wäldern, auf der Heide,
Entfernt von jedem Wohngebäude,
Auf rein botanischem Gebiet,
Weilt jeder gern, der voll Gemüt.
Hier legt sich Bählamm auf den Rücken
Und fühlt es tief und mit Entzücken,
Nachdem er Bein und Blick erhoben:
Gross ist die Welt, besonders oben!
Wie klein dagegen und beschränkt
Zeigt sich der Ohrwurm, wenn er denkt.

Engherzig schleicht er durch das Moos,
Beseelt von dem Gedanken bloss,
Wo's dunkel sie und eng und hohl,
Denn da nur ist ihm pudelwohl.
Grad wie er wünscht und sehr gelegen
Blinkt ihm des Dichters Ohr entgegen.
In diesen wohl erwärmten Räumen,
So denkt er, kann ich selig träumen.
Doch wenn er glaubt, dass ihm hienieden
Noch weitere Wirksamkeit beschieden,
So irrt er sich.—Ein Winkelzug
Von Bählamms Bein, der fest genug,
Zerstört die Form, d. h. so ziemlich,
Die diesem Wurme eigentümlich,
Und seinem Dasein als Subjekt
Ist vorderhand ein Ziel gesteckt.
Sogleich und mit gewisser Schnelle
Vertauscht der Dichter diese Stelle
Für eine andre, mehr erhöht,
Allwo ein Bäumlein winkend steht.
Ein Vöglein zwitschert in den Zweigen;
Dem Dichter wird so schwül und eigen.
Die Stirn umsäuseln laue Lüfte;
Es zuckt der Geist im Faberstifte.
Pitschkleck!—Ein Fleck. Ein jäher Schreck.—
Erleichtert fliegt das Vöglein weg.
Indessen auch der andre Sänger
Verweilt an diesem Ort nicht länger.
Den Himmel, der noch eben blau,
Umwölkt ein ahnungsvolles Grau.
Vor Regen schützt die Scheidewand
Des Schirmes, wenn er aufgespannt.
Verquer durch Regen und Gesträppe
Kommt Krischan mit der scharfen Hippe.
Vom Regen ist der Blick umflort,
Und richtig wird der Schirm durchbohrt.
Betrübend ist und wenig nütze
Das Paraplü mit einem Schlitze;
Doch ist noch Glück bei jedem Hieb,
Wobei der Kopf heroben blieb.
Auch braucht man, lässt der Regen nach,
Ja sowieso kein Regendach.
Und hier, begleitet von der Ziege,
Kommt Rieke über eine Stiege;
Und Bählamm, wie die Dichter sind,
Will diesem anmutsvollen Kind
Als Huldigung mit Scherz und Necken
Ein Sträusslein an den Busen stecken.
Ein Prall—ein Schall—dicht am Gesicht—
Verloren ist das Gleichgewicht.
So töricht ist der Mensch.—Er stutzt,
Schaut dämisch drein und ist verdutzt,

Anstatt sich erst mal solche Sachen
In aller Ruhe klarzumachen.—
Hier strotzt die Backe voller Saft;
Da hängt die Hand, gefüllt mit Kraft.
Die Kraft, infolge von Erregung,
Verwandelt sich in Schwungbewegung.
Bewegung, die in schnellem Blitze
Zur Backe eilt, wird hier zu Hitze.
Die Hitze aber, durch Entzündung
Der Nerven, brennt als Schmerzempfindung
Bis in den tiefsten Seelenkern,
Und dies Gefühl hat keiner gern.
Ohrfeige heisst man diese Handlung,
Der Forscher nennt es Kraftverwandlung.

Siebentes Kapitel

Der Mond. Dies Wort, so ahnungsreich,
So treffend, weil es rund und weich—
Wer wäre wohl so kaltbedächtig,
So herzlos, hart und niederträchtig,
Dass es ihm nicht, wenn er es liest,
Sanftschauernd durch die Seele fliesst?—
Das Dörflein ruht im Mondenschimmer,
Die Bauern schnarchen fest wie immer.
Es ruhn die Ochsen und die Stuten,
Und nur der Wächter muss noch tuten,
Weil ihn sein Amt dazu verpflichtet,
Der Dichter aber schwärmt und dichtet.
Was ist das drüben für ein Wink?
Ist das nicht Rieke Mistelfink?
Ja, wie es scheint, hat sie bereut
Die rücksichtslose Sprödigkeit,
Der Dichter fühlt sein Herz erweichen.
Er folgt dem liebevollen Zeichen.
Er drängt sich, nicht ganz ohne Qual,
In ein beschränktes Stallokal.
Mit einem Mäh, mit einem langen,
Sieht er sich unverhofft empfangen.
Doch nur ein kurzes Meck begleitet
Den Seitenstich, der Schmerz bereitet.
Ein Stoss grad in die Magengegend
Ist aber auch sehr schmerzerregend.
Dass selbst ein Korb in solcher Lage
Erwünscht erscheint, ist keine Frage.
Bedeckung findet sich gar leicht;
Es fragt sich nur, wie weit sie reicht.—
Und grade kommt die Rieke hier,
Der Krischan emsig hinter ihr;
Sie mit vergnügtem Mienenspiel,
Er mit dem langen Besenstiel.
Er schiebt ihn durch des Korbes Henkel
Und zwischen Bählamm seine Schenkel.

Nachdem er sicher eingesackt,
Wird er gelupft und aufgepackt.
Er strampelt sehr, denn schwer im Sinn
Liegt ihm die Frage: Ach, wohin?
Ein Wasser, mondbeglänzt und kühl,
Ist das erstrebte Reiseziel,
Und angelangt bei diesem Punkt,
Wird fleissig auf und ab getunkt;
Worauf, nachdem der Korb geleert,
Das Liebespaar nach Hause kehrt.

Achtes Kapitel

Es tut nicht gut, wenn man im Bad
Und nur die Füsse draussen hat.—
Auch Bählamm hat's nicht wohlgetan.
Es zog ihm in den Backenzahn.—
Das Zahnweh, subjektiv genommen,
Ist ohne Zweifel unwillkommen;
Doch hat's die gute Eigenschaft,
Dass sich dabei die Lebenskraft,
Die man nach aussen oft verschwendet,
Auf einen Punkt nach innen wendet
Und hier energisch konzentriert.
Kaum wird der erste Stich verspürt,
Kaum fühlt man das bekannte Bohren,
Das Rucken, Zucken und Rumoren—
Und aus ist's mit der Weltgeschichte,
Vergessen sind die Kursberichte,
Die Steuern und das Einmaleins.
Kurz, jede Form gewohnten Seins,
Die sonst real erscheint und wichtig,
Wird plötzlich wesenlos und nichtig.
Ja, selbst die alte Liebe rostet—
Man weiss nicht, was die Butter kostet—
Denn einzig in der engen Höhle
Des Backenzahnes weilt die Seele,
Und unter Toben und Gesaus
Reift der Entschluss: Er muss heraus!—
Noch eh' der neue Tag erschien,
War Bählamm auch soweit gediehn.
Er steht und läutet äusserst schnelle
An Doktor Schmurzel seiner Schelle.
Der Doktor wird von diesem Lärme
Emporgeschreckt aus seiner Wärme.
Indessen kränkt ihn das nicht weiter;
Ein Unglück stimmt ihn immer heiter!
Er ruft: "Seid mir gegrüsst, mein Lieber!
Lehnt Euch gefälligst hintenüber!
Gleich kennen wir den Fall genauer!"
(Der Finger schmeckt ein wenig sauer.)
"Nun stützt das Haupt auf diese Lehne
Und denkt derweil an alles Schöne!

Holupp!
Wie ist es? Habt Ihr nichts gespürt?"
"Ich glaub', es hat sich was gerührt!"
"Da dies der Fall, so gratulier' ich!
Die Sache ist nicht weiter schwierig!
Hol———upp!!!"
Vergebens ist die Kraftentfaltung;
Der Zahn verharrt in seiner Haltung.
"Hab's mir gedacht!" sprach Doktor Schmurzel.
"Das Hindernis liegt in der Wurzel.
Ich bitte bloss um drei Mark zehn!
Recht gute Nacht! Auf Wiedersehn!"

Neuntes Kapitel

Dem hohen lyrischen Poeten
Ist tiefer Schmerz gewiss vonnöten,
Doch schwerlich, ach, befördert je
Das ganz gewöhnliche Wehweh,
Wie Bählamm seines zum Exempel,
Den Dichter in den Ruhmestempel.
Die Backe schwillt.—Die Träne quillt.
Ein Tuch umrahmt das Jammerbild.
Verhasst ist ihm die Ländlichkeit
Mit Rieken ihrer Schändlichkeit,
Mit Doktor Schmurzels Chirurgie,
Mit Bäumen, Kräutern, Mensch und Vieh,
Und schmerzlich dringend mahnt die Backe:
Oh, kehre heim! Doch vorher packe!—
Gern möcht' er still von dannen scheiden,
Gern jede Ovation vermeiden,
Allein ihm bleibt bei seiner Fahrt
Ein Lebewohl nicht ganz erspart.
"Meckmeck!" So schallt's aus jener Ecke.
"Meckmeck!" ruft einer durch die Hecke.
"Meckmeck!" So schmettert's in der Näh,
Und Riekens Ziege macht "Mähä!"—
Da wundert sich wohl mancher sehr,
Wie's möglich sei, dass ein Malheur
So schleunige Verbreitung finde.
Der Weise schweigt. Er kennt die Gründe.—
Als Bählamm sein Kupee erreicht,
Wird ihm verhältnismässig leicht.
'ne Frau, 'n Kind und eine Tasche,
Worin die Gummistöpselflasche,
Sind unsers Reisenden Begleiter.
Der Säugling zeigt sich äusserst heiter.
Er strebt und webt mit Händ' und Füssen,
Er lässt sein Mäulchen überfliessen;
Er ist so süss, dass fast mit Recht
Ein Junggesell ihn küssen möcht.
O weh! Die Fröhlichkeit entweicht.
Wohlmeinend wird ihm dargereicht

Das Glas, woraus er sich ernährt;
Er lehnt es ab; er ist empört;
Und penetrant, gleich der Trompete,
Klagt er in Tönen seine Nöte.—
Die Mutter seufzt. Der Trank ist kalt.
Wohl uns! Hier hat man Aussenthalt.
"Ach!" bat sie. "Halten S' ihn mal eben.
Ich muss ihm etwas Warmes geben!"
Sie eilt hinaus ins Restaurant.
Der Zug hält drei Minuten lang.
"Einsteigen! Fertig!"—Pfüt!—Und los,
Mit seinem Säugling auf dem Schoss,
Mit dicker Backe, wehem Zahn,
Rollt er dahin per Eisenbahn
Der Heimat zu und trifft um neun
Präzise auf dem Bahnhof ein.—
Der Säugling, des Gesanges müde,
Ruht aus von seinem Klageliede,
Umhüllt mit einer warmen Windel
Auf Bählamms Arm als stilles Bündel.
Trotzdem hat Bählamm das Bestreben,
Ihn möglichst baldig abzugeben.
Der Schaffner, ohne Mitgefühl,
Bedankt sich höflich, aber kühl.
Desgleichen auch der Bahnverwalter,
Desgleichen auch der Mann am Schalter.
So muss er sich denn wohl bequemen,
Sein Bündel mit nach Haus zu nehmen.
"Der Papa kommt!" So rufen hier
Die frohen Kinder alle vier.
"Und," sprach die Mutter, "gebt mal acht!
Er hat was Schönes mitgebracht!"
Jedoch bei näherer Belehrung,
Wie wenig schätzt sie die Bescherung.
"Oh!" ruft sie. "Aber Balduin!"
Dann wird's ihr vor den Augen grün.
Zum Glück, in diesem Ungemach,
Kommt bald des Knaben Mutter nach.
Zwar ist die Flasche kalt wie nie,
Doch weil's pressiert, so nimmt er sie.—
Der Abschied war nicht sehr beschwerlich,
Was auch bei Bählamm sehr erklärlich;
Denn gerne gibt man aus der Hand
Den Säugling, der nicht stammverwandt.

Schluss

Sofort legt Bählamm sich zur Ruh.
Die Hand der Gattin deckt ihn zu.
Der Backe Schwulst verdünnert sich;
Sanft naht der Schlaf, der Schmerz entwich,
Und vor dem innern Seelenraum
Erscheint ein lockend süsser Traum.—

Ihm war, als ob, ihm war, als wie,
So unaussprechlich wohl wie nie.—
Hernieder durch das Dachgebälke,
Auf rosenrotem Duftgewölke,
Schwebt eine reizend wundersame
In Weiss gehüllte Flügeldame,
Die winkt und lächelt wie zum Zeichen,
Als sollt er ihr die Hände reichen;
Und selbstverständlich wunderbar
Erwächst auch ihm ein Flügelpaar;
Und selig will er sich erheben,
Um mit der Dame fortzuschweben.
Doch ach! Wie schaudert er zusammen!
Denn wie mit tausend Kilogrammen
Hängt es sich plötzlich an die Glieder,
Hemmt das entfaltete Gefieder
Und hindert, dass er weiterfliege.
Hohnlächelnd meckert eine Ziege.
Die himmlische Gestalt verschwindet,
Und nur das eine ist begründet,
Frau Bählamm ruft, als er erwacht:
"Heraus, mein Schatz! Es ist schon acht!"
Um neune wandelt Bählamm so
Wie ehedem auf sein Büro.—
So steht zum Schluss am rechten Platz
Der unumstösslich wahre Satz:
Die Schwierigkeit ist immer klein,
Man muss nur nicht verhindert sein.

Maler Klecksel

Erstes Kapitel

Das Reden tut dem Menschen gut;
Wenn man es nämlich selber tut;
Von Angstprodukten abgesehn,
Denn so etwas bekommt nicht schön.
Die Segelflotte der Gedanken,
Wie fröhlich fährt sie durch die Schranken
Der aufgesperrten Mundesschleuse
Bei gutem Winde auf die Reise
Und steuert auf des Schalles Wellen
Nach den bekannten offnen Stellen
Am Kopfe, in des Ohres Hafen
Der Menschen, die mitunter schlafen.
Vor allem der Politikus
Gönnt sich der Rede Vollgenuss;
Und wenn er von was sagt, so sei's,
Ist man auch sicher, dass er's weiss.

Doch andern, darin mehr zurück,
Fehlt dieser unfehlbare Blick.
Sie lockt das zartere Gemüt
Ins anmutreiche Kunstgebiet,
Wo grade, wenn man nichts versteht,
Der Schnabel um so leichter geht.
Fern liegt es mir, den Freund zu rügen,
Dem Tee zu kriegen ein Vergnügen
Und im Salon mit geistverwandten,
Ästhetisch durchgeglühten Tanten
Durch Reden bald und bald durch Lauschen
Die Seelen säuselnd auszutauschen.
Auch tadl' ich keinen, wenn's ihn gibt,
Der diese Seligkeit nicht liebt,
Der keinen Tee mag, selbst von Engeln,
Dem's da erst wohl, wo Menschen drängeln.
Ihn fährt die Droschke, zieht das Herz
Zu schönen Opern und Konzerts,
Die auch im Grund, was nicht zu leugnen,
Zum Zwiegespräch sich trefflich eignen.
Man sitzt gesellig unter vielen
So innig nah auf Polsterstühlen,
Man ist so voll humaner Wärme,
Doch ewig stört uns das Gelärme,
Das Grunzen, Blärren und Gegirre
Der musikalischen Geschirre,
Die eine Schar im schwarzen Fracke
Mit krummen Fingern, voller Backe,
Von Meister Zappelmann gehetzt,
Hartnäckig in Bewegung setzt.
So kommt die rechte Unterhaltung
Nur ungenügend zur Entfaltung.
Ich bin daher, statt des Gewinsels,
Mehr für die stille Welt des Pinsels;
Und, was auch einer sagen mag,
Genussreich ist der Nachmittag,
Den ich inmitten schöner Dinge
Im lieben Kunstverein verbringe;
Natürlich meistenteils mit Damen.
Hier ist das Reich der goldnen Rahmen,
Hier herrschen Schönheit und Geschmack,
Hier riecht es angenehm nach Lack;
Hier gibt die Wand sich keine Blösse,
Denn Prachtgemälde jeder Grösse
Bekleiden sie und warten ruhig,
Bis man sie würdigt, und das tu' ich.
Mit scharfem Blick, nach Kennerweise,
Seh' ich zunächst mal nach dem Preise,
Und bei genauerer Betrachtung
Steigt mit dem Preise auch die Achtung.
Ich blicke durch die hohle Hand,
Ich blinzle, nicke: "Ah, scharmant!

Das Kolorit, die Pinselführung,
Die Farbentöne, die Gruppierung,
Dies Lüster, diese Harmonie,
Ein Meisterwerk der Phantasie.
Ach, bitte, sehn Sie nur, Komtess!"
Und die Komtess, sich unterdes
Im duftigen Batiste schneuzend,
Erwidert schwärmerisch: "Oh, wie reizend!"
Und wahrlich! Preis und Dank gebührt
Der Kunst, die diese Welt verziert.
Der Architekt ist hochverehrlich
(Obschon die Kosten oft beschwerlich),
Weil er uns unsre Erdenkruste,
Die alte, rauhe und berusste,
Mit saubern Baulichkeiten schmückt,
Mit Türmen und Kasernen spickt.
Der Plastiker, der uns ergötzt,
Weil er die grossen Männer setzt,
Grauschwärzlich, grünlich oder weisslich,
Schon darum ist er löb- und preislich,
Dass jeder, der z. B. fremd,
Soeben erst vom Bahnhof kömmt,
In der ihm unbekannten Stadt
Gleich den bekannten Schiller hat.
Doch grössern Ruhm wird der verdienen,
Der Farben kauft und malt mit ihnen.
Wer weiss die Hallen und dergleichen
So welthistorisch zu bestreichen?
Alfresko und für ewig fast,
Wenn's mittlerweile nicht verblasst.
Wer liefert uns die Genresachen,
So rührend oder auch zum Lachen?
Wer schuf die grünen Landschaftsbilder,
Die Wirtshaus- und die Wappenschilder?
Wer hat die Reihe deiner Väter
Seit tausend Jahren oder später
So meisterlich in Öl gesetzt?
Wer wird vor allen hochgeschätzt?
Der Farbenkünstler! Und mit Grund!
Er macht uns diese Welt so bunt.
Darum, o Jüngling, fasse Mut;
Setz auf den hohen Künstlerhut
Und wirf dich auf die Malerei;
Vielleicht verdienst du was dabei!
Nach diesem ermunterungsvollen Vermerke
Fahren wir fort im löblichen Werke.

Zweites Kapitel

Nachdem die Welt so manches Jahr
Im alten Gleis gegangen war,
Erfuhr dieselbe unvermutet,
Dass, als der Wächter zwölf getutet,

Bei Klecksels, wohnhaft Nr. 3,
Ein Knäblein angekommen sei.—
Bald ist's im Kirchenbuch zu lesen;
Denn wer bislang nicht dagewesen,
Wer so als gänzlich Unbekannter,
Nunmehr als neuer Anverwandter
Ein glücklich Elternpaar besucht,
Wird flugs verzeichnet und gebucht.
Kritzkratz! Als kleiner Weltphilister
Steht Kuno Klecksel im Register.—
Früh zeigt sich seine Energie,
Indem er ausdermassen schrie;
Denn früh belehrt ihn die Erfahrung:
Sobald er schrie, bekam er Nahrung.
Dann lutscht er emsig und behende,
Bis dass die Flüssigkeit zu Ende.
Auch schien's ihm höchst verwundersam,
Wenn jemand mit der Lampe kam.
Er staunt, er glotzt, er schaut verquer,
Folgt der Erscheinung hin und her
Und weidet sich am Lichteffekt.
Man sieht bereits, was in ihm steckt.
Schnell nimmt er zu, wird stark und feist
An Leib nicht minder wie an Geist
Und zeigt bereits als kleiner Knabe
Des Zeichnens ausgeprägte Gabe.
Zunächst mit einem Schieferstiele
Macht er Gesichter und Profile;
Zwei Augen aber fehlen nie,
Denn die, das weiss er, haben sie.
Durch Übung wächst der Menschenkenner.
Bald macht er auch schon ganze Männer,
Und zeichnet fleissig, oft und gern
Sich einen wohlbeleibten Herrn.
Und nicht nur, wie er aussen war,
Nein, selbst das Innre stellt er dar.
Hier thront der Mann auf seinem Sitze
Und isst z. B. Hafergrütze.
Der Löffel führt sie in den Mund,
Sie rinnt und rieselt durch den Schlund,
Sie wird, indem sie weiterläuft,
Sichtbar im Bäuchlein angehäuft.—
So blickt man klar, wie selten nur,
Ins innre Walten der Natur.—
Doch ach! Wie bald wird uns verhunzt
Die schöne Zeit naiver Kunst;
Wie schnell vom elterlichen Stuhle
Setzt man uns auf die Bank der Schule!
Herr Bötel nannte sich der Lehrer,
Der, seinerseits kein Kunstverehrer,
Mehr auf das Praktische beschränkt,
Dem Kuno seine Studien lenkt.

Einst an dem schwarzen Tafelbrett
Malt Kuno Böteln sein Portrett.
Herr Bötel, der es nicht bestellt,
Auch nicht für sprechend ähnlich hält,
Schleicht sich herzu in Zornerregung;
Und unter heftiger Bewegung
Wird das Gemälde ausgeputzt.
Der Künstler wird als Schwamm benutzt.
Bei Kuno ruft dies Ungemach
Kein Dankgefühl im Busen wach.—
Ein Kirchenschlüssel, von Gestalt
Ehrwürdig, rostig, lang und alt,
Durch Kuno hinten angefeilt,
Wird fest mit Pulver vollgekeilt.
Zu diesem ist er im Besitze
Von einer oft erprobten Spritze;
Und da er einen Schlachter kennt,
Füllt er bei ihm sein Instrument.
Die Nacht ist schwarz, Herr Bötel liest.
Bums! hört er, dass man draussen schiesst.
Er denkt: Was mag da vor sich gehn?
Ich muss mal aus dem Fenster sehn.
Es zischt der Strahl, von Blut gerötet;
Herr Bötel ruft: "Ich bin getötet!"
Mit diesen Worten fällt er nieder
Und streckt die schreckgelähmten Glieder.
Frau Bötel war beim Tellerspülen;
Sie kommt und schreit mit Angstgefühlen:
"Ach, Bötel! Lebst du noch, so sprich!"
"Kann sein!" sprach er.—"Man wasche mich."
Bald zeigt sich, wie die Sache steht.
Herr Bötel lebt und ist komplett.
Er ruft entrüstet und betrübt:
"Das hat der Kuno ausgeübt!"—
Wenn wer sich wo als Lump erwiesen,
So bringt man in der Regel diesen
Zum Zweck moralischer Erhebung
In eine andere Umgebung.
Der Ort ist gut, die Lage neu,
Der alte Lump ist auch dabei.—
Nach diesem schon öfters erprobten Vermerke
Fahren wir fort im löblichen Werke.

Drittes Kapitel

Alsbald nach dieser Spritzaffäre
Kommt unser Kuno in die Lehre
Zum braven Malermeister Quast;
Ein Mann, der seine Kunst erfasst,
Ein Mann, der trefflich tapeziert
Und Ofennischen marmoriert
Und dem für künstlerische Zwecke
Erreichbar selbst die höchste Decke.

Der Kunstbetrieb hat seine Plagen.
Viel Töpfe muss der Kuno tragen.
Doch gerne trägt er einen Kasten
Mit Vesperbrot für sich und Quasten.
Es fiel ihm auf, dass jeder Hund
Bei diesem Kasten stillestund.
Ei! denkt er. Das ist ja famos!
Und macht den Deckel etwas los.
Ein Teckel, der den Deckel lupft,
Wird eingeklemmt und angetupft,
So dass er buntgefleckelt ward,
Fast wie ein junger Leopard.
Ein Windspiel, das des Weges läuft
Und naschen will, wird quer gestreift;
Es ist dem Zebra ziemlich ähnlich,
Nur schlanker, als wie dies gewöhnlich.
Ein kleiner Bulldogg, der als dritter
Der Meinung ist, dass Wurst nicht bitter,
Wird reizend grün und gelb kariert,
Wie's einem Inglischmän gebührt.
Ungern bemerkt dies Meister Quast.
Ihm ist die Narretei verhasst;
Er liebte keine Zeitverschwendung
Und falsche Farbestoffverwendung.
Er schwieg. Doch als die Stunde kam,
Wo man die Vespermahlzeit nahm,
Da sprach er mild und guten Mutes:
"Ein guter Mensch kriegt auch was Gutes!"
Er schnitt vom Brot sich einen Fladen.
Der Kuno wird nicht eingeladen.
Er greift zur Wurst. Er löst die Haut.
Der Kuno steht dabei und schaut.
Die Wurst verschwindet allgemach.
Der Kuno blickt ihr schmachtend nach.—
Die Wurst verschwand bis auf die Schläue.
Der Kuno weint der Tränen zweie.
Doch Meister Quast reibt frohbedächtig
Den Leib und spricht: "Das schmeckte prächtig!
Heut abend lass' ich nichts mehr kochen!"—
Er hält getreu, was er versprochen;
Geht ein durch seine Kammerpforte
Und spricht gemütlich noch die Worte:
"Sei mir willkommen, süsser Schlaf!
Ich bin zufrieden, weil ich brav!"
Der Kuno denkt noch nicht zu ruhn.
Er hat was Wichtiges zu tun.
Zunächst vor jeder andern Tat
Legt er sein Ränzel sich parat.
Sodann erbaut er auf der Diele
Aus Töpfen, Gläsern und Gestühle
Ein Werk im Stil der Pyramiden
Zum Denkmal, dass er abgeschieden;

Apart jedoch von der Verwirrnis
Stellt er den Topf, gefüllt mit Firnis;
Zuletzt ergreift er, wie zur Wehre,
Die mächtige Tapetenschere.
Quasts Deckbett ist nach altem Brauch
Ein stramm gestopfter Federschlauch.
Mit einem langen leisen Schnitte
Schlitzt es der Kuno in der Mitte.
Rasch leert er jetzt den Firnistopf
Auf Quastens ahnungslosen Kopf.
Quast fährt empor voll Schreck und Staunen,
Greift, schlägt und tobt und wird voll Daunen.
Er springt hinaus in grosser Hast,
Von Ansehn wie ein Vogel fast,
Und stösst mit schrecklichem Rumbum
Die neuste Pyramide um.
Froh schlägt das Herz im Reisekittel,
Vorausgesetzt, man hat die Mittel.
Nach diesem ahnungsvollen Vermerke
Fahren wir fort im löblichen Werke.

Viertes Kapitel

Recht gern empfängt die Musenstadt
Den Fremdling, welcher etwas hat.—
Kuno ist da. Gedankentief
Verfasst derselbe diesen Brief:
"Geehrter Herr Vater! Bei Meister Quast
Hat es mir leider nicht recht gepasst.
Seit vorigen Freitag bin ich allhie,
Um zu besuchen die Akademie.
Geld hab' ich bereits schon gar nicht mehr.
Um solches, o Vater, ersuch' ich Euch sehr.
Logieren tu' ich auf hartem Gestrüppe.
Euer Sohn, das Hunger- und Angstgerippe."
Der Vater, kratzend hinterm Ohr,
Sucht hundert Gulden bang hervor.
Eindringlich warnend vor Verschwendung,
Macht er dem Sohn die schwere Sendung.
Jetzt hat der Kuno Geld in Masse.
Stolz geht er in die Zeichenklasse.
Von allen Schülern, die da sitzen,
Kann keiner so den Bleistift spitzen.
Auch sind nur wenige dazwischen,
Die so wie er mit Gummi wischen.
Und im Schraffieren, was das Schwerste,
Da wird er unbedingt der erste.
Jedoch zu Nacht, wenn er sich setzte,
Beim Schimmelwirt, blieb er der letzte.
Mit Leichtigkeit geniesst er hier
So seine ein, zwei, drei Glas Bier.
Natürlich, da er so vorzüglich,

Sitzt er zu Ostern schon vergnüglich
Im herrlichen Antikensaale,
Dem Sammelplatz der Ideale.
Der Alten ewig junge Götter—
Wenn mancher auch in Wind und Wetter
Und sonst durch allerlei Verdriess
Kopf, Arm und Bein im Stiche liess—
Ergötzen Kuno unbeschreiblich,
Besonders, wenn die Götter weiblich.
Er ahmt sie nach in schwarzer Kreide.
Doch kann er sich auch diese Freude
An schönen Sommernachmittagen,
Wenn's grade nötig, mal versagen
Und eilt mit brennender Havanna
Zum Schimmelwirt zu der Susanna.
Hier in des Gartens Lustrevier
Trinkt er so zwei, drei, vier Glas Bier.
Daher man denn auch bald erfuhr,
Der Klecksel malt nach der Natur.
Am linken Daumen die Palette,
Steht er schon da vor seinem Brette
Und malt die alte Runzeltante,
Dass sie fast jeder wiederkannte.
Doch eh' die Abendglocke klang,
Macht er den hergebrachten Gang
Zur Susel und vertilgt bei ihr
So seine vier, fünf, sechs Glas Bier.
Da eines Abends sagt ganz plötzlich,
Grad als der Kuno recht ergötzlich,
Dies sonst so nette Frauenzimmer:
"Jetzt zahlen, oder Bier gibt's nimmer!"
Ach! Reines Glück geniesst doch nie,
Wer zahlen soll und weiss nicht wie!
Nach diesem mit Wehmut gemachten Vermerke
Fahren wir fort im löblichen Werke.

Fünftes Kapitel

Ganz arglos auf dem Schillerplatzel
Geht Kunos Freund, der Herr v. Gnatzel,
Ein netter Herr, ein lieber Mann.
Der Kuno pumpt ihn freudig an.
Freund Gnatzels Züge werden schmerzlich.
Er spricht gerührt: "Bedaure herzlich!
Recht dumm! Vergass mein Portemonnaie!
Geduld bis morgen früh! Adieu!"
Von nun an ist es sonderbar,
Wie Gnatzel schwer zu treffen war.
Oft naht sich dieser Freund von ferne,
Und Kuno grüsste ihn so gerne;
Doch kommt er nie zu seinem Zwecke.
Freund Gnatzel biegt um eine Ecke.

Oft sucht ihn Kuno zu beschleichen,
Um ihn von hinten zu erreichen;
Freund Gnatzel merkt es aber richtig,
Grad so, als ob er hintersichtig,
Schlüpft in die Droschke mit Geschick
Und lässt den Kuno weit zurück.
Der Kuno blickt in eine Schenke.
Sieh da! Freund Gnatzel beim Getränke!
Doch schnell entschlüpft er dem Lokal
Durchs Hinterpförtchen wie ein Aal.—
Der Kuno sieht in dieser Not
Nur noch ein einzig Rettungsboot.
Er hat, von Schöpfungsdrang erfüllt,
Verfertigt ein historisch Bild:
Wie Bertold Schwarz vor zwei Sekunden
Des Pulvers grosse Kraft erfunden.
Dies Bildnis soll der Retter sein.
Er bringt es auf den Kunstverein.
Leicht kommt man an das Bildermalen,
Doch schwer an Leute, die's bezahlen.
Statt ihrer ist, als ein Ersatz,
Der Kritikus sofort am Platz.
Nach diesem—ach leider!—so wahren Vermerke
Fahren wir fort im löblichen Werke.

Sechstes Kapitel

In selber Stadt ernährte sich
Ganz gut ein Dr. Hinterstich
Durch Kunstberichte von Bedeutung
In der von ihm besorgten Zeitung,
Was manchem das Geschäft verdirbt,
Der mit der Kunst sein Brot erwirbt.
Dies Blatt hat Klecksel mit Behagen
Von jeher eifrig aufgeschlagen.
Auch heute hält er's in der Hand
Und ist auf den Erfolg gespannt.
Wie düster wird sein Blick umnebelt!
Wie hat ihn Hinterstich vermöbelt!
Sogleich in eigener Person
Fort stürmt er auf die Redaktion.
Des Autors Physiognomie
Bedroht er mit dem Paraplü.
Der Kritikus, in Zornekstase,
Spiesst mit der Feder Kunos Nase;
Ein Stich, der um so mehr verletzt,
Weil auch zugleich die Tinte ätzt.
Stracks wird der Regenschirm zur Lanze.
Flugs dient der Tisch als eine Schanze.
Vergeblich ist ein hoher Stoss;
Auch bleibt ein tiefer wirkungslos.
Jetzt greift der Kritikus voll Hass

Als Wurfgeschoss zum Tintenfass.
Jedoch der Schaden bleibt gering,
Weil ihn das Paraplü empfing.
Der Kritikus braucht eine Finte.
Er zieht den Kuno durch die Tinte.
Der Tisch fällt um. Höchst penetrant
Wirkt auf das Augenlicht der Sand.
Indessen zieht der Kuno aber
Den Bleistift Numro 5 von Faber;
Und Hinterstich, der sehr rumort,
Wird mehrfach peinlich angebohrt.
Der Kuno, seines Sieges froh,
Verlässt das Redaktionsbüro.
Ein rechter Maler, klug und fleissig,
Trägt stets 'n spitzen Bleistift bei sich.
Nach diesem beherzigenswerten Vermerke
Fahren wir fort im löblichen Werke.

Siebentes Kapitel

So ist denn also, wie das vorige
Ereignis lehrt, die Welthistorie
Wohl nicht das richtige Gebiet,
Wo Kunos Ruhm und Nutzen blüht.
Vielleicht bei näherer Bekanntschaft
Schuf die Natur ihn für die Landschaft,
Die jedem, der dazu geneigt,
Viel nette Aussichtspunkte zeigt.
Zum Beispiel dieses Felsenstück
Gewährt ihm einen weiten Blick.
Wer kommt denn über jenen Bach?
Das ist das Fräulein von der Ach,
Vermögend zwar, doch etwas ältlich,
Halb geistlich schon und halb noch weltlich,
Lustwandelt sie mit Seelenruh
Und ihrem Spitz dem Kloster zu.
Zwei Hunde kommen angehüpft,
Die man durch eine Schnur verknüpft.
Der Spitz, gar ängstlich, retiriert,
Das gute Fräulein wird umschnürt.
Der Spitz enteilt, die Hunde nach;
Mit ihnen Fräulein von der Ach.
Der Kuno springt von seinem Steine.
Ein Messerschnitt zertrennt die Leine.
Der Kuno zeigt sich höchst galant.
Das Fräulein fragt, eh' sie verschwand:
"Darf man Ihr Atelier nicht sehn?"—
"Holzgasse 5."—"Ich danke schön!"—
Vielleicht dass diese gute Tat
Recht angenehme Folgen hat!
Nach diesem hoffnungsvollen Vermerke
Fahren wir fort im löblichen Werke.

Achtes Kapitel

Sie blieb nicht aus. Sie kam zu ihm.
Hold lächelnd sprach sic und intim:
"Mein werter Freund! Seit längst erfüllt
Mich schon der Wunsch, ein lieblich Bild
Zu stiften in die Burgkapelle,
Was ich bei Ihnen nun bestelle.
So legendarisch irgendwie.
Vorläufig dies für Ihre Müh!"
Mit sanftem Druck legt sie in seine
Entzückte Hand zwei grössre Scheine.—
Der Kuno, fremd in der Legende,
Verwendet sich zu diesem Ende
An einen grundgelehrten Greis,
Der folgende Geschichte weiss:

Der kühne Ritter und der greuliche Lindwurm

Es kroch der alte Drache
Aus seinem Felsgemache
Mit grausigem Randal.
All' Jahr ein Mägdlein wollt' er,
Sonst grollt' er und radollt' er,
Frass alles ratzekahl.
Was kommt da aus dem Tore
In schwarzem Trauerflore
Für eine Prozession?
Die Königstochter Irme
Bringt man dem Lindgewürme,
Das Scheusal wartet schon.
Hurra! Wohl aus dem Holze
Ein Ritter keck und stolze
Sprengt her wie Wettersturm.
Er sticht dem Untier schnelle
Durch seine harte Pelle;
Tot liegt und schlapp der Wurm.
Da sprach der König freudig:
"Wohlan, Herr Ritter schneidig,
Setzt Euch bei uns zur Ruh.
Ich geb' Euch sporenstreiches
Die Hälfte meines Reiches,
Mein Töchterlein dazu!"
"Mau, mau!" So rief erschrocken
Mit aufgesträubten Locken
Der Ritter stolz und keck.
"Ich hatte schon mal eine,
Die sitzt mir noch im Beine!
Ade!" Und ritt ums Eck.
O altes blaues Wunder!
Da han wir doch jetzunder
Mehr Herz im Kamisol.

Wir ziehen unsre Kappe
Vor solchem Schwiegerpappe
Und sprechen: "Ei jawohl!"
Der Stoff ist Kuno sehr willkommen,
Die zweite Hälfte ausgenommen,
Um ihn mit Kohle zu skizzieren
Und dann in Farben auszuführen.—
Gar oft erfreut das Fräulein sich
An Kunos kühnem Kohlenstrich,
Obgleich ihr eigentlich nicht klar,
Wie auch dem Künstler, was es war.
Wie's scheint, will ihm vor allen Dingen
Das Bild der Jungfrau nicht gelingen.
"Nur schwach, Natur, wirst du verstanden,"
Seufzt er, "wenn kein Modell vorhanden!"
"Kann ich nicht dienen?" lispelt sie.
"Schön!" rief er. "Mittwoch in der Früh!"
Als nun die Abendglocke schlug,
Zieht ihn des Herzens tiefer Zug
Zum Schimmelwirt wie ehedem;
Und Susel macht sich angenehm.
Denn alte Treu, sofern es nur
Rentabel ist kommt gern retour.
Ja, dies Verhältnis hier gedieh
Zu ungeahnter Harmonie.—
Mit zween Herrn ist schlecht zu kramen;
Noch schlechter, fürcht' ich, mit zwo Damen.
Nach diesem mit Zittern gemachten Vermerke
Fahren wir fort im löblichen Werke.

Neuntes Kapitel

Es war im schönen Karneval,
Wo, wie auch sonst und überall,
Der Mensch mit ungemeiner List
Zu scheinen sucht, was er nicht ist.
Dem Kuno scheint zu diesem Feste
Ein ritterlich Gewand das beste.
Schön Suschen aber schwebt dahin
Als holdnaive Schäferin.
Schon schwingt das Bein, das graziöse,
Sich nach harmonischem Getöse
Bei staubverklärtem Lichterglanze
Im angenehmsten Wirbeltanze.—
Doch ach! Die schöne Nacht verrinnt,
Der Morgen kommt; kühl weht der Wind.
Zwei Menschen wandeln durch den Schnee
Vereint in Kunos Atelier.
Und hier besiegeln diese zwei
Sich dauerhafte Lieb und Treu.—
Hoch ist der Liebe süsser Traum
Erhaben über Zeit und Raum.—
Der Kuno, auch davon betäubt,

Vergass, dass man heut Mittwoch schreibt.
Es rauscht etwas im Vorgemach.
O weh! Das Fräulcin von der Ach!
"Herzallerliebster Schatz, allons!
Verbirg dich hinter dem Karton!"
"Willkommen, schönste Gönnerin!
Hier, bitte, treten Sie mal hin!"
Begonnen wird das Konterfei.
Der Spitz schaut hinter die Stafflei.
Der Künstler macht sein Sach genau.
Der Spitz, bedenklich, macht wau, wau!
Entrüstet aber wird der Spitz
Infolge eines Seitentrits.
Die Haare sträuben sich dem Spitze.
Die Staffel schwankt. Aus rutscht die Stütze;
Und mit Gerassel wird enthüllt
Der Schäferin verschämtes Bild.
Nach dieser Krisis, wie ich bemerke,
Geht es zu End' mit dem löblichen Werke.

Schluss

Hartnäckig weiter fliesst die Zeit;
Die Zukunft wird Vergangenheit.
Von einem grossen Reservoir
Ins andre rieselt Jahr um Jahr;
Und aus den Fluten taucht empor
Der Menschen bunt gemischtes Korps.
Sie plätschern, traurig oder munter,
'n bissel 'rum, dann gehens unter
Und werden, ziemlich abgekühlt,
Für längre Zeit hinweggespült.—
Wie sorglich blickt das Aug' umher!
Wie freut man sich, wenn der und der,
Noch nicht versunken oder matt,
Den Kopf vergnügt heroben hat.
Der alte Schimmelwirt ist tot.
Ein neuer trägt das Reichskleinod.
Derselbe hat, wie seine Pflicht,
Dies Inserat veröffentlicht:
Kund sei es dem Hohen Publiko,
Dass meine Frau Suse, des bin ich froh,
Hinwiederum eines Knäbleins genesen.
Als welches bis dato das fünfte gewesen.
Viel Gutes bringet der Jahreswechsel
Dem Schimmelwirte—Kuno Klecksel.—
So tut die vielgeschmähte Zeit
Doch mancherlei, was uns erfreut;
Und, was das beste, sie vereinigt
Selbst Leute, die sich einst gepeinigt.—
Das Fräulein freilich, mit erboster
Entsagung, ging vorlängst ins Kloster.
Doch Bötel, wenn er in den Ferien

Die Stadt besucht und Angehörigen,
Und Meister Quast, der allemal
Von hier entnimmt sein Material,
Wie auch der vielgewandte Gnatzel
(Jetzt schon bedeckt mit einer Atzel),
Ja, selbst der Dr. Hinterstich,
Dem alter Groll nicht hinderlich,
Sie alle trinken unbeirrt
Ihr Abendbier beim Schimmelwirt.—
Oft sprach dann Bötel mit Behagen:
"Herr Schimmelwirt! Ich kann wohl sagen:
Wär' nicht die rechte Bildung da,
Wo wären wir? Jajajaja!"
Nach diesem von Bötel gemachten Vermerk
Schliessen wir freudig das löbliche Werk.

SHORT GRAPHICS AND VIGNETTES

From Diddle-Boom!

Idiosynkrasie

Der Tag ist grau. Die Wolken ziehn.
Es saust die alte Mühle.
Ich schlendre durch das feuchte Grün
Und denke an meine Gefühle.
Die Sache ist mir nicht genehm.
Ich ärgre mich fast darüber.
Der Müller ist gut; trotz alledem
Ist mir die Müllerin lieber.

Die Kirmes

Fest schlief das gute Elternpaar
Am Abend, als die Kirmes war.
Der Vater hält nach seiner Art
Des Hauses Schlüssel wohl verwahrt;
Indem er denkt: Auf die Manier
Bleibt mein Herminchen sicher hier!—
Ach lieber Gott, jaja, so ist es!
Nicht wahr, ihr guten Mädchen wisst es:
Kaum hat man was, was einen freut,
So macht der Alte Schwierigkeit!
Hermine seufzt.—

Dann denkt sie! Na!
Es ist ja noch das Fenster da!
Durch dieses eilt sie still behende
Hierauf hinab am Weingelände
Und dann durchs Tor voll frohen Drangs
Im Rosakleid mit drei Volants.—
Grad rüsten sich zum neuen Reigen
Rumbumbass, Tutehorn und Geigen.
Tihumtata humtata humtata!
Zupptrudiritirallala rallalala!
's ist doch ein himmlisches Vergnügen,
Sein rundes Mädel herzukriegen
Und rundherum und auf und nieder
Im schönen Wechselspiel der Glieder
Die ahnungsvolle Kunst zu üben,
Die alle schätzen, welche lieben.—
Hermine tanzt wie eine Sylphe,
Ihr Tänzer ist der Forstgehülfe.—
Auch dieses Paar ist flink und niedlich,
Der Herr benimmt sich recht gemütlich.
Hier sieht man zierliche Bewegung,
Doch ohne tiefre Herzensregung.
Hingegen diese, voll Empfindung,
Erstreben herzliche Verbindung.
Und da der Hans, der gute Junge,
Hat seine Grete sanft im Schwunge;
Und inniglich, in süssem Drange,
Schmiegt sich die Wange an die Wange.
Und dann mit fröhlichem Juchhe,
Gar sehr geschickt, macht er Schassee.
Der blöde Konrad steht von fern
Und hat die Sache doch recht gern.
Der Konrad schaut genau hinüber.
Die Sache wird ihm immer lieber.
Der Konrad leert sein fünftes Glas,
Die Schüchternheit verringert das.
Flugs engagiert er die bewusste
Von ihm so hochverehrte Guste.
Die Seele schwillt, der Mut wird gross,
Heidi! Da saust der Konrad los.
Zu grosse Hast macht ungeschickt.—
Hans kommt mit Konrad in Konflikt.
Und—hulterpulter rumbumbum!—
Stösst man die Musikanten um.
Am meisten litt das Tongeräte.—
Und damit ist die schöne Fete
Zu jedermanns Bedauern aus.—
Hermine eilt zum Elternhaus
Und denkt, wie sie herabgeklommen,
Auch wieder so hinaufzukommen.
O weh! Da bricht ein Stab der Reben.
Nun fängt Hermine an zu schweben.

Die Luft weht kühl. Der Morgen naht.—
Die gute Mutter, welche grad,
Das Waschgeschirr in allen Ehren
Gewohntermassen auszuleeren,
Das Fenster öffnet, sieht mit Beben
Hermine an der Stange schweben.
Und auch die Jugend, die sich sammelt,
Ist froh, dass da wer bimmelbammelt.
Doch sieh, da zeigt der Vater sich
Und schneidet weg, was hinderlich.
Und mit gedämpftem Schmerzenshauch
Senkt sie sich in den Rosenstrauch.

Romanze

Es war einmal ein Schneiderlein
Mit Nadel und mit Scher,
Der liebt ein Mädel hübsch und fein
So sehr, ach Gott, so sehr.
Er kam zu ihr in später Stund
Und redt so hin und her,
Ob er ihr etwa helfen kunnt
Mit Nadel und mit Scher.
Da dreht das Mädel sich herum!
"Oje, ojemine!
Deine Nadel ist ja schon ganz krumm,
Geh, geh, mein Schneider, geh!"
Der Schneider schrie: "Du falsche Dirn,
Hätt' ich dich nie gekannt!"
Er kauft sich einen Faden Zwirn
Und hängt sich an die Wand.

Der fliegende Frosch

Wenn Einer, der mit Mühe kaum
Gekrochen ist auf einen Baum,
Schon meint, dass er ein Vogel wär,
So irrt sich der.

Sorglos

Selbst mancher Weise
Besieht ein leeres Denkgehäuse
Mit Furcht und Bangen.
Der Rabe ist ganz unbefangen.

SELECTED POETRY

Wer möchte diesen Erdenball
Noch fernerhin betreten,
Wenn wir Bewohner überall
Die Wahrheit sagen täten.

Ihr hiesset uns, wir hiessen euch
Spitzbuben und Halunken,
Wir sagten uns fatales Zeug
Noch eh wir uns betrunken.

Und überall im weiten Land,
Als langbewährtes Mittel,
Entsprosste aus der Menschenhand
Der treue Knotenknittel.

Da lob ich mir die Höflichkeit,
Das zierliche Betrügen.
Du weisst Bescheid, ich weiss Bescheid;
Und allen macht's Vergnügen.

Die Liebe war nicht geringe.
Sie wurden ordentlich blass;
Sie sagten sich tausend Dinge
Und wussten immer noch was.

Sie mussten sich lange quälen,
Doch schliesslich kam's dazu,
Dass sie sich konnten vermählen.
Jetzt haben die Seelen Ruh.

Bei eines Strumpfes Bereitung
Sitzt sie im Morgenhabit;
Er liest in der Kölnischen Zeitung
Und teilt ihr das Nötige mit.

Ach, ich fühl es! Keine Tugend
Ist so recht nach meinem Sinn;
Stets befind ich mich am wohlsten,
Wenn ich damit fertig bin.

Dahingegen so ein Laster,
Ja, das macht mir viel Pläsier;
Und ich hab die hübschen Sachen
Lieber vor als hinter mir.

Sie war ein Blümlein hübsch und fein,
Hell aufgeblüht im Sonnenschein.
Er war ein junger Schmetterling
Der selig an der Blume hing.
Oft kam ein Bienlein mit Gebrumm
Und nascht und säuselt da herum.
Oft kroch ein Käfer kribbelkrab
Am hübschen Blümlein auf und ab.
Ach Gott, wie das dem Schmetterling
So schmerzlich durch die Seele ging.
Doch was am meisten ihn entsetzt,
Das Allerschlimmste kam zuletzt.
Ein alter Esel frass die ganze
Von ihm so heiss geliebte Pflanze.

Lebenslauf

Mein Lebenslauf ist bald erzählt.
In stiller Ewigkeit verloren
Schlief ich, und nichts hat mir gefehlt,
Bis dass ich sichtbar ward geboren.
Was aber nun?—Auf schwachen Krücken,
Ein leichtes Bündel auf dem Rücken,
Bin ich getrost dahingeholpert,
Mitunter grad, mitunter krumm,
Und schliesslich musst ich mich verschnaufen.
Bedenklich rieb ich meine Glatze
Und sah mich in der Gegend um.
O weh! Ich war im Kreis gelaufen,
Stand wiederum am alten Platze,
Und vor mir dehnt' sich lang und breit,
Wie ehedem, die Ewigkeit.

Die Selbstkritik

Die Selbstkritik hat viel für sich.
Gesetzt den Fall, ich tadle mich;
So hab ich erstens den Gewinn,
Dass ich so schön bescheiden bin.
Zum zweiten sagen sich die Leut':
Der Mann ist lauter Redlichkeit.
Zum dritten schnapp ich diesen Bissen
Vorweg den andren Kritiküssen.
Zum vierten hoff ich ausserdem
Auf Widerspruch, der mir genehm.
So kommt es denn zuletzt heraus,
Dass ich ein ganz famoses Haus.

Select Bibliography

Asterisks mark items found especially useful by the editor.

EDITIONS OF WORKS BY BUSCH

Sämtliche Werke. 8 vols. Edited by Otto Nöldeke. Munich: Braun & Schneider, 1943; 2nd ed., 1949; 3rd, abridged ed., 1955.

* *Werke: Historisch-kritische Gesamtausgabe.* 4 vols. Edited by Friedrich Bohne. Hamburg: Standard Verlag, 1959; Zurich: Stauffacher, 1960; Wiesbaden: Vollmer-Verlag, as *Gesamtausgabe in vier Bänden,* 1968, 1974.

Sämtliche Werke und eine Auswahl der Skizzen und Gemälde. 2 vols. Edited by Rolf Hochhuth. Gütersloh: Bertelsmann, 1959–70.

* *Schöne Studienausgabe.* 7 vols. Edited by Friedrich Bohne. Zurich: Diogenes Verlag, 1974 (Diogenes Taschenbücher 60/I–VII).

LETTERS BY BUSCH

Ist mir mein Leben geträumet? Briefe eines Einsiedlers. Compiled and edited by Otto Nöldeke. Leipzig: Gustav Weise, 1935.

* *Sämtliche Briefe.* Kommentierte Ausgabe. 12 vols. Edited by Friedrich Bohne, with Paul Meskemper and Ingrid Haberland. Vol. 1: 1841–92, vol. 2: 1893–1908. Hannover: Wilhelm-Busch-Gesellschaft, Richard Beek, 1968–69.

BIBLIOGRAPHIES

* Vanselow, Albert. *Die Erstdrucke und Erstausgaben der Werke von Wilhelm Busch: Ein bibliographisches Verzeichnis.* Leipzig: Adolf Weigel, 1913.

Abich, Richard. *Wilhelm-Busch-Bibliographie.* Aus der Sammlung des W.-B.-Archivs. *Passim* in *Mitteilungen d. W.-B.-Gesellschaft,* 1933 ff.

Jahrbücher der Wilhelm-Busch-Gesellschaft e.V., Hannover: Wilhelm-Busch-Gesellschaft, *passim.*

* Pape, Walter. *Wilhelm Busch.* Sammlung Metzler, M 163. Stuttgart: J. B. Metzler, 1977. Also listed below under biographies.

BIOGRAPHIES

Nöldeke, Hermann, Adolf, and Otto. *Wilhelm Busch.* Munich: Lothar Joachim Verlag, 1909.

Dangers, Robert. *Wilhelm Busch: Sein Leben und sein Werk.* Berlin-Grunewald: Verlagsanstalt Hermann Klemm AG, 1930.

Nöldeke, Otto. *Chronik von Wilhelm Buschs Leben.* In *Sämtliche Werke,* vol. VIII, pp. 207 ff.

* Bohne, Friedrich. *Wilhelm Busch: Leben, Werk, Schicksal.* Zurich/Stuttgart: Fretz & Wasmuth Verlag, 1958.

* Kraus, Joseph. *Wilhelm Busch in Selbstzeugnissen und Bilddokumenten.* Rowohlts Monographien. Reinbek bei Hamburg: Rowohlt, 1970.

* Pape, Walter. *Wilhelm Busch.* Sammlung Metzler, M 163 (Realien zur Literatur, Abt. D: Literaturgeschichte). Stuttgart: J. B. Metzlersche Verlagsbuchhandlung, 1977. Also listed above under bibliographies.

CRITICISM AND SPECIAL TOPICS

Volkmann, Otto Felix. *Wilhelm Busch der Poet: Seine Motive und seine Quellen.* Leipzig: H. Haessel Verlag, 1910.

Winther, Fritz. "Wilhelm Busch als Dichter, Künstler, Psychologe und Philosoph." *University of California Publications in Modern Philology* 2, no. 1 (1910): 1–79.

Bohne, Friedrich. *Wilhelm Busch und der Geist seiner Zeit.* Ph.D. dissertation, Leipzig, 1931. Hannover: Wilhelm-Busch-Gesellschaft, 1931.

Dorner, Alexander. *Wilhelm Busch, der Maler und Zeichner.* Guide to the WB Centenary Exhibition at the Provinzial-Museum, Hannover, April–July, 1932. Hannover: Wilhelm-Busch-Gesellschaft, 1932.

* Glockner, Hermann. *Wilhelm Busch, der Mensch, der Zeichner, der Humorist.* Tübingen: J. C. B. Mohr, 1932.

* Kramer, Wolfgang. "Busch, Chodowiecki, Daumier." *Zeitschrift für Bücherfreunde* 36 (1932): 173–76.

* ———. "Das graphische Werk von Wilhelm Busch." Ph.D. dissertation, Frankfurt, 1933.

Cremer, Hans. *Die Bildergeschichten Wilhelm Buschs.* Ph.D. dissertation, Munich, 1937. Düsseldorf: G. H. Nolte Verlag, 1937.

Dangers, Robert. *Wilhelm Busch, der Künstler.* Commissioned by the Wilhelm-Busch-Gesellschaft, Hannover. Berlin: Rembrandt-Verlag, 1937.

Nöldeke, Otto. *Wilhelm Busch: Ernstes und Heiteres.* Berlin: Verlagsanstalt Hermann Klemm, 1938.

Stuttmann, Ferdinand. *Der Maler Wilhelm Busch.* In *Sämtliche Werke*, vol. 7 (Nöldeke ed.). 21 color plates.

* Novotny, Fritz. *Wilhelm Busch als Zeichner und Maler.* Vienna: Anton Schroll & Co., 1949.

Heuss, Theodor. "Wilhelm Busch." In *Die grossen Deutschen: Deutsche Biographie,* edited by Heimpel, Heuss, and Reifenberg, vol. 5, pp. 361–67. Berlin: Propylaeen/Ullstein, 1957.

* Kayser, Wolfgang. "Wilhelm Buschs grotesker Humor." *Vortragsreihe der niedersächsischen Landesregierung* 4. Göttingen: Vandenhoek & Ruprecht, 1958.

* Marxer, Peter. *Wilhelm Busch als Dichter.* Ph.D. dissertation, Zurich, 1967. Zurich: Juris, 1967.

Kraus, Joseph. "Ausdrucksmittel der Satire bei Wilhelm Busch." Ph.D. dissertation, UCLA, 1968.

Bonati, Peter. *Die Darstellung des Bösen im Werk Wilhelm Buschs.* Ph.D. dissertation, Basel, 1970. *Basler Studien zur dt. Sprache u. Literatur* 49. Bern, 1973.

* Ueding, Gert. *Wilhelm Busch: Das 19. Jahrhundert en miniature.* Frankfurt a/M: Insel Verlag, 1977.

* Heller, Erich. "Creatures of Circumstance." *The Times Literary Supplement,* no. 3941, October 7, 1977, pp. 1124–26.

Leube, Dietrich, ed. *Das grosse Wilhelm Busch Buch.* Munich: R. Piper, 1979.

Index to English and German Titles

Design and Layout: Laurie Anderson
Mechanicals: John F. Kelly
Compositor: G & S Typesetters, Inc.
Text: VIP Sabon
Display: Phototypositor Sabon
Printer: Malloy Lithographing, Inc.
Binder: John H. Dekker and Sons
Paper: 55 lb. P & S Regular Offset A-50
Cloth: Joanna Oxford 10500